P9-DFH-635

The English Language series

**Series Editors: David Britain and
Rebecca Clift**

World Englishes
An Introduction

GUNNEL MELCHERS and
PHILIP SHAW
Department of English, Stockholm University, Sweden

ARNOLD

A member of the Hodder Headline Group
LONDON
Distributed in the United States of America by
Oxford University Press Inc., New York

First published in Great Britain 2003 by
Arnold, a member of the Hodder Headline Group,
338 Euston Road, London NW1 3BH

http://www.arnoldpublishers.com

Distributed in the United States of America by
Oxford University Press Inc.,
198 Madison Avenue, New York NY 10016

British Library Cataloguing in Publication Data
A catalogue record for this book is available from the British Library

Library of Congress Cataloging-in-Publication Data
A catalogue record for this book is available from the Library of Congress

ISBN 0 340 71887 0 (hb)
ISBN 0 340 71888 9 (pb)
ISBN 0 340 71889 7 (CD)

2 3 4 5 6 7 8 9 10

Typeset in 10 on 13 pt Times by Phoenix Photosetting, Chatham, Kent
Printed and bound in Great Britain by CPI Bath

What do you think about this book? Or any other Arnold title;
Please send your comments to feedback.arnold@hodder.co.uk

Contents

Preface

World Englishes is a linguistic textbook intended for readers who are familiar with basic terms in phonetics and linguistics. It aims to present and describe global variation and change in the vocabulary, grammar, phonology, and pragmatics of English. We also try to give a good deal of context to explain and illuminate the linguistic variation and make the subject more exciting and accessible. By 'context' we mean geographical, historical, social and cultural information, and also linguistic background on topics like indigenous languages and place names. We have aimed to enrich the presentation as much as possible with 'language in use' taken from fiction, popular culture, newspapers, and electronic media.

In writing this book we have been able to draw on our complementary experience: Gunnel Melchers' 20 years of teaching an undergraduate course called 'Global English' at the Department of English, Stockholm University, and work on the dialects of the British Isles, and Philip Shaw's many years of work with speakers of English from every part of the world. The most popular feature of Gunnel's classes has been the live encounters with guest speakers of English from Glasgow, the West Indies, Belfast, Christchurch, etc. In this book the visits are replaced by the voices of 'informants' on the CD – real people from different places, introduced by their real names.

Following the general aims of the series *The English Language*, we have written our book for undergraduate students throughout the world, including those who have English as their first language, second-language users in Africa and Asia, and those like most of our students who use English as a foreign or international language. The Englishes of all three types of user are covered in the book itself.

We have written the book because we think it is important for people to know more about the forms of English and the roles it plays, so that they can better understand the world they live in and the people they communicate with. Any student of English today needs insight into the language's regional and social patterns of global variation.

Each chapter in the book, and each section of the longer chapters, is concluded by suggestions for further reading on its topic. Appendix 2 offers pre-reading questions on each chapter and post-reading questions on each section: readers who wish to can use these to remind themselves, before reading, of what they already know and to check, after reading, that they have remembered a few main points.

We have tried not to present an explicit political stance in our book, and we have tried to make the implicit one as egalitarian and inclusive as possible, but we recognize that we are prisoners of our prejudices and hope that readers can see past them. Similarly, although we have found all varieties rich and fascinating, it is inevitable that our personal knowledge and experience is not evenly distributed. Our base in Europe and Sweden in particular shows through here and there.

Now that the book is finished, we would like to thank many people whose help and support has been invaluable:

Peter Trudgill for first suggesting that Gunnel should write this book, and for teaching us both so much about linguistic variation,

David Britain and Rebecca Clift for their judicious and helpful editing,

Christina Wipf Perry and Lesley Riddle, for their patience and encouragement,

John Wells for providing his excellent framework and teaching us most of what we know about accents of English,

Jack Chambers and Elizabeth Gordon, for sharing their knowledge of Canadian and New Zealand English,

Stanley Ellis and Caryl Phillips for their insights into the importance of non-standard varieties of language,

Efurosina Adegbija and Ebo Ubahakwe, for bringing Nigerian English alive to outsiders,

Magnus Ljung and David Minugh for helpful reading,

Rosemary Morlin for excellent copy-editing, Margareta Olofsson and Joke Palmkvist for support and advice,

the informants from all over the world, for lending their voices to be recorded.

We would also like to thank Matt T. Rosenborg (http://geography.about.com) and Graphic Maps & World Atlas for permission to use the maps,

Harruna Attah of the *Accra Mail* for letting us use the article in 5.4.3.3,

and our students, for many vital insights, and for helpful comments on the manuscript.

The roots of English

And certaynly our langage now vsed varyeth ferre from that whiche was vsed and spoken whan I was borne. . . . Certaynly it is harde to playse euery man by cause of dyuersite & chaunge of langage. (William Caxton, Preface to *Eneydos* (1490))

This view on the state of English, expressed by the legendary printer, editor, and translator who introduced printing in England in 1476 and had considerable influence on the emergence of a standard language, might just as well have been voiced by a contemporary observer of the language. The present-day observer might, for example, react to the sentence *Everyone in the street was shocked when they heard the news*, having learnt that *everyone* should be followed by *he/she*, or be utterly confused by the different vowel qualities in accents of English: the word *pen*, as pronounced by a New Zealander, is easily perceived as *pin* by British speakers.

For a deeper understanding of today's English, with its infinite number of varieties, it is, in fact, worthwhile to travel even further back in history than Caxton's time. In this chapter, we would like to outline the early history of the English language in England, i.e. from its first appearance up to the emergence of a standard language.

About AD 450, when Britain was largely inhabited by Celtic peoples – the last Roman legions having left some 40 years earlier – fair-sized groups of Germanic settlers began coming into the country, driving the indigenous population into 'corners' such as Wales and Cornwall. The invaders, who probably came from Northern Germany and Denmark, represented three main tribes of people known as *Angles*, *Saxons*, and *Jutes*. The Angles, from whose name the word 'English' is derived, settled in the north, the Saxons in the south – their name living on in today's Sussex, Essex and Middlesex – and the Jutes in a small area in the south-east, including Kent and the Isle of Wight. The language of these settlers, later known as Anglo-Saxons, although not documented substantially until about 300 years later, constitutes the roots of English.

On the basis of later evidence and of our knowledge of the mechanisms of language change and diffusion in general, it can be assumed that the distinct groups of settlers produced a dialectally varied language. To some extent this may have been due to differences in the Germanic varieties spoken in their original homelands on the Continent, but it also reflects the distinct communities formed by the groups in various parts of England. Some of these early 'tribal' differences can even be traced in rural dialects today; for example, /f/ and /s/ at the beginning of words or syllables in the standard language correspond to /v/ and /z/ in the south-west of England, (cf. 4.1). 'Cider from Somerset' may, for example, be presented as *Zider vrom Zummerzet* in local advertising. Incidentally, a few of the words featuring this dialectal characteristic have been adopted in the standard language, such as *vixen*, 'female fox' and *vat* (related to German *Fass*, Swedish *fat*).

One of the most important reasons for linguistic variation and change is the degree of contact with speakers of other languages or dialects. When Caxton made his observation on the diversity of English, it had already been exposed to and affected by major influence, in particular from Scandinavian languages and French. Curiously, however, contacts with the indigenous Celtic population have not resulted in many borrowings in English. This is indeed something of a mystery, since the native people would have had a more adequate, traditional vocabulary at their disposal to describe and categorize the world around them. Such evidence as there is survives chiefly in place names: river names such as *Thames*, *Avon*, and *Wye* and place-name elements such as *crag* 'steep and rugged rock' and *cumb* 'deep valley' (cf. *Ilfracombe*). Admittedly, there are also Celtic borrowings of another type in English now, such as *whisky* 'the water of life' and *galore* 'lots of', but these are of a much later date. It should also be added that in some parts of Britain, which are, or have been, Celtic strongholds (parts of Scotland, Cornwall), regional dialects of English have fair-sized elements of Celtic in them. A more thorough account, not restricted to vocabulary, of the impact of this *substratum*, i.e. 'underlying language', will follow in 4.2–4.

In contrast to the meagre evidence of Celtic influence on English, that of Latin is certainly pervasive. To begin with, this influence may be explained by the fact that Latin was not the language of conquered people but of a higher civilization, from which the Anglo-Saxons had a great deal to learn. Some of the early Latin loanwords may actually have been adopted even before the Anglo-Saxons left the Continent. Examples of such early loans are *cheese*, *pepper*, *street*, *pound*, *wall*, and *camp*.

With the introduction of Christianity in 597 the Latin influence made itself noticeable in many spheres of life. Firstly, all the words pertaining to the Church were introduced: *altar*, *angel*, *candle*; also a certain number of words connected with learning and education which reflect another aspect of the Church's influence: *school*, *master*, *grammatical*. Secondly, many words connected with everyday life such as names of articles of clothing and household utensils were introduced: *sock*, *chest*, *sack*, *cap*, as well as words denoting foods: *beet*, *pear*, *radish*. Thirdly, new names for trees, plants, and herbs often replaced the Anglo-Saxon words: *pine*, *lily*, *fennel*.

In fact, the influence of Latin continued to make itself felt until after the Renaissance, affecting scientific and scholarly writing in particular, and it has remained strong to this day. Obviously, since Classical Latin is no longer a living language, its present-day impact could hardly be viewed as 'borrowing'; rather, the Latin element has been integrated into the English system. This integration includes affixes and suffixes productive in word-formation, such as *re-*, *in-*, *inter-*, *-fy* (*reshuffle*, *incapacitate*, *interdisciplinary*, *rectify*).

Towards the end of the eighth century, speakers of English, especially in the north-eastern parts of the British Isles, began to come into contact – of a rather enforced nature – with speakers of yet another language variety, namely the Viking invaders from Denmark and Norway. In spite of the violence and barbarity that characterized many of the invaders and their encounters with the English population, there was a great deal of peaceful settlement and mutual benefit as well. Many individuals became permanent settlers, remaining behind when their ships returned home.

With regard to the language contact in particular, it must have been facilitated by the fact that Anglo-Saxon and Old Norse were fairly closely related; both were Germanic languages and shared a common stock of vocabulary. There were, however, marked differences in the grammatical systems. According to some recent theories, Englishmen and Scandinavians can be assumed to have got round certain communication problems by simplifying the language, e.g. by dropping quite a few inflectional endings. This is, actually, one of the factors that have been brought forward to explain how English developed into the 'ending-less' language it is today.

Although not as massive as that of Latin or French, the Scandinavian influence has been substantial and has affected many everyday words which are close to the core of the language. The very pronunciation of the *k*'s and *g*'s in the following words is a sign of Scandinavian origin: *sky*, *bask*, *whisk*, *skirt*, *kid*, *give*, *egg*. Certain common place name elements are Scandinavian, such as *-by*, *-thorpe*, and *-toft* 'a piece of ground' (cf. *Grimsby*, *Scunthorpe*, *Lowestoft*). Old Norse has even influenced English pronominal usage, which is quite sensational in patterns of borrowing: the pronouns *they*, *their*, *them* are Scandinavian loans, having replaced Anglo-Saxon forms that had grown too similar to other pronouns to keep them distinct.

In certain dialects spoken in typical 'Viking areas', i.e. basically what was known as the *Danelaw*, the influence has been particularly marked; in Yorkshire, for example, the following Scandinavian-based words of an everyday character are widely known: *lake* 'play', *neaf* 'fist', *lathe* 'barn', *teem* 'empty'. Owing to the close relationship between the languages in contact, it can, however, sometimes be quite difficult to determine which words are truly Scandinavian. A case in point is *bairn* 'child', often brought up as an example of a Scandinavian word; yet similar-sounding forms are – or were – found in most Germanic languages. Since the use of *bairn* tends to be restricted to the northern parts of Britain, it is not unlikely that it has been reinforced by the close contacts with Scandinavia.

In Shetland and Orkney, which were under Viking rule up to 1469, well over 95 per cent of the place names and a substantial part of the vocabulary in the traditional dialects is Scandinavian. A few telling examples of Shetland vocabulary, very much alive today, are: *ouskeri* 'tool for baling out water' (cf. Swedish *öskar*), *plagg* for 'garment' (cf. Swedish *plagg*), *scarf* for 'cormorant' (a bird, cf. Swedish *skarv*), *du* as a less formal word of address than *you*.

In 1066 an event occurred which had a greater effect on the English language than any other in the course of its history, possibly with the exception of the quick spread and diversification that we are witnessing in this century. It is certainly worth thinking about that English, the bane of so many other languages, was itself at risk in the two centuries following this event, i.e. the Norman Conquest. During this period, the use of English was socially restricted; it was not used at court, in church, or in government administration. Such restriction generally tends to be an indication that a language variety is endangered. English, however, turned out to be a survivor; although it was seen by many as a crude peasant language, others grew to view it as a marker of ethnicity and national identity. It was formally reinstated in 1362, when the king's speech at the opening of Parliament was delivered in English. In the same year an Act was passed making English instead of French the official language of the law courts.

During its heyday in Britain, however, French had an enormous impact on the linguistic repertoire and on the English language itself. As already suggested, it was the most prestigious language variety. The following is a much-quoted remark made by the late-thirteenth-century chronicler Robert of Gloucester: 'Bote a man conne Frens, me telþ of him lute' ('unless a man knows French, people think little of him').

French was the language of law, administration, business, and sophisticated life, and this is reflected, for example, in the following borrowings, picked from among the 10,000 that were adopted from the time of the Norman Conquest up to about 1500: *judge, cordial, faith, faint, veil*. It is interesting that French words were introduced to denote the meat from certain animals, whereas the names of the animals remained English: *pork* from pigs, *veal* from calves, *mutton* from sheep, *venison* from deer. This is generally explained by the fact that French cooking was seen as superior.

In the period immediately following the conquest, loanwords were from Norman French rather than from a Parisian standard. The same word was later often borrowed in its standard form and came to be used in a slightly different way from its Norman counterpart – another factor which has enriched the English language. Examples of such pairs are *warrant – guarantee* and *warden – guardian*.

It is also worth pointing out that the French influence on the English language has continued over the centuries but has been mostly restricted to certain areas, such as etiquette, literary terminology, fashion, and cookery. The influence has also made itself noticeable in certain grammatical structures and the placement of stress in French-based words such as *canal, hotel, antique*.

In addition to borrowings from the sources mentioned so far, English has, in various periods, been influenced by many other languages: Dutch/Low German, e.g. with regard to boating terms, High German, Spanish, Portuguese, Italian, Yiddish, Hindi, and Afrikaans. Since these influences tend to be connected with certain varieties of English, they will be highlighted in Chapter 4, which will also deal with the considerable historically based regional variation in the British Isles, including the special case of Scots.

Towards the end of the fifteenth century, when English was firmly reinstated as the language of power and the art of printing began to exercise an influence on the style of writing, a standard language began to emerge. Earlier, writing had been clearly dialectal and extremely varied with regard to spelling, vocabulary, and grammar. The developing standard was London-based – in particular, it reflected the language of the prosperous middle-class businessmen who had moved into London from an area north-east of the city. The influential university of Cambridge in that area is also believed to have played an important role here. Not until the eighteenth century, however, was English spelling and grammar codified in a standard form; this happened when the legendary Dr Samuel Johnson published his famous dictionary in 1755. As for a standard of pronunciation, it hardly existed before the latter half of the nineteenth century, when public school usage made a certain southern accent more prestigious than other varieties.

2 The spread of English

English, English everywhere

This motto is the headline in the introduction to a recent account of New Zealand English (Gordon and Deverson 1998). It is difficult not to agree with this claim – walking around Stockholm, for example, we recently observed that well over 80 per cent of the shops in its most fashionable street had English names.

By contrast, consider the following statement made about 400 years ago by Richard Mulcaster, a schoolmaster and linguist: 'The English tongue is of small reache, stretching no further than this island of ours, nay not there over all'. The worldwide expansion of English has, in fact, happened rather quickly, and did not truly escalate until after the Second World War (cf. Crystal 1997a:vii).

When Mulcaster made his pronouncement, English was, however, already embarking on its conquest of the world. With the arrival of the sizeable groups of settlers in Massachusetts in the early seventeenth century, among them the Pilgrim Fathers in Plymouth, the colonization of North America really got under way; in 1640 there were 25,000 English speakers in New England alone. Owing to the prosperity of the colonies and the massive immigration throughout the nineteenth century, the population has increased at an explosive rate; today the USA has 240 million speakers of English as a first language.

The story of English in Canada does not really begin until the latter half of the eighteenth century. In 1763, when Canada became a British possession, it had almost no English-speaking settlers. One part of what is now Canada had, however, been English-speaking long before this, namely the British colony of Newfoundland whose traditional dialect has Irish, Scots, and West Country features as well as a distinct flavour of its own. The number of English speakers in 'Canada proper' increased rapidly after the end of the American War of Independence, when there was a mass migration of civilian and military refugees, the so-called United Empire Loyalists, who moved from the new United States to New Brunswick and Nova Scotia. Today Canada has almost 20 million speakers of English as a first language (out of a total population of 29 million).

Towards the end of the eighteenth century, the first British settlers arrived in Australia and New Zealand. As is well known, a large proportion of the Australian immigrants did not voluntarily move 'down under'; they were prisoners assigned to the penal colonies in New South Wales owing to the fact that the British jails were overcrowded. This convict system operated from 1788 to 1840 and in all some 130,000 prisoners were transported. The early settlers in New Zealand were not prisoners, however. There was an unofficial early settlement of whalers and not until 1840 was an official colony established, when the British government signed the Treaty of Waitangi with the Maori chiefs. Today Australia has well over 15 million speakers of English as a first language and New Zealand about 3.5 million.

In South Africa, English was not established until 1806, when Britain invaded the Cape for strategic reasons. Today there are 3 million speakers of English as a first language in South Africa, but it is only one out of 11 official languages.

Most users of English in the British Isles, the United States, Canada, Australia, New Zealand, a number of major and minor islands in the Caribbean, and other islands and island groups such as the Falkland Islands, St Helena, and Tristan da Cunha, as well as a sizeable proportion of the inhabitants of South Africa are *native* speakers of English and use it as their *first* language. Most of these speech communities have set their own standards, which have been codified in dictionaries and grammar books. They will be presented in detail in Chapter 4, where we call these communities 'the inner circle'.

In other parts of the world, such as many areas in Africa, where English first arrived towards the end of the fifteenth century, and the Indian subcontinent which was first exposed to English in 1600 when the British East India Company was formed, English is used as a *second* language (*ESL*), i.e. quite widely in business and government, often officially recognized and used as the medium of teaching. The English used in these areas often differs radically from inner-circle varieties and is worthy of study on its own account. These varieties of English, especially those with official status, are often referred to as 'the New Englishes' (cf. however Mufwene 2000: 9, who argues that the term *new English* should apply to all varieties identifiable as English today, 'since every spoken language is adapted by its speakers to current communicative needs and contexts'). These varieties will be the subject matter of Chapter 5, where we use the term 'the outer circle'.

English is also widely used today among speakers who have acquired it as a *foreign* language. The massive exposure to and use of English tends to result in a heavy impact on the first language of its users. Some characteristics of English as spoken by various foreign learners as well as examples of its influence are given in Chapter 6, which also discusses the role of English as an international language of communication – its use in the 'expanding circle' created by globalization.

Whereas a number of English varieties fit extremely nicely into one of the three categories, others are characterized by shifting status, e.g. due to the increasing use of English as the medium of instruction in EFL countries, or tend to be viewed differently in the literature. In particular, the distinction between *second* and *foreign* is fuzzy; confusingly, the branch of applied linguistics studying the teaching and learning of foreign languages usually refers to this as *second language acquisition* (SLA).

Not surprisingly, then, the overall statistics for English worldwide appear to be somewhat variable and should be taken with a pinch of salt. Obviously, the EFL category is particularly difficult to pinpoint; it really depends on what level of proficiency a person should have to qualify as a speaker of English. The following figures are quoted from *The Future of English?* (Graddol 1997):

First-language speakers: 375 million
Second-language speakers: 375 million
Foreign-language speakers: 750 million.

The following, taken from the same source, is perhaps even more telling, with reference to the worldwide impact of English:

> One out of five of the world's population speak English to some level of competence. Demand from the other four fifths is increasing. ... By the year 2000 it is estimated that over one billion people will be learning English. English is the main language of books, newspapers, airports and air-traffic control, international business and academic conferences, science technology, diplomacy, sport, international competitions, pop music and advertising. (From the press release for the British Council's English 2000 project in 1995, quoted in Graddol 1997:2)

Whatever source of information we use for our statistics, the figures will be staggering. The story of English and its worldwide spread can, indeed, be said to be the most sensational story of a language ever told. It is true, as the diagram below will show, that Mandarin Chinese, Hindi/Urdu, and Spanish have more native speakers, but they have neither the global sway nor the multi-functional use that characterizes English today. It is also true that Latin in its day was widely diffused in its popular or 'vulgar' forms and that Classical Latin was, for many centuries, the language of scientists and scholars in much the same way as English is now, but, for obvious reasons, this cannot be compared with the worldwide spread and the all-pervasive influence of English that has been witnessed in the latter half of the twentieth century.

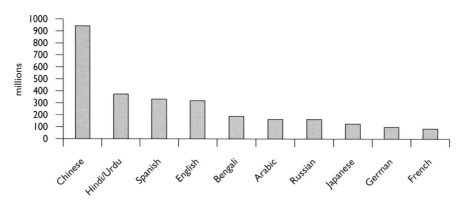

Source: SIL Ethnologue http://www.ethnologue.com/

Fig. 2.1. L1 speakers of major languages

What, then, are the reasons for the success story of English? Some people, including the eminent linguist Otto Jespersen (1860–1943), have actually ascribed the success to inherent, superior qualities in the language itself: it has, for example, been described as 'vigorous', even 'manly'. Whereas such romantic thinking is not very helpful for our understanding of the causes of language change and development, the claim that English is widely used because it is such a flexible language, with few grammatical endings, and has such a cosmopolitan vocabulary, may well contain an element of truth.

Yet the main reason is of another kind; just as the concept of *language* can be clarified by defining it as 'a dialect with an army and a navy', the special position of English in a worldwide perspective should be related to political/economic power and historical coincidence. In other words: the fact that English is now an influential world language is not really due to its superiority as a language, but is a result of the activities of its speakers over the centuries.

A leading textbook in this field, David Crystal's *English as a Global Language* (1997a), was recently severely criticized for political naïvety. In presenting our own account of World Englishes we inevitably lay ourselves open to the same kind of criticism, although throughout the presentation we have tried to account for conflicting political stances reflected in the linguistic literature. We are, of course, fully aware of the oppression and suffering caused by colonialism, and to some extent we also sympathize with anxiety felt with regard to cultural imperialism. Our main driving force in writing this book is, however, of a truly positive kind: a fascination with the endless strength, expressivity, variation, and changeability of this world language.

Before looking more closely at its many varieties, however, we should clarify our framework for classifying and describing them; this is the purpose of the following chapter.

Variation in English

A dialect is – er – a different way of speaking – from the same place – different areas – they have different accents – yes ... (laughter) (A London girl interviewed for the BBC radio series *Locally Speaking*, produced by Brian Redhead and Malcolm Petyt (early 1980s))

The main purpose of this chapter is to provide a framework for the presentations of varieties of English around the globe. Throughout the chapter, any examples illustrating terms and concepts are directly related to the subject matter of this book. The first section is devoted to a discussion of the character and possible causes of linguistic variation and change. The following section presents types of variation at various levels of language, setting up the structure for detailed descriptions of individual varieties in Chapters 4–6. Finally, the classification of world Englishes is discussed along several dimensions.

3.1 LINGUISTIC DIVERSITY AND DIFFUSION

3.1.1 Models and explanations

The diversity of language can, at least to some extent, be accounted for by using models such as 'language family trees', suggesting genetic relationships and temporal as well as spatial divergence. This tree model, a typical expression of nineteenth-century German philology, is essentially adopted by the influential twentieth-century linguist Ferdinand de Saussure as well. He envisages the emergence of 'dialect splits' in the following way: a language, originally quite uniform, existing on two isolated islands, will eventually and gradually split into two dialects. This is said to be 'purely a function of time', although it obviously also points to spatial causation, e.g. relative isolation due to physical barriers such as water, forests, and mountains.

The reasons for the development of regional linguistic differences are, however, rather more complex and not completely understood. Whereas the traditional line of thinking described above clarifies a great deal of linguistic diversity, it also fails to account for many phenomena. Why is it, for example, that regional linguistic variation is comparatively limited in Australian English, despite the vastness of the country and the existence of major geographical barriers? Conversely, neighbouring villages in many European countries, including Britain, may have clearly distinctive dialects, to the point of unintelligibility.

The branch of modern linguistics known as sociolinguistics has made great strides towards a more sophisticated understanding of linguistic differentiation. Whereas some features can probably only be explained as independent innovations, others are the results of social rather than purely geographical phenomena: the strong sense of togetherness in certain speech communities and the search for a marked identity; the possibility and frequency of contacts with other groups of people; social mobility; linguistic accommodation; urbanization. Recent linguistic innovation and spread can, indeed, to a large extent, be ascribed to the last-mentioned phenomenon.

In Chapter 4 we will take a closer look at some linguistic scenarios where urban centres seem to play a crucial role in the diffusion of innovations, such as the impact of London English and the 'Northern Cities vowel shifts' in the USA.

In attempting to account for the causes and effects of language change, a distinction is usually made between *internal (endogenous)* and *external (exogenous)* explanations, i.e. 'whether change is brought about by pressures internal to the linguistic system itself, or whether it is the speakers who can be held responsible, adopting forms from other varieties' (Foulkes and Docherty 1999:10). Clearly, however, linguistic changes may also be brought about by social factors *within* the same variety (cf. Hickey 1999, describing the impact of 'fashionable Dublin').

3.1.2 Some basic concepts: language, dialect, accent

Without further specification, the terms *language, dialect* and *accent* have already been used in this book but as the motto at the head of this chapter suggests, they are not so easily defined. Here we discuss these terms and introduce some other concepts that are relevant for our presentation of world Englishes.

The difference between *language* and *dialect* is not clear-cut. It is often suggested that languages are *autonomous*, whereas dialects are *heteronomous*; in other words: we can say that 'X is a dialect of language Y', or 'Y has the dialects X and Z', but never 'Y is a language of dialect X'. There is a great deal of truth in this distinction, but it is contentious in borderline cases such as the status of Scots (4.3.2.2).

The most realistic distinction is probably 'A language is a dialect with an army and a navy', as famously formulated by the linguist Max Weinreich, i.e. it is *extra-linguistic*, not based on language itself but on the political situation in the real world.

The names of languages tend to be related to the names of independent political entities, 'polities': Danish, for example, is the language spoken in Denmark. Yet this distinction obviously does not apply to English, considering that it is the sole official language of more than 20 nations.

Another difference is said to be that dialects, in contrast with languages, are mutually intelligible. Yet this is not always the case, as exemplified in the following conversation, quoted by the sociolinguist Lesley Milroy (1994:161), where cross-dialectal miscomprehension is due to differences in tense systems:

A: How long are yous here?
B: Till after Easter.

(2.00 seconds pause: A looks puzzled)
C: We came on Sunday.
A: Ah yous are here a while then.
(Contextual note: A is a native of Donegal, Republic of Ireland; B and C are Standard English speakers resident in Ireland.)

It is also true that dialects are characteristically spoken and do not, like languages, have a *codified* written form, laid down in dictionaries and grammar books. Regional/social or *nonstandard* dialects are, however, frequently reflected in writing: in fiction, though usually restricted to the dialogue, in local publications and in school essays, at least in speech communities where dialect writing is encouraged. It is true that nonstandard written representation can but rarely rely on set grammatical rules or systematic spelling conventions, and therefore tends to be idiosyncratic, incomplete and inconsistent (cf. Taavitsainen and Melchers 1999:1–26). In this book, the text samples that are included in Chapters 4 and 5 represent different varieties of Standard English, but we have also included samples of nonstandard language to illustrate characteristic regional/social features.

Dialects are also said to be used only in certain 'domains', whereas languages show maximal variation or 'elaboration of function'. This has to do with the situational use of language in a society. The term *domain* simply stands for 'a recurring situation type', 'a definable context of life in a society'. Typical domains are the school, the family, work, local as well as national administration, the Church, and the media. Nonstandard dialects may, for example, be restricted to family life, possibly to work and – marginally – to the school. A vigorous living dialect or language is characterized by use in several domains; loss of a domain is often an indication that the dialect is endangered, as studies of a Scottish Gaelic dialect have shown (Dorian 1981).

In order to avoid the notoriously difficult dialect/language distinction, linguists tend to prefer a more neutral term, namely *variety*, which covers both concepts and is not clouded through popular usage. This term, as the reader will already have noticed, is generally used in referring to World Englishes.

The difference between *dialect* and *accent* can be formulated in a very simple way: *accent* refers to the pronunciation of a variety and *dialect* to its grammar and vocabulary. It should, however, be borne in mind that speaking a particular dialect usually implies using a particular variant of pronunciation as well. In particular, this refers to 'word-based', 'nonsystemic' or *lexical-incidential* pronunciations (Wells 1982:5–6), i.e. those spread over the vocabulary in an unpredictable way. They can usually be explained historically, but will definitely seem nonsystemic if viewed synchronically. Nor do they show a regularity of correspondence with the standard accent; the lexical items *night, fight, mice, find*, for example, are all pronounced with the /aɪ/ diphthong in Received Pronunciation (RP), the Standard English English accent, whereas in traditional West Yorkshire speech their vowels are all different: /niːt/, /fɛɪt/, /maɪs/ and /fɪnd/.

In an introductory textbook aiming to describe worldwide variation in English, it is obviously not conceivable to include very localized regional dialects or fine social distinctions. Rather, the focus will be on the standard varieties, such as Standard Canadian English and the various accents associated with them. Whenever regional/social variation is considerable, however, and when it has played a part in the shaping of 'transported' Englishes, it will be accounted for. Since regional linguistic diversity is clearly related to a development over time, it is – not surprisingly – above all in the sections on the British Isles that we will have occasion to take a closer look at regional, nonstandard features.

3.2 TYPES OF VARIATION IN FORM

If we imagine a large sample of written texts and tape-recordings of English from all over the world, we will find that the published written texts are generally very similar, with almost identical grammar, spelling that varies in a few well-defined areas, and limited variation in lexis. Of course we will find a few written texts in other dialects, like this extract from a poem which represents the pronunciation (*gorra* = 'got to'), and lexis (*cannit* = 'can't', *bairn* = 'child') of the Geordie dialect of Newcastle in north-east England:

A hev gorra bairn
an a hev gorra wife
an a cannit see me bairn or wife
workin in the night

(Tom Pickard, from Horovitz, M. (ed.) 1969 *Children of Albion*: 259)

But such texts will be extremely rare, with the majority much more uniform. This reflects the fact that most published written texts are in the same dialect, the one we call Standard English above. On the basis of small variations in spelling, lexis, and grammar, we will be able to group these texts into varieties of Standard English.

The spoken texts will vary widely in pronunciation and more widely in grammar and lexis than the written ones. Spoken language (and private written language, as in e-mails) is generally less influenced by the standard than written. These differences mean that we will be able to divide the spoken texts up into a fairly large number of varieties, with common features within the groups and predictable differences between them. However we would not expect every speaker to use one and only one variety, because of the effect of context; we know that speakers often use one variety at work and another with their friends, for example. Nor would we expect all the texts in a group to have identical features, even at the same level of formality; we know there is variety 'inside' varieties.

Variation in world Englishes can thus be found at all levels of language, i.e. spelling, phonetics/phonology, morphology, syntax, the lexicon (vocabulary), and discourse. In the following presentation we give an introduction to this variation and outline our descriptive framework. We begin with the smallest units in writing and speech and end with discourse, in the sense of 'a series of connected utterances, a unit of potential analysis larger than a sentence' (Wales 1989:130).

3.2.1 Spelling

Most written texts, at least those that are published, are produced in codified, standard varieties, where spelling is regulated by authoritative dictionaries. Although varieties of (World) Standard English are generally characterized by great similarity at this level of language, there are some well-known exceptions, such as the British-American diversity, mostly rule-governed as in *travelled* vs *traveled*, *centre* vs *center*, *colour* vs *color*, but also lexical-incidental as in *grey* vs *gray*, *tyre* vs *tire*. Most of the American spelling conventions were created by Noah Webster, who in 1789 proposed an 'American Standard'. It was partly a matter of honour 'as an independent nation . . . to have a system of our own, in language as well as government' (Crystal 1995:80).

In some transported Englishes, especially Canadian English, which is generally characterized by conflicting loyalties, i.e. to Britain vs the USA, there is great variability in spelling and usage varies for regional, social, and political reasons (4.6.3.1). An ongoing worldwide survey for a prospective international style guide, *Langscape*, reports on the language preferences of supraregional reading/writing communities, and on their affiliations to the British/American divide (Peters 2001). McArthur (2001:5) claims that 'we already have a single print standard for world English, which consists of dual institutions for spelling and punctuation . . .'.

As already mentioned, Scots, with its long written tradition, holds a special position, arguably as a language in its own right, (cf. 4.3.2.2). Those who argue that Scots is a language distinct from English claim that it therefore merits a distinct orthography (McClure 1995:41). The exact character of this orthography, however, is subject to endless debate, if not controversy. The most serious attempt to supply a codification and formal recommendation for Scots spelling is the *'Makars' Style Sheet'*, created in 1947 by a group of writers, but according to McClure (1995:43), '. . . the prospect of an officially-recognised standard orthography for Scots is as remote in 1995 as it was ten years previously . . .'.

Finally, although English-based pidgins and creoles are only marginally treated in this book, it is worth noting that they but rarely as yet have standardized orthographies (cf. Romaine 1988:111). Broadly speaking, written representations of these varieties are characterized by a wish for closer relationship between spelling and pronunciation than in standard orthographies, e.g. *bilong* for 'belong', *kwin* for 'queen' (Tok Pisin, Papua New Guinea).

3.2.2 Phonetics/phonology

This level of language is the most distinctive in the characterization of varieties of English; in fact, the distinction and divergence in English accents appears to be increasing continuously, whereas at other levels, such as syntax, varieties are rather converging (Trudgill 1998b).

We assume that you are familiar with basic phonetics such as the speech organs, the difference between vowels and consonants (including the concept of approximants), the general classification and description of speech sounds and some aspects of prosody such as the structure of the syllable and forms and function of intonation. Similarly, you are expected to be familiar with the elements of phonology, especially the concept of *phoneme*. If you feel a need to brush up on any of these topics, you are referred to one of the standard textbooks (Davenport and Hannahs 1998, Gimson 1994, Ladefoged 1993, Roach 2001).

We have included the latest IPA (International Phonetics Association) chart (on the inside front cover), but have tried to avoid using extremely narrow phonetic transcription with an array of diacritics. If an accent of English is characterized by very special phonetic realizations, this will usually be described in words rather than by adding a number of additional symbols. As is customary, // is used to indicate phonemic transcriptions, whereas [] is used for allophonic transcriptions (cf. the description of the /ɑː/ phoneme in RP and Australian English below) and occasionally also for impressionistic notation without relying on phonological analysis. Any symbols (letters) enclosed in <> refer to spelling, not pronunciation.

Below, we also list and exemplify a few terms that are often used in the book but may not be familiar to you if your phonetic training has been exclusively based on Received pronunciation (RP) or General American (GA):

glottal: a sound produced in the larynx, due to the closure or narrowing of the glottis, as in the initial consonant [h] of *happy* and in the **glottal stop** [ʔ], which is stereo-typically connected with London Cockney but actually found in various accents around the English-speaking world.

retroflex: a position slightly further back than alveolar, with the tip of the tongue bent or 'curled' backwards, as generally in *r*'s produced by Americans and speakers from England's West Country (the south-west).

tapped: refers to consonants that are related to trills; the difference is that it is momentary: there is only one beat (tap), which is usually produced by the tip of the tongue. A tapped /r/ which is represented as [ɾ] and sounds almost like a [d], is common in some accents of British English, especially between vowels, as in *very, hurry*. This sound is also characteristic of most varieties of American English, but then as a realization of intervocalic /t/, as in *city, latter*.

trilled (rolled): refers to certain types of /r/ and stands for the rapid, repeated tapping of one speech organ against another. It is something of a stereotype that front trills – in which the tip of the tongue is used – are characteristic of Scottish English (cf. 4.3.3.2). According to Catford (1994:70), 'the apico-alveolar trill [r] is . . . a type of *r* traditionally used by stage Scotsmen'.

uvular: the back of the tongue against the uvula. Unlike many European languages, English does not generally have uvular, 'back' /r/, but there is a recessive pocket in north-east England where it can be heard under the name of the 'Northumbrian Burr', and some Scottish speakers use it variably, as for example the Glasgow speaker included in the accompanying CD.

wide: a term used about diphthongs that are characterized by a relatively long distance from the starting-point to the finishing-point. Some Broad Australian diphthongs, for example, are typically wider than their correspondences in the reference accent (RP) as in [saɪ] rather than [seɪ] for *say* (cf. 4.7.2.3).

In comparing accents of English around the globe, we should consider the *phonemic inventory*, i.e. the set-up of distinctive units, as well as the *phonetic output*, i.e. the various *allophones*. The average listener will no doubt find the most striking differences in the actual output; variation in vowel quality, in particular, is enormous. Two accents, such as RP and General Australian English, may have exactly the same number of distinctive units (phonemes), and yet sound very different indeed. Both accents, for example, have an /ɑː/ phoneme, as in *palm*, *father*, which is realized as [ɑː] in RP but as a front [aː] by most Australian speakers. To take another example: the minimal pair *bed/bad* will apply to all native-speaker varieties of English, but the actual contrastive sounds vary drastically in quality: in New Zealand English they approximate to *bid/bed* as pronounced by an RP speaker. Not surprisingly, such differences will lead to cross-dialectal misunderstandings, such as the unfortunate pronunciation of *Shetland* as ['ʃɪtlənd] by a New Zealand visitor to the islands.

There are, however, also important differences among world Englishes with regard to the phonemic inventory. Comparing RP and the somewhat constructed 'average' accent General American, which may be referred to as the two *reference accents*, we find that the vowel systems differ quite substantially. The most striking difference is that American English has fewer diphthongs, generally lacking centring ones and having a monophthong in words such as *goat*. Scottish English has even fewer diphthongs and African as well as Caribbean English varieties tend to have restricted vowel systems with many mergers.

We wish to emphasize that the only reason for our frequent comparisons made to the reference accents, especially RP, is that they are well defined and, above all, generally well known to students of English. In using them as yardsticks we are not saying that they are superior to other accents, nor that they are the original sources from which all other accents have developed.

A very useful and widely quoted attempt at a worldwide classification of English accents was made by Trudgill and Hannah for their pioneering textbook *International English*, first published in 1982. It should be pointed out that this 'typology' relates to fairly standardized, first-language varieties only. The classification identifies four main types of English: 1) 'English-based', including English as spoken in England and Wales, but also in South Africa, Australia, and New Zealand; 2) 'American-based', including English as spoken in the USA and Canada; 3) 'Scottish-based', including Scotland and Northern Ireland; 4) 'Irish-based', exclusively found in the Republic of Ireland.

Trudgill and Hannah (1994:5–6) give 11 criteria distinguishing accents of English and identifying the four types. Some of the most important criteria are:

- the quality of the vowel (/ɑː/ vs /æ/) in words such as *bath, half, dance*
- the absence (in *non-rhotic* accents) or presence (in *rhotic* accents) of /r/ in final position or before a consonant (*non-prevocalic /r/*), as in *hear, work*
- the degree of closeness in the front vowels, as in *pen, pan*
- a front or back vowel in words such as *father, part*
- absence or presence of contrast in length and vowel quality in word pairs such as *cot–caught*
- absence or presence of voice in intervocalic /t/, as in *later, letter.*

Absence of non-prevocalic /r/, for example, is characteristic of 'English-based' accents, whereas voicing of intervocalic /t/ is found in 'American-based accents', and the lack of contrast in *cot–caught* is typical of Scottish-based accents but also found in Canada.

Wells (1982:181ff.), setting up a typology for accents of English based exclusively on vowels, suggests virtually the same four types, namely Type I: provincial southern Irish English; interestingly, also valid for Jamaica and Barbados; Type II: RP, Australia, New Zealand, South Africa, 'and indeed most accents of England and Wales'; Type III: General American and Canada; Type IV: Scotland and Northern Ireland. His two main factors are systemic differences in the vowel system and the phonological distribution of these vowels, particularly in words such as *near* and *square*. As a shortcut in assigning accents to types, the following table is suggested (Wells 1982:183):

	I	II	III	IV
1. Does *lawn* rhyme with *corn*?	No	Yes	No	No
2. Does *mirror* rhyme with *nearer*?	No	No	Yes	No
3. Does *good* rhyme with *mood*?	No	No	No	Yes

1–3 exemplify differences in historical phonology. As we have seen earlier, Type II accents are characterized by absence of non-prevocalic /r/; hence *lawn* rhymes with *corn*. Type III accents only have undergone a change in which nonsyllabic [ə] disappeared between a vowel and a following /r/, thus making *nearer* rhyme with *mirror* and *sharing* with *herring* (Wells 1982:244). In Type IV accents, Middle English /u/ and /uː/ have merged. It would appear, then, that Type I accents, having undergone none of these changes, are the most traditional.

In the detailed presentation of accents to follow in Chapters 4 and 5, we will use the framework provided in Wells 1982, i.e. the so-called 'standard lexical sets' which are by now well established in the literature.

Throughout the work, use is made of the concept of **standard lexical sets**. These enable one to refer concisely to large groups of words which tend to share the same vowel, and to the vowel which they share. They are based on the vowel correspondences which apply between British Received Pronunciation and (a variety of) General American, and make use of **keywords** intended to be unmistakable, no matter what accent one says them in. Thus 'the KIT words' refer to 'ship, bridge, milk …'; 'the KIT vowel' refers to the vowel these words have (in most accents, /ɪ/); both may just be referred to as KIT. (Wells 1982:xviii)

In other words: since the actual phonetic quality of the KIT vowel may vary (in New Zealand English, for example, it approximates to /ə/), the KIT word is a much better reference point than the /ɪ/ vowel.

The 24 standard lexical sets are shown in Table 3.1:

Table 3.1. The 24 standard lexical sets

GA	RP	Key word	Wells' examples
ɪ	ɪ	KIT	ship, sick, bridge, milk, myth, busy
ɛ	e	DRESS	step, neck, edge, shelf, friend, ready
æ	æ	TRAP	tap, back, badge, scalp, hand, cancel
ɑ	ɒ	LOT	stop, sock, dodge, romp, quality
ʌ	ʌ	STRUT	cup, suck, budge, pulse, trunk
ʊ	ʊ	FOOT	put, bush, full, good, look, wolf
æ	ɑː	BATH	staff, brass, ask, dance, sample, calf
ɔ	ɒ	CLOTH	cough, broth, cross, long, Boston
ɜr	ɜː	NURSE	hurt, lurk, urge, burst, jerk, term
i	iː	FLEECE	creep, speak, leave, feel, key, people
eɪ	eɪ	FACE	tape, cake, raid, veil, steak, day
ɑ	ɑː	PALM	psalm, father, bra, spa, lager
ɔ	ɔː	THOUGHT	taught, sauce, hawk, jaw, broad
o	əʊ	GOAT	soap, joke, home, know, so, roll
u	uː	GOOSE	loop, shoot, tomb, mute, huge, view
aɪ	aɪ	PRICE	ripe, write, arrive, high, try, buy
ɔɪ	ɔɪ	CHOICE	adroit, noise, join, toy, royal
aʊ	aʊ	MOUTH	out, house, loud, count, crowd, cow
ɪr	ɪə	NEAR	beer, sincere, fear, beard, serum
er	eə	SQUARE	care, fair, pear, where, scarce, vary
ɑr	ɑː	START	far, sharp, bark, carve, farm, heart
ɔr	ɔː	NORTH	for, war, short, scorch, born, warm
or	ɔː	FORCE	four, wore, sport, porch, borne, story
ʊr	ʊə	CURE	poor, tourist, pure, plural
(ə	ə	schwa	comma)

Note that the standard lexical sets are exclusively designed to provide a framework for variation in vowels. On the other hand, it is of course true that some sets, such as NEAR and SQUARE, are very much conditioned by consonants in the phonetic environment. Needless to say, our presentation of accents will also include characteristic consonantal features. There is, for example, considerable variation in the quality of /r/ and /l/ and in the realization of /θ/ and /ð/.

So far, our description of English phonetics/phonology has been restricted to segments, i.e. individual sounds (vowels, consonants, approximants). All accents are however also characterized by prosodic (suprasegmental) features, which function over longer stretches of speech than phonemes. These include not only stress, rhythm, and intonation, but also syllabic and phonotactic structure, i.e. the specific sequences of sounds that occur in a language.

The most important phonotactic difference among accents of English has, in fact, already been described in connection with the account of typologies, namely the distribution of /r/. Another issue has to do with sequences (clusters) of consonants. In most accents of English, a word or syllable may be initiated by a sequence of three adjacent consonants, but only if the first of these is /s/. A great variety of combinations is found in initial two-consonant clusters, yet all possible combinations are not exploited. The historical initial cluster /kn/ in words such as *knee, knock* was lost in the south of England in the late seventeenth century, but can still be heard in varieties of Scots, as in Shetland dialect, where *knee* may be realized as [kniː] or [kəˈniː]. The latter exemplifies a common strategy in pronouncing unusual and problematic clusters: the cluster is actually avoided through the insertion of a so-called *epenthetic* vowel. A well-known historical example of this is the name *Canute*, the English version of the Scandinavian name *Knut*.

Epenthetic vowels of this kind are common in other accents of English, especially second-language and foreign-language varieties, to handle consonant clusters not found in the speaker's first language: 'sakool' for *school* as pronounced by Punjabi speakers (McArthur 1992:376), 'sukuru direba' for *screw driver* by Hausa speakers in Africa (Wells 1982:641) and [suturaɪku] for *strike* by Japanese speakers. Medial and final clusters may also be avoided by epenthesis, as in Hausa 'silik' for *silk* and 'crisipusi' for *crisps* (produced by EFL speakers from various countries); this strategy is also well known from 'inner-circle' varieties, e.g. Irish English [ˈfɪləm] for *film*, [ˈdʌbəlɪn] for *Dublin*. Epenthesis is not the only strategy used in avoiding consonant clusters, however. Reduction (deletion) is often found in initial as well as final clusters, as in [kratʃ], [traŋ], [tʃaɪl] for *scratch, strong, child* recorded in Jamaican Creole (cf. 4.11); this is also a characteristic of varieties of African English and of African American Vernacular English (AAVE).

Prosodic features of speech no doubt play an important part in the recognition of individual speakers as well as accents, e.g. rising tones in statements produced by Northern Irish English speakers, the Welsh 'lilt', and the characteristic rhythm perceived in Indian English. Regrettably, a coherent account or typology based on stress, rhythm, and intonation is not yet available (but cf. www.phon.ox.ac.uk/~esther/ivyweb/ for information on a British typology project). The following should therefore be seen as an unpretentious listing of a few prosodic features that in our experience appear to be salient.

A characteristic of Received Pronunciation is the very marked difference between stressed and unstressed syllables, in particular with regard to vowel quality; unstressed syllables are generally reduced to [ə] as in [kənˈsɪdə] for *consider*, [ˈɪnvəntəri] for *inventory* (according to Wells (2000), italicized schwa indicates that the vowel may be left out altogether). Whereas unstressed Latin prefixes are largely realized in the same way in General American, medial syllables are not: the American variant of *inventory* is given in Wells 2000 as [ˈɪnvəntɔːri]. On the other hand, certain accents in the north of England are characterized by a different rhythmical pattern, giving much more prominence to prefixes. Instrumental analysis of realizations of the word *consider* by RP and Yorkshire speakers showed that the first vowel was more than twice as long in the Yorkshire recordings (Melchers 1972:57).

Conversely, some accents of English surpass RP in having extremely marked stresses to the degree of near-exclusion of unstressed syllables. This is amusingly illustrated in the *Jimmy Carter Dictionary* (Maloney 1977), a popularly written handbook to facilitate the understanding of the president's southern accent, where *Urp* indicates his way of pronouncing *Europe*, and *Prezdet* indicates his title. Interestingly, a similar kind of rhythm is found in England's East Anglia (Wells 1982:341), as illustrated in Dickens' rendering of East Anglian speech in *David Copperfield*, e.g. *gen'l'm'n, Mas'r, Em'ly* (cf. Poussa 1999:33ff.).

Most accents of English as a first language are generally described as *stress-timed*, i.e. 'a general rule of English rhythm is that we take an equal amount of time from one stressed syllable to the next' (Cruttenden 1997:20), whereas Asian and African varieties are said to be *syllable-timed*, which means that an equal amount of time is taken over each syllable; it follows that much less use is made of reduced syllables (cf. 5.2.2.2).

Accents of English also vary a great deal with respect to word stress, both in groups of lexical items, e.g. words having the suffix *-ize*, and lexical-incidentally (3.1.2).

There is, of course, also variation in intonation patterns (cf. the website recommended above). Cruttenden (1997:133, 136) states that the most noticeable variation within British English is the extensive use of rising tones in many northern cities; nowhere in the English-speaking world is the difference in tonal inventory as great as that between RP and Belfast or Liverpool.

In addition to the rising tones used routinely in certain regional accents, a particular type of rising statement intonation is increasingly used in what are traditionally falling-tone accents. This phenomenon, known as HRT (high rise terminal) was first observed in young people's speech in New Zealand and Australia in the 1960s, but is found in many other English-speaking countries, such the USA, Canada and the UK. Some further information about its possible origin and its social and conversational functions is given in 4.8.3.2.

An excellent literary representation of HRT in US speech is given by Jane Smiley in her campus novel *Moo* (1995):

The undergraduate student approached him as soon as he got off the elevator. "I'm Lyle Karstensen, sir?" he said, and he held out the portfolio he had under his arm. "I'm leaving school? I'm going to work for a year or so and come back? It's not like I'm flunking out or anything? It's just so expensive, you know?"

Dr. Cates said, "Is there a problem with your grade?" He pushed the key into the lock of his office.

"No, sir? You gave me an A? See, that was the only A I've ever gotten here? Because I really liked your course? So when I was thinking of someone to give these to, I thought of you?"

Finally, a few words should be said about *voice quality*. This refers to the overall characteristics of speech, including pitch and loudness ranges, which are not only individually but also socially and regionally determined and clearly function as salient features. Voice quality tends to be described in rather vague terms such as 'harsh' or 'loud'. Laver 1980, however, has provided an excellent framework for description, on which Wells (1982:92ff.) bases his claims that a high and wide pitch range is associated with AAVE, whereas a Texan tends to have a low pitch range and a Scottish Highlands accent is characterized by generally low volume.

A pioneering sociophonetic study identified a specifically working-class Glaswegian voice quality but also found that it is justified to talk about a special 'Glasgow voice', since all the speakers in the investigation shared a particular constellation of articulatory settings (Stuart-Smith 1999:215).

3.2.3 Grammar

This section, which deals with morphology and syntax, the two main domains of grammar, is – for various reasons – considerably shorter and less detailed than the previous one. For one thing, we find that students are generally more familiar with the relevant terminology, and our treatment of grammar is quite straightforward and traditional (following Quirk *et al.* 1985).

More importantly, morphological and syntactic variation – at least among standard varieties of English – is not as striking as phonological, nor has it been as thoroughly studied and described. After presenting their typology of English accents (cf. 3.2.2), Trudgill and Hannah (1994:6) write:

> Lexically and grammatically, the split between the 'English' and 'American' types is somewhat neater, with USEng and CanEng being opposed on most counts to the rest of the English-speaking world.

As the following section in this chapter will indicate and the accounts of 'inner-circle' varieties in Chapter 4 will further corroborate, this is indeed very true as regards the lexicon. Considering morphology and syntax, Trudgill and Hannah are also right, yet the differences are few and can often be described as tendencies rather than absolute distinctions. In addition, English English is presently undergoing certain changes that may be attributed to the influence of American English: the use of *hopefully* as a sentence adverbial (*Hopefully, you will find this chapter useful*), the use of *do*-support in constructions such as *Do you have any money?*, *Did they use to do that?* and the increasing use of 'bare' infinitival complements after *help*, as in *My mum used to help cook the meals for the children* instead of *help **to** cook* (cf. Cramley 2001:79). On the other hand, according to Trudgill (1998b:32) there is also some indication that grammatical innovations may be spreading from Britain to the USA, e.g. the use of *do* in sentences such as *I don't know if I'm going to the party tonight, but I might do.*

There exists as yet no neat, comprehensive typology of grammatical variation in world Englishes. However, attempts have been made at describing worldwide variation in certain salient features such as tag questions (Crystal 1995:299), which may be *variant* as in *You didn't see him, did you?* or *invariant* as in *You didn't see him, is it?* (cf. Cramley 2001:161ff. and 5.2.3 in this book). Other syntactic and morphological features that are clearly variable and would lend themselves particularly well to typological descriptions are:

- concord with collective nouns
  (e.g. *the government/audience is/are*: the plural is used much less frequently in American English than in English English; Australian English has a pattern of its own, etc.).
- tense and aspect
  (the past and perfect tenses are, for example, used differently, as in American English *Did you call her yet?* corresponding to English English *Have you called her yet?* (cf. also the Irish English example quoted in 3.1.2); in a number of varieties around the world the progressive form is used with stative verbs, as in Irish English *This is belonging to me*).
- the use of auxiliaries
  (variation in the use of *shall* and *should* with first-person subjects, the development of new auxiliaries such as *gotta* in certain varieties; cf. also the changing use of *do*-support described above).
- pronominal usage
  (there are, for example, two distinct second-person pronouns in some varieties of English, signalling different degrees of formality such as sg. *you* vs pl. *yous(e)* in Irish English, also found in some American and Australian English (again, consider the example quoted in 3.1.2)).
- irregular verb forms
  (e.g. the well-known 'American' past tenses *dove* (instead of *dived*) and *snuck* (instead of *sneaked*); in non-standard varieties, variation is particularly striking).

3.2.4 Lexis

3.2.4.1 Processes of lexical differentiation
All varieties of English share the overwhelming majority of their abstract and generalized vocabulary, because it derives from a common body of knowledge and a

common set of texts. We will use the term General English for words which are non-local in this way. However, it is common experience that the names of some everyday things vary across varieties of English. What the Americans call a *closet* the British call a *cupboard* or *wardrobe*, and the Indians an *almirah*. This variation is usually accommodated in the notion of Standard English – that is Standard English has US, British, Indian, etc. variants with some different lexis.

One source of different lexis in present-day varieties is *separate inheritance*. Two variants may have existed in the norm at the time when the varieties separated and the two varieties may have happened to adopt different ones as the unmarked word. This is said to be the origin of the contrast between British *autumn* and US *fall*, for example. Similarly, both *railroad* and *railway, sidewalk* and *pavement* were in use in Britain in the nineteenth century and *railroad* and *sidewalk* have happened to become the norm in the USA as against *railway* and *pavement* in Britain.

The second source of difference in lexis is *word-formation* (coining) in one or both varieties. There are many different word-formation processes. Perhaps the most common is the simple application of an old word to a new concept. Thus North Americans use the word *robin* to refer to a different bird from the one called *robin* in Britain, and a *hawker* in Singapore and Malaysia is someone who keeps a stall in the market, while a British *hawker* goes from door to door selling his or her wares (5.2.4). A particular variant of this is *conversion*: shift of word class with retention of meaning, as in West African *to off* – 'to switch off'.

A new word may be formed by *compounding* or giving a specialized meaning to a combination of English words. In the US the compound *washcloth* corresponds to the British forms *face flannel,* or just *flannel.* West Africans have produced the combination *chewing stick* for the stick with a chewed end that is used for toothcleaning.

Another intralingual process is *derivation*, where a new word is created by adding affixes to an old one. When cars acquired noise-reduction devices the suffix *-er* was used in Britain to create *silencer* and in the US to create *muffler.* In West Africa a chief sits on a stool just as a king sits on a throne, so the words *destool* and *enstoolment,* have been derived by analogy with *dethrone, enthronement.* In Australian English, the suffixes *-ie* and *-o* are particularly productive (*roughie* for 'outsider in a horse race', *arvo* 'afternoon', *smoko* 'a break for smoking').

The third main source of lexical difference is *borrowing*. Meeting the new vegetable *cucurbita ovifera*, the British gave the word *marrow* a new meaning, while the early US settlers, meeting the related *cucurbita pepo,* borrowed Narragansett Indian *asquutasquash* and shortened it to *squash.* Borrowing has been a common way of dealing with new phenomena in newly settled areas – *koala* bear, *billabong* in Australia – and of referring to local institutions where English is a second language – *Dalit* 'caste name', *namaskar* 'type of prayer' in India.

There are various degrees of borrowing: *squash* exemplifies radical reforming to suit the borrowing language, whereas the borrowings for 'small/young *cucurbita ovifera* fruit' – British *courgette* from French and US *zucchini* from Italian – retain more of their source-language form. Borrowed forms are often combined with native ones to make hybrids like Indian English *generator-wallah* 'man who supplies generators'.[1] The elements of source language compounds or idioms can be translated literally to produce a *loan-translation* or calque like West African *long legs* 'influence in high places'.

Variety difference often results from a combination of these processes: US English has coined the compound *eggplant* for the vegetable, but British English has borrowed the word *aubergine* and Indian and South African English have borrowed *brinjal.*

3.2.4.2 Types of lexical difference and similarity

Following Deverson (2000:33), we can use two dimensions to classify variation in lexis: variation of form and variation of meaning. In terms of form, we can distinguish forms which are unique to a particular variety (such as IndE *dalit* 'untouchable'*)* from those which occur in other varieties (such as *muffler,* which occurs in both British and American (perhaps old-fashioned) English meaning 'scarf' and in US English meaning 'car silencer'). In terms of meaning we can distinguish between meanings which are unique to a particular culture or area, and those which are lexicalized in several or all varieties. We can subdivide the unique meanings into those which are inherently local, referring to an aspect of local culture, fauna, etc., that is unique, and those which are local lexicalizations of concepts which could arise anywhere. We can also subdivide the forms that occur in other varieties by whether they only have their characteristic local meaning, or whether the local meaning co-exists with a more widespread one.

As Table 3.2 shows, this gives us nine possible categories. Cells 1 and 2 contain *localisms*, that is, words whose form and meaning are both unique to a particular variety. Cell 3 contains *heteronyms* (Figure 3.1), that is, local words for generally available concepts (Görlach 1995a). Cells 4, 5, 7, and 8 contain *tautonyms* (Figure 3.2), that is, words which have the same form but different meanings in different varieties. Finally cells 6 and 9 contain words which are simultaneously heteronyms

Table 3.2. Types of lexical variation

		Exclusively local meaning		Meaning shared with other varieties
		Exclusively local referent: foreignism	Local lexicalization	
Exclusively local form		1 Localism	2 Localism	3 Heteronym
Form shared with other varieties	Both local and general meaning in this variety	4 Partial tautonym	5 Partial tautonym	6 Partial tautonym + heteronym
	Only local meaning in this variety	7 Tautonym	8 Tautonym	9 Tautonym + heteronym

1 *Tribune of India* 7 August 2002.

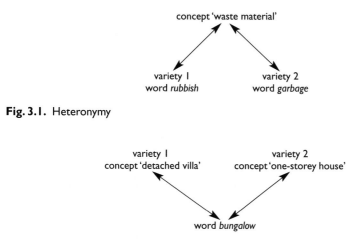

Fig. 3.1. Heteronymy

Fig. 3.2. Tautonomy

and tautonyms, such as *pavement*, which is a tautonym in that it means 'sidewalk' in Britain but 'road surface' in the US, and a heteronym in that British *pavement* and US *sidewalk* mean the same thing.

Starting with the exclusively local forms, in cell 1 we have *foreignisms* (Figure 3.3): the names of institutions, natural organisms, artefacts, etc., which are unique to the culture in question. These are often on a cline from words borrowed from a particular local language and only comprehensible to speakers of that language, via genuinely English words for local referents which are genuinely only known to locals, to General English terms for referents which do not occur everywhere.

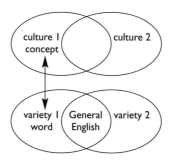

Fig. 3.3. Foreignism

Thus *interdining* 'eating with members of a different caste' is probably only known to speakers of Indian English and presupposes Indian culture (rules for caste behaviour). *Aga saga* 'middlebrow novel about middle-class English rural life' is probably only known to speakers of British English and presupposes British culture (the type of people who have an Aga-brand cooker).

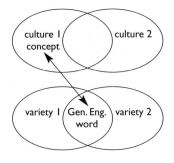

Fig. 3.4. General English word for a local item

In describing local vocabulary, however, attention needs to be paid to another type of relationship between variety and culture. If the referent is widespread or becomes well known, the foreignism becomes simply the General English name for a non-universal item or concept (Figure 3.4 above), like *home run* (baseball term), *wicket* (cricket term), *rambutan* (tropical fruit), *obeche* (tropical hardwood), *sarong* (South East Asian garment), or *sharia* (Islamic law). In fact General English often has names for phenomena and institutions outside the geographical regions and cultural domains where being monolingual in English is the norm. Thus the English of anthropology includes terms like *bride price* (gifts are given to the bride's family on marriage, rather than the groom's, as with a traditional European or Indian *dowry*). Several writers on different African Englishes cite *bride price* as a foreignism, but it would be more appropriate to regard it as a General English term with an extended stylistic range due to the local culture.

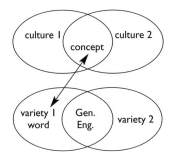

Fig. 3.5. Local lexicalization of generally available concept

In cell 2 of Table 3.2 (Figure 3.5 above) there are cases where the unique local word represents a concept which could exist in any variety but has not been lexicalized in all: British (etc.) *fortnight* 'two weeks', *stone* '14 pounds, as a measure of weight', Indian *crore* 'ten million, mainly for money sums', Yorkshire *lake* 'play as a leisure time activity (as opposed to *play* as in *play a game*)'.

In cell 3 we have one type of heteronym (Figure 3.1). For example, the concept 'flea' is represented by *flea* in General English but by *lop* in traditional Yorkshire speech. Similar heteronyms differentiate dialects in the USA: what is a *paper sack* in some places is a *paper bag* in others. The heteronyms that differentiate varieties worldwide are mostly fairly new. Many refer to physical objects, particularly those that have come into prominence in the last two centuries (British *drawing pin* = US *thumb tack).* As British and other terms are replaced by their American equivalents (older British *wireless* has been replaced by *radio,* for example), the number of heteronyms tends to diminish. New technology does not throw up heteronyms to the same extent as railways, roads, motor cars, etc., did. However, US *cellphone* and *urban legend* vs British *mobile phone* and *urban myth* are exceptions to this rule.

In cell 4 we have partial tautonyms (Figure 3.2), where one meaning of a form is shared among varieties while another is exclusively local. Deverson (2000) cites New Zealand *elder* as an example, where the word refers both to the plant it refers to in General English, and to a different local one. In cell 5 there are partial tautonyms where the local meaning could be used anywhere, like *backbencher* which in General English means 'member of the legislature outside the government', but in Indian English only also means 'lazy/uncommitted student', a concept for which (we are arguing) there is, by chance, no lexicalization in other standard varieties. In cell 6 there are partial tautonyms which are also heteronyms. For example *darning needle* is said to refer not only to a type of needle, as in General English but also to a dragon-fly in some US varieties, and conversely the concept 'dragon fly' is related to the forms *dragon fly* and *darning needle* in different varieties. Similarly New Zealand *mob* refers both (as in General English) to a mob of people and (uniquely in New Zealand) to a flock of sheep. Conversely the concept 'flock' is related to the forms *mob* and *flock.*

In cell 7 there are full tautonyms, which unambiguously refer to different (local) things in different varieties. These are not particularly common, and the examples seem to be mostly transfers of species names. An example is North American *robin,* which refers only to a local species, but is tautonymous with British *robin* referring to a different species. Cell 8 may be empty.

Cell 9, on the other hand, represents a frequent situation. It is illustrated not only by *pavement* above but also by *potato chip* which is tautonomous in that it refers to 'crisps' in the USA but 'french fries' in Britain, and heteronymous as part of the set US *potato chip* = Brit *crisp* = older Indian *wafer.*

Görlach (1995a) points out that when a variety adopts a heteronym from another it can replace the original form (as *radio* has basically replaced *wireless*), it can become a synonym within the new variety (as *garbage* and *rubbish* seem to have done in many varieties) or the two words can become specialized. British English has adopted formerly US *can* for drinks (*a can of beer/coke)* and metaphorical uses (*canned music)* but kept *tin* for other products (*a tin of beans/meat).*

3.2.5 Pragmatics

Pragmatics is concerned with language in use: how we use language in particular circumstances to achieve particular ends. It is concerned with appropriacy rather than correctness. Some aspects of pragmatic difference are linguistic, in that a different form is used for a similar purpose across varieties.

Thus it is a common feature of many varieties of English that terms of endearment are used to establish solidarity between strangers in certain circumstances. Assistants in small shops often address customers as *dear* or an equivalent. But there are strict pragmatic rules for who can address who in these terms and varieties differ in the terms used. In Britain terms of endearment can be used from men to women, and vice versa, and among women. In London *love*, *dear*, and *darling* are heard, all over the North *love,* in Newcastle *pet* and *dear,* and in Devon one can hear *my lover.* In small towns in the USA one might hear *honey* and in Louisiana *cher.*

However, pragmatic differences are cultural or social as well as linguistic. From a male taxi-driver to a male customer in Britain *mate* would establish solidarity, and *sir, guv,* or *squire* would establish social distance with varying degrees of respect. In Australia *mate* might be the only possibility. In the USA *man* might be equivalent to *mate* and *sir* might be similar in implication to its British equivalent, but there would be no equivalent to *squire*. Different societies call for different systems of address, different types of politeness, and provide different occasions when it is necessary to say something.

3.2.6 A note on the linguistic variable

It goes without saying that our descriptions of individual varieties of English given in the two following chapters will not cover complete grammars or sound systems, let alone vocabularies. For one thing, our scope is limited, but more importantly, it would make the presentation very repetitious and tedious. It follows that we have tried to focus on characteristic features, highlighting the differences between the main varieties, but also social/regional variation within these varieties.

The term *linguistic variable*, which was originally developed by William Labov (1972) in his pioneering sociolinguistic studies, refers to a feature in which variation has been observed to occur, where that variation can be related to social variables or to other linguistic variables. The feature could be taken from any of the five categories described in this section, but so far most studies have been devoted to phonology and grammar.

Some well-known examples of socially/regionally significant linguistic variables – at least in part of the English-speaking world – are rhoticity, present-tense verb endings, and the realization of *-ing*.

3.3 VARIATION IN HISTORICAL ORIGIN

A linguistic-history criterion for classifying varieties would look at where their characteristic features come from historically. Although these distinctions are controversial, some writers would suggest three categories:

autonomous varieties, whose features are due to developments inside the variety. Thus rhotic and nonrhotic varieties differ because an innovation starting in London in the seventeenth century – loss of preconsonantal /r/ – has spread to some but not all other dialects. When cars were introduced the Americans chose to call the part that controls noise the *muffler*; the British called it the *silencer*.

substratum varieties, some of whose features can be attributed to another language which the population spoke or still speaks. As we will see in Chapters 4 and 5, some grammatical features of Irish English and phonological ones of Indian English are due to Irish and Hindi respectively (even though most speakers of Irish English are native speakers of English). Of course there are autonomous features in these varieties as well: what the Americans call a *ballpoint* (and some British people a *biro*) is what some Indians call a *jotter*. If we chose to recognize Swedish English or Japanese English we would expect virtually all their distinguishing features to be due to the mother-tongue substratum.

postcreole varieties, which are descended from pidgins and retain vocabulary and morphology or syntax from that stage. Pidgins are limited languages used for trade between people with different mother tongues; creoles are traditionally regarded as pidgins which have been extended to full languages usable for all purposes, often as a result of their becoming the native language of a generation of children. English-based pidgins and creoles are usually too remote from English to be considered varieties of the language, but where a creole has been in contact with English, as in Jamaica, Trinidad or, especially, Barbados, it has often become decreolized and can be described as a postcreole variety, that is, a variety which retains creole features but is now clearly a variety of English.

These distinctions have been criticized (Mufwene 2001) because they make the differences between the types of variety sound too great. Actually, it is argued, all varieties are recreated by children from the pool of features available to them in each generation. This means that 'autonomous' American or Australian varieties arose because children selected from a pool of features created by their parents' generation, coming from a mixture of British varieties and from some non-native speakers (indigenous locals and immigrants from other countries). Substratum varieties arise in exactly the same way but from a pool that contains a large number of features coming from non-native speakers of English with a particular mother tongue, and creoles arise from a pool that includes many pidgin features along with others deriving from nonstandard British varieties and from non-native varieties.

3.4 DIMENSIONS OF CLASSIFICATION

We have shown above that we can group samples of language by linguistic characteristics: spelling, pronunciation, grammar, lexis, and pragmatics. The groups of samples with similar features in these areas would represent varieties like Afro-American Vernacular English (AAVE), Australian, Indian, Jamaican Creole, Nigerian, Singapore, RP + Southern British, Northern US.

These varieties differ in a number of ways other than their linguistic or code features, and this section looks at ways of classifying varieties, their speakers, or the countries in which they are used (Gupta 1997). The terminology in the area is confused, and we will try to produce a clear set of terms for our own use and at the same time point out other possible uses of the category-labels.

3.4.1 Ideological frameworks of discussion, by political stance

We start with a grossly over-simplified *political classification of the ideological stances* one can have towards the phenomenon of the globalization of English. Given that everyone agrees that there are many varieties of English in the world, some associated with powerful nations and social groups, and others with less powerful ones, we could distinguish between three broad ideologies:

conservative: people in this group (Quirk 1990, Honey 1997) emphasize that it is valuable for members of less powerful groups to gain respect and credibility by assimilating to more powerful groups' language practices.

liberal: people in this group (Crystal 1997a, Kachru 1983, MacArthur 1998) emphasize that all varieties are linguistically equal and deserve equal recognition.

radical: people in this group (Phillipson 1992, Pennycook 1994, Tollefson 1992) emphasize the inequalities among groups who use different languages and the tendency of English to exacerbate some of these inequalities.

Our assumption here is that the three ideologies are essentially different interpretations of the same facts. The conservatives consider the best course of action for individuals given the present balance of power, the liberals strive to ensure 'equal opportunities' within the present system of widespread use of English, and the radicals seek to alter the balance of power by government policy.

3.4.2 Varieties, by standardization

We can now try to group these linguistically-defined varieties in informative ways. First of all, we attempt to define more closely what we mean by terms like 'norm' and 'standard'. We try to provide coherent definitions of terms in Global English studies, making clear *what is being classified*: a language variety, a country, or a speaker for example, and *what criteria are used* for the classification: sociolinguistic, linguistic, psycholinguistic, etc. The reader will see that the same cake can be cut up many different ways for different purposes.

3.4.2.1 Norm

We suppose that any community which uses a variety of English has a linguistic norm for its use. That is, we use the term *norm* for the implicit set of rules speakers appear to use for what it is appropriate to say in what grammatical or social context. When we say that Northern Irish English tends to use the base form of the verb with *they* as subject but the *-s* form with plural nouns (*the girls does that, they do that* (Milroy and

Milroy 1985)) we are describing the norm for Northern Irish English. In terms of the norm of the relevant Northern Ireland community, *the girls does that* is correct and unmarked, and *the girls do that* would be the mark of an outsider (D'Souza 1998).

In practice we will expect the type of agreement we find in an individual Northern Irish speaker to vary both because of the influence of the standard norm, and because speakers do not always conform to the norm. That is, individuals may only intend to follow the standard norm in some situations, for some people, or for some of the time, and even so they may not always manage what they intend (3.4.3).

Linguistically the norm thus represents the variety typical of most of the given community in a given situation most of the time. Sociolinguistically it is the variety that signals membership of the group in question in a given situation. The term *norm*, as we shall use it, implies nothing in terms of acceptance by schools, publishers, or social elites.

3.4.2.2 Standards and Standard English

As we have noted above, varieties are often classified by the *sociolinguistic criterion of relation to Standard English*. As we described in Chapter 1, during the eighteenth and nineteenth centuries publishers and educationalists defined a set of grammatical and lexical features which they regarded as correct, and the variety characterized by these features later came to be known as *Standard English*. Since English had, by the nineteenth century, two centres, Standard English came to exist in two varieties: British and US. These were widely different in pronunciation, very close in grammar, and characterized by small but noticeable differences in spelling and vocabulary. There were thus two more or less equally valid varieties of Standard English – British Standard and US Standard.

Subsequently there has been a demand for other local standards – Australian, Indian, South African, Nigerian, Jamaican, etc. This has been accommodated by saying that varieties that vary from one another and from British/US Standard English in the way that British and US vary from each other can be counted as standard English, while varieties that vary more are nonstandard (Trudgill and Hannah 1994, 1–4) . According to this definition Standard English is a dialect, not an accent, and no particular accent is (in theory) attached to it. A variety of Standard English can have almost any accent, but can only have a very small range of grammatical difference from others. Norfolk dialect or AAVE, which say *I do, he do,* are 'non-standard' (but mainly spoken by natives), while Indian Standard or Nigerian Standard, which say *I do, he does* are 'standard' even though they may not have the 'typically English' /θ/ and /ð/ sounds (and are mainly spoken by non-natives).

Three implications are worth emphasizing. First, there is no such thing (at present) as a Standard English which is not British or American or Australian, etc. There is no International Standard (yet), in the sense that publishers cannot currently aim at a standard which is not locally bound. Second, the implication of Trudgill's distinction is that one can very well speak some variety of Standard English with a Chinese or Spanish accent. Third, Standard English is only defined by the elite publishers and journalists. It has no official status, and so can change and there can be disagreement about what is now standard and what is not (yet).

We shall use 'Standard' to refer to a norm which is linguistically within Trudgill's definition. In a given territory there may therefore be several local norms, not all of which are Standard varieties. Some writers call all these norms 'standards' (with a small 's') but we will not do so.

If speakers in a country look to one of the norms in their own society as standard, we can call them *endonormative*. If they look to a norm outside their own country we can call them *exonormative*. If Nigerians start to appeal to a Nigerian standard rather than a British one, they become more endonormative. In the seventeenth century Scottish people started to look to London rather than Edinburgh for 'correct language' and thus became more exonormative (4.3.2.2).

3.4.2.3 Codification and use in writing

There are at least four stages in language standardization: *selection* of language conventions, their *acceptance* by an influential group, their *diffusion*, and their *maintenance* by some authoritative institutions. In the first stage, one norm is *selected* by some powerful group from the various norms existing in a particular area, typically a state. This is based on the prestige of the norm rather than any linguistic feature – standard varieties are usually based on the norm of the capital, the educated classes, the dominant ethnicity, etc. For example, as what was later to be called Standard English started to emerge, initially as a norm for writing, in the fifteenth and sixteenth centuries it was based on the language of the court in London, the London publishers, the social and educational elite at Oxford and Cambridge, etc. As the rules are being formulated, *acceptance* for them must be sought from influential groups like religious authorities, civil servants, publishers, teachers, the social elite, and in the seventeenth century particularly the royal court. Once they are accepted they are *diffused* and *maintained* by agencies like the church, schools, and publishing houses. Diffusion is typically accompanied by *elaboration of form and function*; for example, at the same time as Standard English was developing it took over a great deal of Latin and Greek vocabulary that allowed it to fulfil functions in science, theology, and philosophy previously performed by Latin.

At a fairly late stage in the standardization process *codification* becomes possible and seen as desirable. In the course of the eighteenth century English grammar books and dictionaries started to be produced defining what they called 'correct' usage for both speech and writing. Once the standard norm is codified, *prescription* becomes possible. 'Correct' can now mean 'according to an abstract principle of correctness' rather than 'conforming to an observed norm'. One such principle might be that one should pronounce words according to their (now standardized) spelling and speak according to the written standard. This meant that the books recommended pronouncing words like *hunting* with /ɪŋ/ according to their spelling rather than /ɪn/ and saying *isn't* rather than *ain't* even though most people of all classes said /ɪn/ and *ain't*. At some point in the process it becomes possible to condemn people for not following the rules, and social discrimination on a linguistic basis becomes possible.

Many varieties are little used in writing and there are no prescriptive rules for correct grammar, spelling, or vocabulary: correct usage, the norm, is just what people say. Other varieties, like Caribbean Standard English, Indian Standard English, or Nigerian Standard English are at a fairly early stage of standardization where some selection has taken place and the selected norm is accepted in some quarters, but not yet generally. As Banjo (1993) shows, Nigerian writers have to rely on their intuitions about what educated Nigerians would or would not say. There is a dictionary of Indian English (Nihalani, Tongue, and Hosali 1979) but its authors state specifically that their list is descriptive, not prescriptive, and they may include usages which are not Indian Standard. Görlach (1995b) shows that provincial Indian newspapers in English include much Indian English grammar which seems to fall outside the definition of the standard based on British and American publishers' practice. It is possible that the definition of standard needs rewriting to allow more grammatical variation, but the point is that at present it is impossible to say whether a particular usage is part of Indian Standard or not. By contrast, in the codified standards (3.1.2), a writer can check, in authoritative and accepted reference material, whether usages are accepted or not. Although *ain't* is widespread in spoken usage, it is clearly excluded from Standard English, for example. This codification is not complete, universally accepted or rigid, but it is considerably more complete than that for other norms.

Standard English, as defined by Trudgill, allows any pronunciation, and prescriptions on pronunciation are not widely enforced nowadays. However, it is worth noting that the British prestige accent called RP (for Received Pronunciation) is extremely well codified (for foreign-language teaching purposes, among others), and was at one time prescribed for broadcasting and diffused by elocution teachers, as described in Tony Harrison's poem *Them and [ʊz]* (Harrison 1986). The trend over the last 40 years has been to reduce or abandon attempts to standardize English English pronunciation.

3.4.2.4 Varieties, by type of prestige

Another sociolinguistic criterion for classifying varieties would be the type of prestige the variety gives its speakers. Here we would need to distinguish between *overt* and *covert* prestige (Labov 1972). Some varieties might give no prestige of any kind, for example perhaps dying traditional rural dialects. Others might be stigmatized and called 'ugly' or 'low-class' but actually give covert status (make their speakers appear warm, 'cool', humorous, masculine, or tough). Examples might be Cockney, Afro-American Vernacular English, or Jamaican Creole. Third there are standard or near-standard varieties which seem to give both overt and a kind of covert prestige. These are varieties like Educated Scots, Standard Singapore English, Nigerian Standard English. In their own areas they give their users overt prestige (make them sound educated, powerful, cultured, polite, etc.), but at the same time they express loyalty to or solidarity with their own community. Scots, Singaporeans, or Nigerians do not want to sound like Englishmen or Americans. Finally there are varieties which give overt prestige worldwide – principally US Standard with a General American accent and British Standard with an RP accent. Because speakers may not wish to identify entirely with one group we will find mixed varieties – particularly in the area of accent, with some pronunciations signalling membership of one group and some of another.

In many societies (Jamaica, Singapore, for example) there is a continuum of speech forms from a local standard, used by educated people on formal occasions, through a range of intermediate forms, to a very nonstandard variety used by uneducated people in informal situations. The terms *acrolect, mesolect,* and *basilect* can be used for the 'high', 'middle', and 'low' ranges of the continuum in these circumstances. It is often the case that the more informal the situation the more basilectal the speech, so one person may speak mesolect at home and acrolect at work, and another may speak basilect at home and mesolect to the boss.

To sum this section up, we can say that a variety is defined by characteristics of its phonology, morphology, syntax, lexis, semantics, and (perhaps) pragmatics. Some varieties have covert prestige and some overt. Varieties which share most features of morphology, syntax, and lexis with the varieties used by British and American publishers can be called standard (and they typically have overt prestige). Some standard varieties are codified, that is there are accepted grammars and dictionaries which define them and create a (fairly) clear boundary between standard and nonstandard usage. Other standard varieties are less codified, so that it is more difficult to produce standardized texts in these varieties.

We can relate this section to the ideologies in the following way. Conservatives will tend to emphasize the importance of knowing and using one of the codified standards. Liberals will emphasize that every variety is of equal communicative efficiency and that the important thing is to use a variety appropriate to the situation and the people one is talking to. Radicals may argue that the institution of a standard language creates inequalities, disadvantages those who cannot use it, and thus increases the concentration of power in the hands of the already powerful.

3.4.3 Texts, by degree of standardization

Standardization normally is the process of developing a norm into a standard language. But it is worth noticing that many of the texts we encounter, at least in print, have gone through a process of standardization – editing.

Informal conversation is not and should not be edited, but when we hear unedited formal spoken language, we quite often notice lapses. For example, an (Irish) aircraft cabin crew member has been heard to announce *your cooperation with these measures **are** essential if we are to prevent the spread of foot-and-mouth disease.* We can assume that the target here was standard agreement, and the failure to hit it was not a result of a different norm, but a 'lapse' of some kind.

We meet lapses less often in writing, because books have mostly been edited by publishers' editors, newspaper articles have been checked by subeditors, and in the past letters and circulars had been typed by secretaries. They have undergone a standardization process which makes the texts conform to a set of prescriptions: the publisher's or newspaper's house style rules backed by the editor's intuition. The effect is to eliminate from our reading most signs of the variability of writers' codes. This variability may come from other norms – usages associated with regional dialect for example – or from changes in the norm of the standard not yet recognized by the prescriptions, or from lapses. Lapses are often to be seen in unedited notices, (cf. also Krishnaswamy and Burde 1998:75) but the ease of electronic publication means that more unedited written text is becoming publicly available. For example, this is an e-mail circular issued by a British university's internal security staff:

> **Dear all**
> All depts please be aware of sneak thiefs / sus characters, now is the time with lots of student activity about that these people are likely to strike, they obviously blend in well, but do act differently. Reports of suspicious youths in student health, description although vague are as follows: – 2 persons (youths) both 17ish spotty, casual appearance, base ball caps, puffa jackets, trainers, short dark hair one, has curly hair with a possible broken tooth These guys were seen off by vigilant staff so please be aware.

The availablility of e-mail means that the notice has been written out and published in five minutes, instead of going through a process of typing by a professional secretary, duplicating on paper, addressing, etc. A by-product of this technical progress is that the message now emerges as first conceived, without editing to eliminate failures of punctuation, agreement (*description . . . are* presumably influenced by *reports*), and even morphology (*thiefs*). There is also some mixture of style (*these guys were seen off by vigilant staff, so please be aware*). The last sentence also shows that the logical connections are of a spoken type.

Such texts are interesting because they show that the standard is artificial in its regularity. The text-standardization process eliminates most lapses from our reading, making the standard language a more predictable and transparent vehicle of meaning. We should never have let edited language create the illusion that a uniform and well-regulated language code is normal and natural, but this illusion is likely to be less easy to maintain in the future as electronic media tend to destandardize English and other languages.

Hence in discussing varieties we have to pay attention to the type of text we are dealing with, the extent to which it has been standardized, and the particular prescriptions that have been applied.

Our three caricatures of language ideologies will interpret the text standardization process as follows: the conservatives will welcome it as eliminating errors and illogicalities; the liberals will emphasize that the standardized texts are no 'better' than the unstandardized ones, but recognize the appropriacy of standardized texts in many functions; the radicals will emphasize the power that the process gives to those who have internalized the forms of the standard, probably as a result of elitist education.

3.4.4 Countries

3.4.4.1 Countries, by domains of English use

We can classify countries by *domains of English use*, following (and adapting) a well-known three-circle model developed by Kachru (1985). Those in which virtually all public and private interaction takes place in English for a majority of the population are what Kachru (1985) calls *inner-circle* countries: Australia, Canada, the USA, the UK, Barbados, etc.[2] These countries were either settled predominantly by English-speaking people or settled in such a way that English-speaking people provided a linguistic model, as described in Chapters 1 and 2. In the process local languages, regarded as uncivilized, were eliminated or marginalized, often along with their speakers.

Many countries were colonized by Britain (or the USA) without massive settlement or the accompanying destruction of languages and peoples. At decolonization English was often retained, for reasons discussed in Chapter 5. The result has been countries where English co-exists with other languages. Those countries in which private inter-action typically does not take place in English for the majority, but public interactions in fields like the law, secondary education, national politics, and business often use English belong in Kachru's *outer circle*: India, Nigeria, Singapore, and many other ex-colonial countries. This situation, where one language is used for 'high' functions and another or others for 'low' ones, can be called *diglossia*. Notice that the definition used here makes South Africa clearly an outer-circle country, since less than 10 per cent of the population uses English for all purposes, and Canada an inner-circle one, since a majority (about two-thirds) of the inhabitants do so.

In the majority of other countries in the world English is an important school subject and increasingly used for international communication, particularly in science and business (Chapter 6). These countries, in which English is taught as a school subject and used predominantly for interaction with foreigners, are put in the *expanding circle* by Kachru. But the category covers a wide range from countries like the Scandinavian ones, where English is an everyday presence in the media and even on the street, to Russia and Japan, where actual use of spoken English is a remote and obviously 'foreign' phenomenon.[3,4]

2 Görlach (1991) points out that there is a subset of the inner circle in which much private interaction takes place in one particular variety which is very different from Standard English. Thus in Jamaica and Scotland Standard English may be a second dialect learnt at school by people who use Creole or Scots as their home language.

3 Most countries outside the inner and outer circles probably fall into this category. Though one can imagine that countries which belong to the outer circles for Russian and French (such as Kazakhstan or the Congo) tend to use those languages for international communication, there seems to be increasing interest in learning English even there.

4 An interesting expanding-circle subgroup is the countries where a minority group speaks a low-status variety of English, like the English creole speakers in Honduras and Nicaragua. Here we have non-standard varieties which are not in contact with a standard variety in schools, etc. English is the low member of a diglossia with Spanish.

The definition we have given here takes no account of the legal status of the language as official or otherwise, since it appears that there are countries like Kenya where English plays most of the roles typical of the outer circle without being official, and ones like Rwanda where the official status of English does not indicate widespread public use (outside sections of the elite).

There are expanding-circle countries (Sweden, Denmark, the Netherlands, the Flanders region of Belgium) where English is increasingly being used in tertiary, and even secondary, education, in business, and in the media. In some of these countries it is common for companies to nominate English as 'company language', so that a proportion of written internal communication among, for example, Swedes in the Volvo company takes place in English. One can imagine that these communities might develop towards outer-circle status, but none are close yet.

3.4.4.2 Countries, by proportion of efficient speakers of some variety of English
The domains in which English is used are not directly related to the proportion of people who are proficient in English. Kachru's model says nothing about the amount of individual bilingualism in the countries classified. We could try to classify countries by a demographic criterion: the *proportion of speakers with the ability to speak on a range of topics in some variety of English* in the population. No reliable or comparable figures could be obtained for such a vague criterion, but it is clear that such a classification would not parallel the three-circle one. In outer-circle India, for example, it is said that only five per cent of the population is proficient in English, while in some expanding-circle countries, such as the Netherlands and the Scandinavian countries much higher proportions of the population – up to 60 or 70 per cent – may have a comparable level of proficiency (Preisler 1999a,b). In fact, since levels of literacy and completed primary education are low in some outer-circle countries one could speculate that there are many rich expanding-circle countries where knowledge of English is more widespread than in some poor outer-circle countries.

3.4.4.3 Summary
This section thus shows that countries can be divided according to the functions or domains of English within them, but the categories 'outer circle' and 'expanding circle' do not correlate with the proportions of the population who can use English, or with the status of the language as official or unofficial.

It can be connected to the previous sections in the following way: the prestigious codified standard varieties are associated with inner-circle countries, which are countries in which a large majority of the people can use English, though probably only a minority use a fully standard variety. The uncodified standards are associated with outer-circle countries, in some of which only a small proportion of people have more than very limited proficiency in English, and again a minority of the English speakers use a standard variety. As Krishnaswamy and Burde (1998:13) say of India: 'English is used only by a few, typically in the urban areas of each region, and that too only in certain domains, and hardly ever as the language of intimacy'.

Conservatives will be concerned that the low proportion of speakers of Standard

English in the outer circle threatens intercomprehensibility and correctness. Liberals will emphasize that all these countries are in some sense 'English-speaking' and deserve equal treatment. Radicals will be concerned that the low proportion of speakers of standard English in the outer circle means that power (and education) is concentrated in the hands of a minority elite.

3.4.5 Official language, by political function

Fishman (1968) makes a distinction between an official language which has a *nationalist* function (as a symbol of national identity) and one which has a *nationist* function (as a practical means of communication in administration, for example).[5] Since most countries which use English intranationally do so because they were at one time or another colonies, English can be problematic as a nationalist language. The USA solved this early on by establishing its own variant of Standard English, and some inner-circle countries like Australia are following this route. In other inner-circle territories attempts can be made to maintain a minority language as a nationalist symbol. Ireland is an extreme case where the nationalist language – Irish – is little used and the nationist one – English – is for many a reminder of oppression and loss of identity. Maori in New Zealand and Welsh in Wales are supported as nationalist symbols, but monolingual English speakers in these countries may be nationalistic without identifying with the language.

Many other postcolonial states have the same kind of opposition between symbol and practicality. In multilingual countries like Singapore or Nigeria the choice of English as administrative language has been made for nationist reasons, and local languages may be used to arouse loyalty. In India the nationist solution – English – has survived partly because the local languages Hindi, Tamil, etc., are the focus of rival nationalisms. In all these cases nationalist sentiment encourages the recognition of local norms and local varieties of Standard English, usually alongside maintenance of (or lip-service to) local languages.

To relate this to previous sections we can say that there is a general (more or less acute) political problem of national identity associated with carrying out public functions in a nonlocal language. The conservatives might see this in terms of the inferiority of the local language for 'modern' functions. The liberals might see it as an argument for developing the local languages so that they can take over nationist functions, or for establishing an independent local (codified) variety of English as a focus for nationalism. The radicals might see the survival of English as evidence of betrayal of the nationalist cause by the English-speaking elite, and the recognition of local norms and variants of the standard as a subtle way of making the neocolonial language locally acceptable.

---

5 This could be related to Crystal's distinction (1997a) among the languages in an individual's repertoire between 'languages for identity' – nationalist languages in a sense, and 'languages for intelligibility' – nationist languages in a sense.

3.4.6 Speakers

3.4.6.1 Speakers, by type of proficiency

Speakers of English or any other language can be classified by a *psycholinguistic criterion – the type of proficiency* they have. Language acquisition researchers seem to be confident that a language learnt very early in life is known in a different way from one learnt later on.[6] So we can distinguish first-language speakers who have learnt the language at a young age in the home, from second-language speakers who have encountered it later. This gives us the categories *native speaker* (of a particular variety) and *non-native speaker* (of a particular variety).[7] Note that there are increasing numbers of native speakers of varieties associated with the outer circle, such as Nigerian pidgin (Schaefer and Egbokhare 1999) and Singaporean (Gupta and Yeok 1995).

It is often difficult to tell who is to count as a native speaker. Some people have used English as their main language since they were three or four, but did not speak it 'first'. Others speak no language except a strongly nonstandard version mostly spoken by non-natives. Others spoke English to their mothers from infancy but no one else, and did not speak the language at all between the ages of five and 15. The way in which these ambiguities are solved by society reveals that the category 'native speaker' is partly a social construction. The main criterion seems to be accent: an accent associated with a variety mainly used by native speakers (particularly white native speakers) qualifies the speaker as a native. Correspondingly an accent associated with a variety mainly used by non-native speakers (Indian, for example) qualifies one as a non-native, however one acquired it. Nevertheless, regarded as a psycholinguistic category describing someone's personal history, 'native speaker' seems as valid as any other category surrounded by a grey area of hard cases.

3.4.6.2 Speakers, by scope of proficiency

An alternative classification of speakers which emerged in the 1990s (Mufwene 2000, Modiano 1999a,b) uses *a functional criterion – the scope of proficiency.* Here we could distinguish four levels. At the highest the speaker is *internationally effective –* able to use communication strategies and a linguistic variety that is comprehensible to interlocutors from a wide range of national or cultural backgrounds. An American, an Indian, or a Swede who can use English to communicate with Arabs, Singaporeans, or Australians would have a proficiency of this scope. The next level is *nationally effective* proficiency: what a South African would need to communicate with other South Africans with different mother tongues, or an Alabaman would need to talk to a Vermonter. The third level, *local proficiency*, is the proficiency someone needs to deal with people in his or her own area: a working-class Glaswegian or Detroiter talking to

---

6 Thus it has been found in studies of the sign language of the deaf that 'native signers' sign much better than the 'non-native signing' parents from whom they learnt to sign, and in creole studies that a pidgin is transformed by becoming the language of native creole speakers. See also Paradis 1998.

7 We might well also want to distinguish those who have learnt and used the language under some threshold age – say ten or, as Mohanan suggests in Singh *et al.* (1998), five – from those who have not learnt – or not used – English until after that age.

his or her peers. The fourth level – *ineffective* – is the level of the language learner who knows some English but cannot communicate in it.[8]

The functional criterion takes no account of the psycholinguistic one (and vice versa). Thus there is no reason to believe that natives (as here defined)[9] will necessarily be internationally effective communicators: their accent, lexis, or, most likely, communication strategies and cultural presuppositions may make them ineffective. Non-natives may well have developed better communication strategies and a better knowledge of what is culturally specific; on the other hand, given the bias of broadcasting, their accent is more likely to be unfamiliar to their interlocutor. A separate issue is that native speakers may tend to use their linguistic confidence to dominate interactions and thus be effective in a different sense.

The distinction between type and scope is important because in ordinary usage to call someone a non-native speaker of a language implies that he or she is less than fully competent in the language. Thus non-native speakers are condemned to being 'perpetual learners' (Kandiah 1998) whose usage never acquires any authority. For skilled users of well-established standard varieties like Indian English this is a ridiculous affront.

The conservatives may argue that only native competence is true proficiency, and that non-natives speak a less perfect variety of the language. The liberals may argue that all proficient speakers are equal regardless of their personal history and that scope of proficiency is the key criterion. Some radicals will agree in rejecting the 'nativeness' criterion but point out that access to the wider scopes of proficiency is limited to the richer and more powerful in all communities. Other radicals may emphasize the special status of the mother tongue, and the human right to use it in domains like education and politics.

3.4.7 Overview

In this section we have argued that we can only understand variation in English worldwide if we separate the classification of countries, language varieties, speakers' personal histories, and speakers' personal competence from one another. By analogy with other languages, we often bundle together speaker's nationality, the variety spoken in the country of origin, being a native speaker of that variety, and highly proficient use of that variety. We assume that being American, British, or Australian, being a native speaker of English, speaking Standard English, and being highly proficient are interchangeable. But as English becomes an international language we have to take account of all sorts of other possibilities: non-native speakers of Indian

---

8 It will be noted that local proficiency is mainly of use to native speakers and immigrants to English-speaking communities, since non-natives will usually communicate with their peers in their mother tongue.

9 Singh (1998:48) suggests a definition of 'native speaker' which makes it a proficiency category rather than one based on psycholinguistics or personal history: 'one who shares with others in the relevant speech community relatively stable well-formedness judgements on expressions used or usable in the community'.

English who are Indian citizens with internationally effective proficiency, native speakers of Singapore English who are British citizens with internationally effective proficiency, non-native speakers of American English who are American citizens with only nationally effective proficiency, native speakers of British English who are British citizens with only locally effective proficiency, and all other combinations of the four parameters.

4 The inner circle

This chapter deals with mother-tongue Englishes throughout the world, from Standard English English to Jamaican creoles. It is organized along a regional, i.e. country-by-country, and to some extent historical, dimension rather than a typological one. It is true that linguistically, especially with regard to phonology, English English is closer to Australian, New Zealand, and South African English than to Scottish or Irish English. From a cultural and societal point of view, however, the relationships may be rather different; this is why the first sections will deal with varieties in the British Isles. Both the order of presentation and the distribution of pages in this chapter may give the impression that we favour Britain at the expense of the USA. We do of course fully recognize the status of US English as the most influential variety today. This is particularly obvious in our account of the 'expanding circle' and in our discussion of trends and prospects (Chapters 6 and 7).

A country-by-country approach is unproblematic in a case like New Zealand, where a variety of English is used in a well-defined geographical area which is also a political unit, but we are very much aware that this is not always the case. The sections describing varieties in the UK, for example, clearly do not deal with different countries in the sense of 'states' and, on the whole, all these varieties look to Standard English English as the norm for the written language throughout the area. Furthermore, Northern and Southern Irish English are both dealt with in the section on Ireland, which cannot be said to be a political unit; the reason is partly historical but mainly linguistic, considering the Celtic substratum and – disregarding phonology – the close affinity between the varieties. You will also notice that South Africa as a linguistic area is dealt with in more detail in Chapter 5; yet it deserves a section here, too, even if only 10 per cent of the population use English as their first language. South African English is a variety in its own right, with its own codified standard. The Caribbean, too, features inner-circle as well as outer-circle varieties of English; on a great number of the West Indian islands, such as Jamaica, St Kitts and Montserrat, a variety of English is the only existing native language. Finally, we regret that – for lack of space – it has not been possible to include descriptions of a number of smaller English-speaking communities such as the Falkland Islands and Tristan da Cunha.

The sections are introduced by maps providing the necessary background to settlement history and regional variation. Some basic facts on geography and history, with special reference to demography, are provided, followed by an outline of the language situation. We have also tried to think of an appropriate 'motto' for each section which should capture some essential aspect of the language used or an attitude characteristic of a certain regional identity. Sometimes the mottoes reflect popular, folk-linguistic stereotypes, which – like all stereotypes – contain an element of truth but also express interesting attitudes.

The bulk of the presentation is devoted to a descriptive account of linguistic features, in accordance with the principles and terminology laid out in Chapter 3. Each section/variety consequently features a table of the Wells' standard lexical sets (cf. 3.2.2), indicating local realizations – in some cases two or more variants – as compared to at least one of the reference accents (RP and General American). The data included in the tables is mostly taken from Wells (1982); any change and variation is described in some detail in the following text. While it is feasible to give a fairly complete picture of the sound system in this way, this is clearly not the case when it comes to giving a useful, structured account of the lexicon. We have tried to exemplify – although not necessarily spell out – the processes, such as borrowing and derivation, and types, such as heteronomy, of lexical differentiation described in 3.2.4. The passages on spelling (if included) and grammar are comparatively short, since – at least in standard Englishes – the differences are not striking and varieties tend to be converging rather than diverging. Pragmatic characteristics, if any, are often incorporated in the section on grammar.

At the beginning of the linguistic description of most varieties we suggest a 'shortlist' of particularly salient features. The purpose of this is simply to provide some cues or markers for 'variety-spotting'. To take an example: Australian and South African speakers of English share a great many vowel qualities, but are easily distinguished by the vowel in *father*: South Africans have the RP-like back [ɑː], whereas Australians typically use a front [aː]. Inevitably, the salient features are somewhat subjective, but they are largely based on experience from students' perceptions.

A limited selection of works suggested for further reading is given at the end of each section.

The length of the sections varies to some extent. Although they may enjoy a special status, at least from a historical and normative point of view, the reference varieties have not been particularly favoured, partly because they are more familiar and exhaustively treated in general linguistic textbooks, but also because they are not viewed as 'major' or 'better'.

4.1 ENGLAND

... the copiousnesse of our language appeareth in the diversitie of our Dialects, for wee have Court and we have Countrey English, wee have Northerne, and Southerne, grosse and ordinarie, ...

(from *The Excellencie of the English Tongue* by Richard Carew (1555–1620))

Fig. 4.1. The United Kingdom and Ireland

The United Kingdom
Area: 245.000 sq.km
Population: 59.5 million (of which 98 per cent speak English as their first language)
Capital: London

The Republic of Ireland
Area: 70.000 sq.km
Population: 3.8 million (of which about 3.5 million speak English as their first language)
Capital: Dublin

4.1.1 An introductory note

English English (EngE) as a variety sometimes seems, as it were, to be taken for granted; it is not even the declared official language of the UK. It is symptomatic that some descriptions of World Englishes do not include a section on EngE and that the two records brought out by the BBC in the 1970s with the titles *English with a Dialect* and *English with an Accent* do not include samples of RP/Standard EngE (they do include General American).

Here we certainly devote a section to England as a linguistic area, but for various reasons, the character of the presentation will differ somewhat from the other sections. Since Standard EngE and RP constitute well-known norms to which other varieties are compared for reference, it is neither meaningful to highlight salient features nor is it desirable to provide a detailed description of such a standard variety in a book of this kind. A similar approach is adopted in the section on American English (4.5).

Instead, some attention is paid to nonstandard/regional variation in England. There are two reasons for this: first, as pointed out in 3.1.2, this is where we find the most striking regional variation in the English-speaking world and second, as many of the following sections will show, regional varieties of EngE have provided a considerable input in the so-called 'transported Englishes'.

4.1.2 The country and its people

England today is a heavily urbanized country, with well over 90 per cent of the population living in towns. Textbooks in geography generally emphasize the contrast between northern and southern England, not just because of different landscape types but also because of the industrialized north as opposed to the more rural south. This distinction is widely perceived, as demonstrated, for example, in the use of regional accents in television commercials. Studies of attitudes to accents (cf. Wales 2002:61ff.) confirm the picture of northerners as, for example, more reliable, friendly, and down-to-earth ('tell 'em Yorkshire, tell 'em straight'). The north–south distinction is also the best known and most striking with regard to regional variation in language (cf. 4.1.3). 'From a linguistic point of view, the population of England is about equally divided between the north and the south.' (Wells 1982:349).

The early history of England as outlined in Chapter 1 tells us that its population is composed of a variety of peoples, whose languages have all left their stamp on Standard EngE and on the regional dialects. In recent times the structure of England's population has changed through large-scale immigration, especially from the Caribbean and south Asia. The immigrants have mostly settled in urban centres, forming significant communities in the major cities. The writer Caryl Phillips, whose voice can be heard on the accompanying CD, represents this category. He was born on the island of St Kitts in the West Indies and grew up in Leeds, which can be heard from his accent.

Caribbean English varieties known as 'patois' or 'creole' (cf. 4.11), as represented, for example, in the songs written and performed by Linton Kwesi Johnson (*A Cockney Translation*, *Inglan is a bitch*), have had considerable impact on young people's speech and play an important role in marking identity.

In England today, ethnicity is indeed an important factor in the study of linguistic change and variation, as is still social class. Yet many recent studies have identified gender as prior to class and there is also evidence of general changes in social structure and behaviour, resulting in linguistic levelling (cf. Foulkes and Docherty 1999:14f).

4.1.3 Regional variation in language – an overview

The phonology, grammar, and lexicon of traditional dialects in particular, but to some extent also of modern varieties, show that a major division is into dialects north and south of the river Humber. There is a clear historical background to the existence of this boundary (cf. Chapter 1). Early written sources confirm that the speech of northerners was perceived as different in the south:

> All the language of the Northumbrians, and specially at York, is so sharp, piercing, and harsh, and shapeless, that we Southerners can scarcely understand that language.
>
> (A modern version of John Trevisa's translation of *Polychronicon*, 1385)

Although north–south, admittedly with a less rigid boundary line, remains the most significant distinction, further subcategorization is called for. In describing regional variation in England, the medieval text quoted above actually also mentions the speech of the 'men of myddel Engelond', i.e. the Midlands.

In Wells 1982, the description of EngE accents contains four main sections, devoted to RP, London, the south (highlighting East Anglia, the West Country, and Bristol) and the north (highlighting Merseyside and Tyneside). This means that 'the linguistic north' according to Wells also comprises most of the Midlands. Some linguistic differences between speakers representing different dialect areas are presented in 4.1.5.

In reality, dialect areas are seldom fixed and absolutely distinctive or discrete but tend to form a continuum. It is, for example, not easy to establish where 'Yorkshire dialect' turns into 'Lancashire dialect' and varieties can be distinguished *within* 'Yorkshire dialect'. The following transcript of a recording of a sheep farmer from Askrigg in Northern Yorkshire demonstrates that characteristic, regional features may be variable, not only among the speakers of a community, but also in individual speakers. The speaker, who has been asked to describe the art of 'dry stone walling' naturally uses the word *stone* several times. The word is sometimes realized as a typically northern form, /steːn/, but just as often as a more southern variant, /stoːn/.

> Well, first of all, you sort your /steːns/ out, you see
> you level your ground
> and you get your biggest /stoːns/
> your foundation /steːns/
> you've an eye for t' /stoːns/
> it's a gift, is dry stone /stoːn/ walling
> . . .
> you finish off wi' your top /steːns/
> now your top /steːns/ is t' /steːns/ . . .

4.1.4 Standard English English/Received Pronunciation – a 'reference variety'

The emergence and status of Standard EngE was outlined in Chapters 1 and 3. The codification and propagation of this dialect is maintained and updated in major publications such as the *Oxford English Dictionary (OED)* as well as a number of general dictionaries and grammar books written for native and non-native users of English.

The dialect which we call Standard EngE is not necessarily linked to a standard pronunciation; it could just as well be pronounced with a localized Manchester or Norwich accent. It has been estimated that 12 per cent of the population of England are speakers of Standard English; nine per cent speak Standard English with a regional accent (cf., for example Trudgill 2002). In EFL teaching, however, Standard EngE is often still inextricably linked to Received Pronunciation (RP) (cf. Chapter 6).

The concept of Received Pronunciation (where *received* is used in the sense of 'approved', 'accepted') was developed by Daniel Jones (1881–1967), Professor of Phonetics at University College London, the real Professor Higgins. It is worth mentioning that he did not view this accent as 'better' than any other. Rather, its great advantage was, as he saw it, that it was 'widely understood'. Today, the description and codification of RP, which has a southern bias but is a social rather than a regional accent, is above all maintained through the *Longman Pronunciation Dictionary (LPD)* (Wells 2000).

Like all other accents, RP is not static but subject to change, e.g. influenced by features of Cockney, a variety 'often overtly despised, but covertly imitated' (Wells 1994:205). A popular, loosely defined term for a south-eastern, London-influenced accent of this kind is Estuary English. Opinions vary as to its status and character. Trudgill (2001) rejects the idea that it is a new variety. Similarly, Foulkes and Docherty (1999:11) consider it to be a levelled form rather than a unitary, well-defined variety, spreading because the features represent neither the standard nor the extreme nonstandard poles of the RP–Cockney continuum.

A rich documentation on Estuary English and its relationship to RP and Cockney can be found at www.phon.ucl.ac.uk/home/estuary.

The inevitable change of RP is reflected in the latest edition of *LPD*, which includes 'a number of pronunciations that diverge from traditional, "classical" RP'. In fact, *LPD* now also includes some regional variants, not given as first alternatives, and marked with a special symbol, e.g. northern forms of BATH (Wells 2000:xiii). A great number of entries also bear witness to the impact of American pronunciation, e.g. *harass*, which is shifting its stress to the second syllable.

4.1.5 English English (EngE) – a descriptive account with special reference to regional variation in phonology

General differences between EngE and AmE are not dealt with at length but outlined and exemplified in Chapter 3 and highlighted in the descriptions of varieties which are characterized by competing norms, such as CanE (4.6), where, for example, you will find an account of some spelling differences.

4.1.5.1 Phonology

We begin by presenting the lexical sets, contrasting RP with the accent of Leeds (the data are from Wells (1982)) and three recently analysed localized accents (Foulkes and Docherty 1999), namely Norwich (East Anglia), West Wirral (near Liverpool), and Derby (between Birmingham and Sheffield). Traditionally, Norwich is classified as a southern accent, whereas Leeds, West Wirral, and Derby are northern.

Table 4.1. Lexical sets contrasting RP and four other English accents

Leeds	Derby	West Wirral	Norwich	Key word	RP
ɪ	ɪ	ɪ	ɪ	KIT	ɪ
ɛ	ɛ	ɛ	ɛ > e	DRESS	e
a	a	a	æ – æɛ	TRAP	æ
ɒ	ɒ	ɒ	ɑ > ɒ	LOT	ɒ
ʊ	ʊ	ʊ	ɐ	STRUT	ʌ
ʊ	ʊ	ʊ	ʊ	FOOT	ʊ
a	a	ɑ – aː	aː	BATH	ɑː
ɒ	ɒ	ɒ	ɔː	CLOTH	ɒ
ɜ	əː > ɨː	əː – ë	əː	NURSE	ɜː
iː	iː – ɪi	iː	ɪi	FLEECE	iː
eː (– ɛɪ)	ɛɪ	eɪ –ï –ɛɪ	æi > ẹ	FACE	eɪ
aː	ɑː – ɒː	aː	aː	PALM	ɑː
ɔː	ɔː	ǫː	ɔː	THOUGHT	ɔː
oː (– ɔʊ)	əʉ – ou	əʊ –ʌʊ–əʊ –ou	ʊu > ʊ	GOAT	əʊ
uː	ʉː > uː – ɨː	ʉː	ʉu > ʊu	GOOSE	uː
aɪ	aɪ – ɑɪ – ɒɪ	aɪ	ɑɪ	PRICE	aɪ
ɔɪ	ɔɪ	ɒɪ	ɔɪ	CHOICE	ɔɪ
aʊ	aː	ɑʊ	æʉ	MOUTH	aʊ
ɪə	ɪː – ɪ(j)ə	iə	ɛː	NEAR	ɪə
ɛː	ɛː	ëː – əː	ɛː	SQUARE	ɛə
aː	ɑː – ɒː	aː	aː	START	ɑː
ɔː	ɔː	ǫː	ɔː	NORTH	ɔː
ɔː (–ɔə)	ɔː	ǫː	ɔː	FORCE	ɔː
ʊə (ɔː)	jɔː > jʊːə	jǫː >jʉ(w)ə	əː	CURE	ʊə

(When variants are given, > indicates difference in currency, whereas – indicates roughly equal currency. The Derby GOOSE vowel, for example, is mostly centralized and rounded, but has less frequent variants, either back, rounded, or centralized, unrounded. For the significance of the diacritics see the IPA chart.)

In Table 4.1, you may well object, we deviate from our policy of not using 'extremely narrow phonetic transcription with an array of diacritics' (3.2.2). We have made an exception here because we want to show the kind of flux the vowel systems in the dialects of England are currently undergoing, which is richly demonstrated in Foulkes and Docherty (1999), a more sociolinguistically oriented work than Wells (1982). The lexical sets with variants are generally socially sensitive variables. The Derby GOAT vowel, for example, is traditionally back and rounded in the speech of older working-class males, but centralized and (partly) unrounded variants predominate in young speakers and older middle-class speakers (Docherty and Foulkes 1999:49). The Norwich LOT vowel is traditionally unrounded (as in American English) but changing towards the rounded vowel found in RP and accents further south. Trudgill (1999:138) refers to it as an exogenous (cf. 3.1.1) change, an example of dedialectization, which is indeed a powerful factor in language change today. Some of the variation in the Norwich vowels, on the other hand, exemplifies endogenous change (the diphthongization of TRAP, the fronting of the first element in GOAT, the merging of NEAR and SQUARE).

As Table 4.1 shows, northern and southern accents are clearly distinguished by the pronunciation of the STRUT vowel, which in the north is identical with FOOT. Northern STRUT represents an older form; hence Wells refers to the 'FOOT–STRUT Split' (Wells 1982:350ff.), which took place in southern England in the eighteenth century. This meant that the phonemic inventory was increased to six distinctive short vowels instead of five, as can be deduced from Table 4.1 above. Unsplit FOOT–STRUT 'has to be, along with the vowel in BATH, one of the most salient and the most symbolic markers of Northern English pronunciations today' (Wales 2002:49). Evidence of the salience of unsplit FOOT–STRUT is given in the Tony Harrison poem mentioned in 3.4.2.3 ('We say [ʌs] not [ʊz]'). The northern accents of Leeds and Derby clearly show so-called 'flat' [a] vowels in BATH as well. A striking difference in northerners' attitudes to these markers is reported:

> There are many educated northerners who would not be caught dead doing something so vulgar as to pronounce STRUT words with [ʊ], but who would feel it to be a denial of their identity as northerners to say BATH words with anything other than short [a]. (Wells 1982:354)

The high awareness of unsplit FOOT–STRUT has resulted in intermediate forms, such as [kəp] for cup, and also in hypercorrect realizations of FOOT, e.g. ['ʃʌɡə] for *sugar*.

In addition to STRUT, northern accents (cf. especially the Leeds system) generally reflect a more old-fashioned, monophthongal pronunciation in FACE and GOAT. In Devon and Cornwall, too, FACE may be pronounced in this way.

In RP and the south-east generally (Estuary English) a shift in the quality of DRESS and TRAP is taking place to the effect that these vowels are lowered to [ɛ] and [a] respectively. TRAP is thus approximating to STRUT and there is already anecdotal evidence of miscomprehension:

> One day in the early 1990's a judge is reported to have said in court: 'I'm afraid we'll have to adjourn this case, I have written my judgment out but I left it in my cottage in Devon and I can't get it sent here until tomorrow.' 'Fax it up, my Lord,' the helpful barrister suggested, to which his Lordship replied, 'Yes, it does rather.' (cf. Crystal 1995:255)

Interestingly, in other Englishes, notably AusE, NZE, SAfE and AmE, short front vowels are moving in the opposite direction, i.e. getting closer.

A distinctive feature not included in the table is the so-called *happY* vowel, i.e. final, unstressed *i*. The symbol used in *LPD* is [i], signalling that in RP it has become clearly different from KIT. Its changing quality is ascribed to Cockney influence. Most northern accents do not have this so-called 'happY tensing'.

A characteristic of East Anglia and adjoining areas is so-called yod dropping, a well-known feature of US English, i.e. words like *due* and *few* are realized as [duː], [fuː]. Yod dropping is increasingly found in RP as well (*super, suit,* etc.) but not as generalized as in East Anglia.

In Scouse (the Liverpool dialect/accent), there is no contrast between NURSE and SQUARE; both can be represented as [ɛː] (cf. the West Wirral data above). Consequently, *stare* and *stir, fair* and *fur* are homophones, and true Liverpudlians like The Beatles happily rhyme *aware* with *her* (Trudgill 1999a:72f). This feature is reminiscent of Irish English, at least as spoken in Dublin and Belfast (cf. 4.4.3.1).

In traditional Geordie (the Newcastle dialect/accent), on the other hand, NURSE has the same vowel as NORTH, which means, for example, that *shirt* and *short* are homophones. Another characteristic feature of Geordie is that a number of words belonging to the THOUGHT set, especially those with the spelling <a> followed by <l>, are pronounced with [aː]. The following well-known Geordie joke illustrates its unusual vowel system:

> A local man goes to see the doctor (who apparently is not local) about his hurt knee; the doctor bandages it up and asks him: 'Do you think you can walk [wɔːk] now?', to which the Geordie man replies: 'What do you mean, can I work? I can hardly walk [waːk]!' (cf. Wells 1982:375)

It is in the vowel systems that we find the most striking examples of variation and change, but varieties of English in England are also characterized by distinctive consonantal features, some of which are also highly significant from a social point of view. Initial /h-/, a notorious prestige marker, shows significant social variation. H dropping, which is quite a natural phenomenon owing to the 'elusive' character of [h] and known from varieties of many languages, is particularly well-known from traditional Cockney. In present-day RP and Estuary English, non-stigmatized h dropping occurs only in function words in unstressed position, but in most non-standard accents content-word h dropping is the rule rather than the exception. Only

Geordie and East Anglian speakers do not tend to drop their h's. In all h dropping areas, hypercorrect forms are common, such as ['hæpl] for *apple* , ['hɔːdi] for *Audi*.

In some areas, particularly in the West Midlands, syllable-final <-ng> is characteristically realized with retained final [g]. The local pronunciation of *Birmingham* is ['bœːmɪŋgəm].

Like RP most accents in England today are nonrhotic, but there is an 'r-ful' pocket in Lancashire and a rhotic area in the south-west, where /r/ is retroflex. There are, in fact, several types of /r/ in England with regard to quality: most commonly a weakly articulated postalveolar approximant [ɹ], tapped [ɾ], especially in medial position, and increasingly a [w]-like approximant. In Northumberland, uvular /r/ can still be heard (cf. 3.2.2).

As mentioned in Chapter 1, initial fricatives are typically voiced in the south-west, as in *finger* [v-], *saddle* [z-], *shepherd* [ʒ]. Admittedly, this feature is recessive.

A characteristic of RP and Estuary English in particular is the striking allophonic variation in /l/, which is 'clear' before a vowel, as in *love* but 'dark' – even vocalized – before a consonant or in word-final position as in *milk, fall*. Since the position of the back of the tongue in dark /l/ approximates to [o], a natural phonetic process has resulted in so-called L vocalization, e.g. [mɪok] for *milk*. A famous regional characteristic of /l/ is found in Bristol, where it is used intrusively at the end of words ending in [ə], i.e. not quite like RP intrusive /r/, which is a linking phenomenon, as in *Panorama-r-interview, Arlanda-r-Airport*. Bristol /l/, which is stigmatized, often features in jokes, such as the somewhat 'constructed' account of a family with three daughters, called *Idle, Evil*, and *Normal*. It is, however, very much alive. Stanley Ellis, an expert on English dialects, reports that a Bristol lady talked about having been to the *'operal'* where the heroine wore a beautiful *'tiaral'* (personal communication).

For some information on prosodic characteristics we refer you back to 3.2.2, where a useful website on a current project was also suggested.

By way of summarizing this section we display some of the characteristic features discussed above on a map, focusing on the following regions: Central Yorkshire and Lancashire, Tyneside, Merseyside, the south-west, and East Anglia (Fig. 4.2).

4.1.5.2 Grammar

In line with our presentation of phonology, we would like to draw your attention to some characteristics of nonstandard grammar. Some of these are widespread, such as double or multiple negation (*I couldn't find none nowhere*), 'nonstandard *never*' (using *never* for *not*), seemingly 'switched' concord as in *we sees, he go*, and a wider variety of relatives than used in the standard (*the man what was driving the car, the man as was driving the car*). We referred to the nonstandard verb forms as 'seemingly switched' because we want to emphasize that they are only ungrammatical if seen as representations of Standard English. Nonstandard, regional grammar is as rule-governed, if not yet as well described, as the standard language. An important step forward towards remedying the lack of adequate description has been taken in the

Fig. 4.2. Phonological features of dialects in England

publication of *Real English, The Grammar of English Dialects in the British Isles* (Milroy and Milroy 1993).

Some more regionally restricted grammatical features are listed below.

Pronouns: the use of 'three-dimensional' demonstratives, i.e. with a further degree of remoteness, as in *this/that/yon* in the north, and *thease/that/thik* in the West Country; access to two forms of address, signalling different degrees of formality, i.e. *you* and *thou* (*tha*) in the north; 'pronoun exchange', i.e. using subject instead of object forms and vice versa, in the West Country (*Her told I*).

Verbs: 'invariant' forms, i.e. used for all persons, of BE, such as *is* or *am* in the north and – particularly well retained – *be* in the West Country, where another characteristic is the use of *do* as a marker of aspect: *I see* refers to a single event, whereas *I do see* (pronounced with the emphasis on *see*) refers to a habitual or repeated action (cf. Trudgill 1999a:103).

4.1.5.3 Lexicon

There are few examples of specific words used in specific urban areas, yet Trudgill (1999a:109ff.) shows that regional variation can exist in the naming of fairly recent phenomena, such as words for *gymshoes*. Cockney is known to have many Yiddish loanwords, such as *nosh* for *eat*, and, in particular, to make use of so-called 'rhyming slang', in which a two-term phrase is used for a single, everyday word with which it rhymes: *trouble and strife* for *wife*, *apples and pears* for *stairs*. The second element in the phrase may be dropped: *butcher's* for *look* (from *butcher's hook*), i.e. 'take a butcher's', *loaf* for *head* (from *loaf of bread*).

On the whole, it is difficult to generalize about regional lexical variation. Word maps showing distributions of traditional dialect words, e.g. Upton and Widdowson (1996), based on material from the *Survey of English Dialects*, roughly confirm the dialect areas outlined in the phonology section. There is also a clear link to the different early settlements. The Scandinavian-based word *lake* for *play*, for example, mentioned in Chapters 1 and 3, is firmly located in an area north of the Humber, but there are also indications of the extended 'linguistic north', e.g. in the distribution of another word of Scandinavian origin, namely *teem* for *pour*. Cornwall had a Celtic-speaking population only a few centuries ago, and this still shows in the vocabulary of the local dialects: *fuggan* for *pastry-cake*, *gook* for *bonnet*, and *muryans* for *ants* are all Celtic loanwords (rather 'remnants' or 'relics', in fact). In East Anglia, immigrants from the Low Countries (Flemish weavers, Dutch canal builders) have influenced the local dialects, as exemplified in the (recessive) word *dwile* for *dishcloth*.

In the modern dialects there is much less differentiation between dialect words, although the vocabulary used in certain areas of social life, such as food and drink, is still regionally variable and quite confusing. Trudgill (1999a:125) accounts for regional differences in words for making tea: *make, mash, mask, wet, brew*. In a heated debate on what constitutes a *tea-cake*, a Lancashire lady recently gave her firm definition: 'It's a sweet thing, is tea-cake' (personal experience).

Not surprisingly, studies have shown that the knowledge of traditional dialect words is decreasing at an alarming rate. There are several reasons for this so-called 'lexical attrition'. For one thing, a great number of words used to refer to artefacts and ways of life, especially rural, which are no longer there. Another reason is clearly the ever-increasing exposure to Standard English. When Stanley Ellis, field-worker for the Survey of English Dialects in the late 1950s, interviewed an informant in Lancashire, she mentioned an ordinary Standard English word, characterizing it as hilarious and deviant; this could hardly be experienced today (personal communication).

4.1.6 Further reading

Foulkes, P. and G. Docherty (eds) (1999) *Urban Voices. Accent Studies in the British Isles*. London: Arnold.

Trudgill, P. (1999a) *The Dialects of England*. (2nd edn). Oxford: Blackwell.

Wells, J.C. (1982) *Accents of English, Vol. II. The British Isles*. Cambridge: Cambridge University Press.

4.2 WALES/CYMRU

It's the crowning glory for anybody to play [pleɪ] for Wales [weːlz]. (Welsh informant from Carmarthen recorded by J. C. Wells for *Accents of English*)

4.2.1 The country and its people

Wales (called Cymru in Welsh) is a principality of the UK. It has a population of about three million, unevenly distributed over its almost 21,000 sq.km. Whereas most of the country is mountainous and sparsely populated, the south-east, especially the so-called 'Valleys' of Glamorgan and Gwent have been densely populated ever since the Industrial Revolution. Almost two-thirds of the population live in this area, in a belt around the industrial centres of Cardiff, Swansea, and Newport.

It is believed that the indigenous population of Wales was overrun by Celtic peoples, the original 'Britons' or 'Brythons', in the Bronze and Iron Ages. From the first to the fifth century the Romans ruled the country. After the Roman withdrawal, the Celtic population maintained independence against the Anglo-Saxons who had established themselves in England. In 1282 Edward I took over Wales completely and bestowed the title of Prince of Wales on his first-born son; hence the title 'Prince of Wales'. The integration of Wales into the administrative system of England was confirmed through the Acts of Union of 1536 and 1543, which had explicit linguistic consequences in that English was made the official language of law, education, and trade; the Church was to remain a Welsh domain. (Incidentally, the Tudors, who then ruled England, were of Welsh origin themselves.) These statutes preceded the corresponding Acts of Union in Scotland and Ireland by 150 and 250 years respectively.

The Industrial Revolution led to drastic changes in the structure of the population. To begin with, there was massive emigration of Welshmen looking for jobs in England; later, there was considerable immigration of Englishmen for work in the mining and smelting industries of South Wales (Crystal 1995:334).

In comparison with Scotland and Ireland, the two other 'Celtic countries' which are much more or totally independent politically, Wales has been quite successful in preserving its Celtic language and cultural heritage. Welsh, the Celtic language, is spoken by about one-sixth of the population, most of whom live in the north-west and centre of the country. All children living in Wales are obliged to learn Welsh at school. There is a Welsh-medium television channel and a number of Welsh-dominated song and poetry festivals, such as the National Eisteddfod [aɪˈstedfəd], dating from the twelfth century and revived in the late nineteenth century. An important role in the maintenance of Welsh language and culture has been played by Plaid Cymru, the Welsh Nationalist party. Nevertheless, because of restrictions in domains, Welsh is regarded as an endangered language (cf. Crystal 2000 and 4.2.2.1 below).

The words *Cymru* [ˈkəmri], the indigenous name of the country and *Cymraeg*, the name of the language, are derived from the older Celtic word *Combroges* 'compatriots'. The etymology of *Wales/Welsh* is obscure but the leading theory is that its original meaning is related to a word meaning 'foreigner'. It was the Anglo-Saxons who named the country *Wealas* (a plural form).

4.2.2 Wales as a linguistic area

4.2.2.1 A note on Welsh and its current status
Welsh belongs to the Celtic languages, which are distantly related to English and other Germanic languages in that they are all Indo-European. Some basic Welsh vocabulary indicates this relationship; also, Welsh and English share a number of early borrowings from Latin (cf. Chapter 1): *ysgol* 'school', *eglwys* 'church', *stryd* 'street', *pont* 'bridge', *cwningen* 'rabbit'. For further examples, cf. www.bwrdd-yr-iaith.org.uk/. Because of the substratum effect, some other Welsh features are mentioned in the presentation of Welsh English below.

Welsh and Gaelic (spoken in Ireland and Scotland) represent the two main branches of Celtic that are still extant: Brythonic and Goidelic, respectively. The two branches are sometimes referred to as 'p-Celtic' and 'q-Celtic', since a distinction between them is found in the consonants of a great number of words, e.g. Welsh *pren*, Irish *crann* 'tree'. The closest relative of Welsh today is Breton, spoken in Brittany, France. Cornish, once spoken in Cornwall and subject to revival, is another p-Celtic variety.

Although Welsh is 'unquestionably in the strongest position of any Celtic language today' (Nettle and Romaine 2000:136), its general decline, especially from the end of the nineteenth century to the 1970s, is referred to by the same authors as 'a catastrophic collapse'. During the last 20 years, the process has actually slowed down and there are indications that it may even reverse. Crystal (1995:334) illustrates, with the help of a map, the evidence from twentieth century census data (the percentages refer to the total population):

Welsh-only (monoglot) speakers: 1891 – 30%; 1931 – 4%; 1961 – 1%; 1981 – 0.8%

(It is unthinkable that this particular development will reverse.)

Welsh-English bilingual speakers: 1891 –54%; 1931 –37%; 1961 –26%; 1981 –19%; 1991 –18.7%

At the time of writing this text, data from the 2001 census are not yet available.

There are striking differences between the different counties; in Gwynedd (northwest): according to the 1991 data, 61 per cent of the people over three years of age (!) claimed that they could speak Welsh.

The rapid decline in the twentieth century can be illustrated by the following observation recently reported by a Swedish tourist: a tombstone in the village churchyard in Goginan near Aberystwyth dedicated to the memory of a sister and brother has the inscription referring to the sister, who died in 1903, in Welsh, whereas the text referring to her brother runs 'and her brother the Rev. Richard Arnold James, died Sept. 9th, 1953, aged 86 years'.

For an informative study of attitudes to bilingualism in Wales, see Baker (1992), who reports research conducted among 11–18-year-olds in three schools in three regions representing different degree of 'Welshness'. The results show, for example, overall agreement with the statements 'It is important to be able to speak English and Welsh', 'Knowing Welsh makes people cleverer' and 'Road signs should be in English and Welsh', but disagreement with 'Knowing both Welsh and English gives people problems' and 'People only need to know one language' (Baker 1992:81ff.).

4.2.2.2 Welsh English – an overview

In general classifications of world Englishes, mainly according to phonological criteria (cf. 3.2.2), Welsh English (WelshE) is placed in the 'English-based' category. The reasons why WelshE differs from Irish and Scottish English in this respect are historical; it is simply not a variety that has had a chance to develop its own character over the centuries.

> Although ordinary Welshmen have had some acquaintance with English since the Middle Ages, they have not had it as their mother tongue, as their first language, until quite recently – a matter of a century or two. In looking at the pattern of English in Wales today, one must remember that North America, for instance, has had a substantial body of native English speakers for longer than Wales has. Welsh English, as a native language, is mostly not much older than South African English. (Wells 1982:377)

As pointed out in 3.1.1, regional linguistic variation is clearly, though not exclusively, a function of time. WelshE, although – on the whole – a 'young' dialect, nevertheless shows considerable phonological variation. Wells (1982:378) draws attention to three areas influenced by three different regions in England: South Wales (the west of England, e.g. Bristol), mid-Wales (the Midlands, e.g. Birmingham), and North Wales (the north of England, e.g. Liverpool). To some extent, this regional division is related to the topography of Wales, which has made north–south communication somewhat difficult. Another obvious factor is the varying use of Welsh and the history of English in the respective areas. There are, in fact, pockets in Pembrokeshire (south-west Wales) which were anglicized as early as the Middle Ages. The Gower peninsula in the south is another well-known example of early anglicization. The distinctiveness of WelshE is most noticeable in the north-west where Welsh is strong.

The regional dialects spoken in the industrial south and in the east have strong affinities with the dialects in England that have provided an input through contact and immigration. These dialects were once superimposed on distinct substratal Welsh influences but it is believed that they are gradually losing their Welshness (Thomas 1994:112).

Like many other regional accents in the UK, WelshE today is heavily influenced by accents spoken in the south of England. A striking example of this influence is given by Mees and Collins in their study of ongoing glottalization in Cardiff. Interestingly,

'... in Cardiff and the adjacent area, where many people appear to look away from Wales towards England, glottal stop is a prestige feature' (Mees and Collins 1999:201).

4.2.3 Welsh English (WelshE) – a descriptive account

A 'shortlist' of particularly salient features:

- the 'sing-song' or 'lilting' intonation, particularly in the 'Valleys'
- long medial consonants as in *ready, happy, knitting* ['nɪtːɪŋ]
- schwa in STRUT words, making *a large untidy room* homophonous with *a large and tidy room* and *seagull* rhyming with *eagle* (Wells 1982:381). Welsh typically has a very similar vowel. On the other hand, schwa does not occur in final checked (= followed by a consonant) syllables, as in *Welshmen* ['wɛlʃmɛn].
- a Welsh consonant: voiceless /l/ when the spelling has <ll>, as in *Lloyd, Llangollen,* used in place- names, personal names and a few Welsh-based words.
- the invariant tag *isn't it?*, as in *You are enjoying yourself, isn't it?*
- the fronting of sentence constituents, e.g. *Singing they were.*

4.2.3.1 Phonology

The WelshE lexical sets (Table 4.2) are taken from Wells (1982:380). This system is said to be typical of the south-east. Aspects of regional/social variation will be highlighted in the commentary.

As we have already seen, WelshE differs from RP in the phonemic inventory because of the STRUT–schwa merger (cf. the salient features listed above). As Table 4.2 shows, NEAR can be quite distinctive, with a final element merging with NURSE.

SQUARE is not a diphthong, but RP, too, has a monophthongal variant (Wells 1982:305). START (and to a lesser degree PALM) words are socially sensitive, varying from the front vowel seen in the table to a more prestigious RP-like back vowel. A close fronted variant is found in Cardiff working-class speech; stereotypical representations of class-related speech are ['kɛːdɪf] vs ['kɑːdɪf].

Although not shown in the table, NURSE is often rounded in south-east Wales, giving it the quality of [œː] or [øː]. There is no corresponding vowel to NURSE in Welsh, and Wells (1982:383) makes the interesting observation that the rounded versions are reminiscent of slightly inaccurate attempts made by EFL learners. PRICE and MOUTH are characterized by a centralized first element having the schwa-like quality of STRUT.

The diphthongs in FACE and GOAT are typical of the south-west, but as our motto for Wales shows, FACE has a monophthongal variant, occurring, for example, in the south-west where the speaker comes from. Similarly, GOAT may be realized as [goːt]. These realizations are different because the corresponding vowels were different in the Middle Ages. As the motto also shows, there is a split in the FACE set: monophthongal variants occur in words where the corresponding spelling is <a>,

Table 4.2. Welsh English lexical sets

WelshE (SE)	Key word	RP
ɪ	KIT	ɪ
ɛ	DRESS	e
a	TRAP	æ
ɒ	LOT	ɒ
ə	STRUT	ʌ
ʊ	FOOT	ʊ
a – aː	BATH	ɑː
ɒ – ɔː	CLOTH	ɒ
ɜː	NURSE	ɜː
iː	FLEECE	iː
ei	FACE	eɪ
aː	PALM	ɑː
ɔː	THOUGHT	ɔː
ou	GOAT	əʊ
uː	GOOSE	uː
əi	PRICE	aɪ
ɔi	CHOICE	ɔɪ
əu	MOUTH	aʊ
jɜː – iːə	NEAR	ɪə
ɛː	SQUARE	ɛə
aː	START	ɑː
ɔː	NORTH	ɔː
ɔː	FORCE	ɔː
uːə	CURE	ʊə

making minimal pairs such as *made–maid*, *pane–pain*. Similarly, *throne* /θroːn/ and *thrown* /θroun/ constitute a minimal pair.

The most striking consonantal feature is the extended duration of medial consonants as described above. Welsh voiceless /l/ (its IPA symbol is [ɬ]), an alveolar lateral fricative or approximant, also included among the salient features of WelshE, is not common among the world's languages and not found elsewhere in Europe (Ladefoged and Maddieson 1996:203). Non-Welsh speakers sometimes replace it by [l], [θl], [fl] or [kl]. Except for the anglicized areas in the south-east, /l/ does not exhibit allophonic variation, but tends to be clear in other areas in the south and dark in the north.

One reason why WelshE is firmly placed among the English-based varieties like

AusE and NZE is the fact that it is non-rhotic. This is something of a mystery, since Welsh is rhotic and so were the varieties of EngE spoken by the early settlers. Wells (1982:380) speculates that it may be ascribed to the kind of English imposed by schoolteachers. The quality of prevocalic /r/ is variable, ranging from rolled to tapped to approximant, depending on region as well as phonetic environment (cf. Wells 1982:390).

A characteristic of northern WelshE phonology is the nonexistence of /z/, making, for example, *price–prize* and *seal–zeal* homophonous.

As our first salient feature we chose the characteristic intonation. 'Sing-song' is a very vague designation, often used about any accent that sounds unfamiliar. Unfortunately, an adequate account of Welsh intonation is not yet available, but an observation formulated by Wells (1982:392) provides useful guidance: in ordinary statements where standard accents would have a simple fall, e.g. *It's no longer `valid*, WelshE would have a rise-fall *(^valid)*.

4.2.3.2 Grammar

Like other Englishes, WelshE is less distinctive at this level of language than in phonology. The following presentation refers to informal – mostly spoken – language, and includes a number of nonstandard features.

To a great extent, these features are shared with other varieties in the British Isles (cf. 4.1.5.2): double (multiple) negation, 'nonstandard *never*', participles preceded by *a-* (*a-doing*), the relatives *as* and *what*, generalization of verb forms (*I sees, they likes*), 'unorthodox' forms of strong verbs (*He was took bad*), the pronoun *her* used in the subjective, possessive pronominal forms such as *yourn, theirn*.

In addition to the invariant tag *isn't it?,* referring to the whole sentence, north-western WelshE has the tag *yes?*, as in *You're studying World Englishes, yes?*

The following characteristics, more specific to WelshE, relate to the Welsh substratum and/or to traditional dialects in western England. Most of the data is taken from Thomas (1994).

The fronting of a constituent was included among the particularly salient features (*Singing they were*). Fronting is a strategy for focusing on a constituent and is accompanied by emphatic stress. In Standard English, focusing is often expressed through pseudo-clefting, i.e. *What they were doing was singing*, or clefting, e.g. *It's now that they are going*. In Welsh there is no distinction between clefting and pseudo-clefting; both correspond to fronting, which is commonly used. The WelshE correspondence to the cleft sentence exemplified above would simply be *Now they're going*, with the emphasis on the first word.

WelshE has characteristic ways of expressing aspect through use of periphrastic *do* as in *I do go to chapel every Sunday*. Similar constructions are found in England's West Country (cf. 4.1.5.2) and believed to 'represent an older Celtic substratum' (Thomas 1994:192). *Be + -ing*, used as a habitual marker as in *I'm going to chapel every Sunday*, also has parallels in Welsh and other Celtic languages.

Another feature which has its parallel in Welsh, is 'expletive there', used in exclamations such as *There's strange it was!* corresponding to Standard English *How strange it was!*

4.2.3.3 Lexicon

There are surprisingly few borrowings from Welsh in WelshE. We have already mentioned the widely used *eisteddfod*. Other borrowings include *del* and *bach* [baːx], used as terms of endearment, *hwyl* [hʊil] 'enthusiasm', and *bara brith* [briːθ] 'bread loaf made with currants'.

WelshE dialects further contain words that are found in certain dialects in England. A well-known example is *clem* 'starve', found in the west Midlands and as far north as Lancashire.

There are also many characteristic idioms, some of which can be ascribed to the Welsh substratum, whereas the origins of others are obscure. An example of the latter category is the repetition of an adjective for intensification, as in *She was pretty, pretty.*

According to Thomas (1994:145ff.), 'Welsh English, as a distinct dialect, is a transitional phenomenon'; increasingly, WelshE will exclusively be characterized as a distinct *accent*.

4.2.4 Further reading

Thomas, A. R. (1994) 'English in Wales'. In R. Burchfield (ed.), *The Cambridge History of the English Language, Vol. 5* . Cambridge: Cambridge University Press, 94–147.

4.3 SCOTLAND

'I'm not an English girl, I'm a wee Scots girl' (quoted from a Glasgow informant recorded by Caroline Macafee for *Traditional Dialect in the Modern World* (1994))

4.3.1 The country and its people

Scotland is the northernmost part of the UK (map Fig. 4.1), comprising about a third of its area but not even a tenth of its population. Its main distinctive areas are: the Highlands in the north and north-west ; the more populous Lowlands in the south with the capital Edinburgh; the Western Isles (Outer and Inner Hebrides) and the Northern Isles (Orkney and Shetland).

The founder population of Scotland can be viewed as consisting of:

- Celts from Ireland, representing the Goidelic (Gaelic) language group, settling in the west in the fifth century.
- Anglo-Saxons, in particular the 'tribe' known as Angles, expanding northwards from Northumberland into southern Scotland and gradually spreading westwards to south-western Scotland (seventh century).
- Scandinavian (especially Norwegian) Vikings who conquered Orkney, Shetland, and part of the Scottish mainland (Caithness) in the ninth century.

■ Anglo-Normans from England at the invitation of Scottish kings who gave them lands partly in the hope of strengthening the monarchy. Their retainers and servants were English-speaking.

4.3.2 Scotland as a linguistic area

Scotland as a linguistic area is as varied as its topography. Three main language varieties can be recognized, each of which in turn includes a number of dialects: (Scottish) Gaelic, Scots, and Scottish English (ScotE). Although obviously not a variety of English, Scottish Gaelic deserves inclusion in this overview presentation, owing to its importance as a substratum language. Whether Scots is a variety of English or not will be subject to further discussion below (cf. also 3.1.2).

4.3.2.1 Scottish Gaelic – its history and status

Scottish Gaelic, the Celtic language of Scotland, which in Scotland is usually simply referred to as *Gaelic* ['gælɪk], belongs to the q-Celtic branch (cf. 4.2.2.1). In the tenth century Scotland was largely Gaelic-speaking, but during the eleventh century this language lost its pre-eminence at court and among the aristocracy who spoke Norman French. In eastern and central Scotland it was largely replaced by Scots. By the seventeenth century, Gaelic had retreated to the Highlands and Hebrides. After 1745, when the highland chieftains were defeated during a rebellion, Gaelic began losing its position as a first language throughout most of the Highlands.

From the late fifteenth century into the eighteenth, the decline of Gaelic was precipitated by a number of acts of the Scottish and British Parliaments, aimed at promoting English-language education. The neglect of Gaelic resulted in the language surviving as an oral rather than a written medium (MacKinnon 1998:176ff.).

The latest census figures available (1991) tell us that 58.9 per cent of Scotland's 65,978 Gaelic speakers claimed to read Gaelic and 44.6 per cent to write it.

Nancy Dorian's famous study of the process of language death in east Sutherland (north-east Scotland) confirms the picture of a diglossic situation (3.4.4.1), with Gaelic being used in high domains, particularly the Church, whereas it was undergoing rapid and conscious loss in the important home domain. One of Dorian's informants characterizes his parents' use of language in the following way: 'They wanted to speak Gaelic so that we couldn't understand them' (Dorian 1981:104). Virtually all Gaelic speakers are today functionally bilingual.

The Western Isles traditionally constitute a stronghold for Gaelic, together with some areas in the north-west of mainland Scotland. The 1991 census results also show that there seems to be a growing proportion of Gaelic speakers in the Lowlands, especially in the Glasgow area.

In recent years, a number of Gaelic-medium primary schools have been set up. In places, Gaelic is also taught as a second language. Recent years have also seen an increase in Gaelic radio and television broadcasts, where various genres are represented, e.g. soap operas. There is a Gaelic publishing house and a film unit.

4.3.2.2 The history and status of Scots

As has already been hinted at, a great number of people, linguists included, might resent the inclusion of Scots in a book entitled *World Englishes*, arguing that it is a language in its own right. On the other hand, this variety certainly deserves a place in a section describing 'language in Scotland'. Also, even if its status is that of a language, it is nevertheless more closely related to English than any other language, and it is descended from Old English. Its impact on ScotE is undisputed; in fact, it can be argued that Scots–ScotE constitutes a linguistic continuum (cf. Aitken 1984).

There is a wealth of early written sources, giving evidence of a distinct variety of language, as exemplified in the following extract from a schoolboy's letters dating from the 1540s. A striking feature of early forms of Scots is initial *quh-*, corresponding to present-day *wh-*.

> Father, I requist yow for crystis schaik [sake] till hauie pitie vpon your pour brother villam, quhilk is now beth [both] modderles and fatherles, and guie ye tack [take] a chair [care] of him, and bring him vill up ... (quoted from Meurman-Solin 1999:309)

Yet, throughout the growth of Scots it remained close to northern varieties of English and Scots and English were generally intelligible (Romaine 1982:57). Many written sources, in fact, are characterized by a mixture of Scots and English features.

Between the fourteenth and seventeenth centuries all Scots of all ranks (with the exception of monolingual Gaelic speakers) spoke a form of language that is known as 'Older Scots'. Aitken, expressing some doubt as to the exact status of present-day Scots, does not hesitate to call Older Scots 'an autonomous national language, with its own distinctive pronunciations, grammar, vocabulary and, very strikingly, spelling ...' (Aitken 1985:42).

After the joining of the crowns of England and Scotland in 1603, written as well as spoken language in Scotland became more and more anglicized. A less formal and conservative variety of Scots, based on the spoken language, was used in some genres, especially poetry, e.g. by Robert Burns (1759–96). Scots as a spoken language was used by the rural population and the working classes.

Written Scots was revived and promoted in the so-called 'Scottish Renaissance' in the twentieth century, led by a group of influential writers. Drawing on previous literary and dialect usage from the Lowlands, this group came up with an 'eclectic variety' (Crystal 1995:333), sometimes scathingly referred to as 'synthetic Scots', but generally known as *Lallans* (= Lowlands). A style sheet for spelling was set up in 1947 (cf. 3.2.1).

There is today abundant writing in Scots, in localized forms such as Shetland dialect as well as more regionless variants. Mostly, writers do not seem to look to the style sheet for guidance, but set up their own rules for spelling. It is likely that dictionaries such as *The Concise Scots Dictionary* (1985), supplying spelling variants, are also consulted. Virtually all genres are represented, from private letters, notes, and radio scripts to fiction, Bible texts, and scholarly articles.

The following text is a recent example of the last genre:

> Ither efforts 50 year syne were direckit at the braidcast media. David Abercrombie (supportit be ithers, includin Jack Aitken) was raxin for the preevilege o hearin *Scottish accents* on the radio, never min the Scots leid.
> [Other efforts 50 years ago were directed at the broadcast media. D.A. (supported by others, including J.A.) was demanding the privilege of hearing *Scottish accents* on the radio, never mind the Scots language.] (Caroline Macafee, *Scots: Hauf Empty or Hauf Fu?* (Macafee 2001))

In support of the claim that Scots is a language in its own right, the following arguments are usually brought forward (cf. McArthur 1998:139):

- It has a historically based, highly distinctive sound system, grammar, and vocabulary.
- It has a varied and unbroken orthographic and literary tradition.
- It has dialects of its own.
- It is now recognized as a language by the European Bureau of Lesser Used Languages, an agency of the European Union.

For further information about Scots, cf. e.g. www.scots-online.org ('Pittin the Mither Tongue on the Wab!').

4.3.2.3 Scottish English (ScotE)

ScotE can simply be defined as Standard English pronounced with a Scottish accent and with a few scotticisms in grammar and vocabulary, e.g. *wee* for 'little', as used in our motto. This variety, often referred to as Standard Scottish English, has been the official language of Scotland for at least three centuries. It is 'the mother tongue of a large minority of native-educated Scots (mainly the middle classes and those who have received a higher education) and the public language of most of the remainder (mainly the working class of the Lowlands)' (McArthur 1992:903). Note that the major Scottish dictionaries do not constitute a codification of this standard variety but rather focus on Scots.

It is worth mentioning that 'RP does not enjoy the same status in Scotland as it does in England and Wales; a Scottish accent can be prestigious in a way that a local English accent is not' (Wells 1982:393). It could even be claimed that Scotland has its own RP in the so-called Edinburgh 'Morningside' accent, stereotypically represented in the film *The Prime of Miss Jean Brodie*.

4.3.2.4 Regional variation in Scotland

In the Highlands, Gaelic began being displaced by English in the mid-eighteenth century. Since Scots was never spoken there, the language variety used is Scottish English (with some substratum effects from Gaelic). Scots has always been connected with the Lowlands (cf. the term *Lallans* mentioned above), including the cities of Glasgow and Edinburgh, but has also been extended to the Northern Isles (Orkney and Shetland) and to the north-eastern part of mainland Scotland. The Aberdeen area is known for its marked accent. Compare also the variety known as Ulster Scots, described in 4.4.

Among the regional varieties of Scots, Shetland, Orkney and – to a lesser extent – Caithness, occupy a distinctive position in that here Scots has been 'planted' on a Scandinavian substratum. Until the year 1469, these areas were part of a Viking earldom. The language used was a Scandinavian variety known as Norn, which was the first Germanic language to be spoken in the area. The shift from Norn to Scots must have been gradual, and – owing to the scarcity of written sources – it is not possible to determine the time of the actual demise of Norn (cf. Waugh 1996 for a heated debate on this issue). It is definitely misleading to label present-day Shetland dialect (a Scots dialect) as Norn, as is done, for example, in Crystal 1995 but also by many Shetlanders and Orcadians themselves, taking a romantic view.

As seen from the following extract from a letter, Shetlanders are generally bidialectal, mastering Shetland dialect as well as Standard English as discrete varieties.

> Diss is twaartree lines aleng wi' da peerie booklet o' Frisle wirds . . . I toitht du wid likk ta höy een o' dem . . . Am been skrivan a lokk a auld wirds diss winter, and hiv gottin aboot a thoozan doon.
> I think I had better write in English! I have been meaning to write for a while but being me I never got down to it.
>
> [This is just a few lines together with the little booklet of Fair Isle words . . . I thought you would like to have one . . . I have written down a lot of old words this winter, and have got about a thousand] (Alexander Stout, Barkland, Fair Isle, in a letter to Gunnel Melchers, 1985)

By contrast, most other Scottish varieties display a complex interplay between two language varieties, i.e. there is continuous rather than discrete variation. Along this continuum, speakers have access to features from both linguistic systems and adapt their speech according to context and audience. A sociolinguistic study of Edinburgh and Glasgow speakers indicates that Edinburgh speakers are more oriented towards standard varieties than their Glasgow counterparts (Chirrey 1999:223ff.).

In the following description of linguistic features, we take account of the Scots/Scottish English continuum, but it is impossible to do justice to the richness and variation found in Scots.

4.3.3 Scots/Scottish English (ScotE) – a descriptive account

A 'shortlist' of particularly salient features, found in all varieties, but in most cases to a higher degree in Scots:

- the retention of the voiceless velar fricative /x/ in words spelt with <gh> or <ch>, such as *loch, bright, dreich* 'dull', *Waugh.*

- dark /l/ in all positions, which in Scots has resulted in L vocalization, evidenced in spellings such as *fu* 'full', *ca* 'call', *saut* 'salt', *aa* 'all' (cf. the title of Macafee's article quoted above).
- a characteristic distribution of vowel length as compared to RP, which makes 'expected' short vowels sound quite long and 'expected' long vowels rather shorter (consider, for example, the representation of *privilege* in the Macafee text).
- the firm rhoticity which explains the non-existence of centralized diphthongs, i.e. words such as *cheers* and *care* are pronounced with monophthongs.
- the Scots component in the vocabulary, as already exemplified in *wee, dreich, syne*.

4.3.3.1 The spelling of Scots

As pointed out in 3.2.1 and 4.3.2.2, Scots spelling is highly variable in spite of access to a style sheet and various dictionaries, which, however, tend to allow for a number of variants, e.g. *breid, brede, bread, braid* for 'bread' according to the *Concise Scots Dictionary*. Some further observations on the orthographic representation of certain phonological features can be made by looking at the Scots texts above. Present-day writers of fiction who use Scots regularly, at least in dialogue, tend to indicate 'long' vowels, as in *jaykit* for 'jacket' (Irvine Welsh). This should only be necessary if the text is written for a non-Scottish readership.

4.3.3.2 Phonology

The Scots vowel system is regionally variable, but has at least eight phonemes: /i e ɛ a ɪ u o ʌ/. The number of distinctive vowels could vary between eight and twelve, to which should be added two or three diphthongs (Wells 1982:397ff.).

The lexical sets given below (Table 4.3) represent, according to Wells, 'a Scottish accent of English'.

As pointed out in 3.2.2, the Scottish vowel system, including Northern Irish English, is distinct typologically from other accents of English (Type IV). An obvious difference from RP is that ScotE has a smaller phonemic inventory which can be seen from the lexical sets displayed in Table 4.3. One reason for this has to do with rhoticity as explained in the list of salient features. Another reason, also apparent from the salient features, is that ScotE (and Scots) does not have some vowel contrasts that are found in RP. FOOT and GOOSE are identical, which means that word pairs such as *full–fool, pull–pool* are homophonous. The quality of FOOT/GOOSE is subject to social variation: the quality suggested in Table 4.3 above represents an 'elegant' realization, but the usual quality is close, rounded, central [ʉ]. Similarly, front [a] vowels in BATH and PALM are associated with higher status than back [ɑ]. A Morningside accent, in fact, is characterized by [æ] or even [ɛ]. As in CanE (4.6.3.2) and varieties of AmE (4.5.5.1), LOT and THOUGHT are identical.

As seen from the ScotE lexical sets, no vowel is indicated as long; any differences are in quality only. Yet all vowels, with the exception of /ɪ/ and /ʌ/ (which are always short), have long or short allophones in complementary distribution. The rule for this

Table 4.3. Scottish English lexical sets

ScotE	Key word	RP
ɪ	KIT	ɪ
ɛ – ë	DRESS	e
a	TRAP	æ
ɔ – ɒ	LOT	ɒ
ʌ	STRUT	ʌ
u	FOOT	ʊ
a – ɑ	BATH	ɑː
ɔ – ɒ	CLOTH	ɒ
ər ɛr ʌr . . .	NURSE	ɜː (BIRD [bərd] HEARD [hɛrd] WORD [wʌrd])
i	FLEECE	iː
e	FACE	eɪ
a – ɑ	PALM	ɑː
ɔ	THOUGHT	ɔː
o	GOAT	əʊ
u	GOOSE	uː
ae, ʌi	PRICE	aɪ
ɒɪ	CHOICE	ɔɪ
ʌu	MOUTH	aʊ
ir	NEAR	ɪə
er	SQUARE	ɛə
ar, ɑr	START	ɑː
ɔr – ɒr	NORTH	ɔː
or	FORCE	ɔː
ur	CURE	ʊə

distribution, known as Aitken's Law or the Scottish Vowel Length Rule (SVLR), says that vowels are short unless they are followed by /r/, a voiced fricative, a morpheme boundary, or are final in an open syllable (cf. Wells 1982:400, Chirrey 1999:224). A few examples of the workings of SVLR: the vowels in *heed* and *hid*, *mace* and *mess*, and the stressed vowel in *Peter* have the same (short) duration, whereas those in *seethe*, *sleeve*, *maze* would be longer (cf. also the short duration of *take* represented as *tack* in the Older Scots text above). The importance of the morpheme boundary can be illustrated by word pairs such as *greed–agreed* and *need–kneed* (past tense of the verb *knee*) where the first word would have a relatively short vowel and the second a rather longer one. The rule operates in diphthongs, too: the realization of *tide* will be different from *tied*, for example. In concluding our brief presentation of the SVLR, we have to mention that, according to recent research (Scobbie *et al.* 1999), it is susceptible to considerable pressure from non-Scottish varieties and may play a smaller role in Scottish phonology than claimed by Aitken and Wells.

A few further comments on ScotE vowels and diphthongs:

The quality indicated for KIT applies to an 'educated' Scottish accent; in most accents it is centralized or even further retracted and more open. This may explain why the word *fingers* pronounced by a Shetlander was perceived as *fungus* by a Lancashire lady.

As we have seen, PRICE is variable in quantity according to the SVLR. It is also socially variable: the first variant in the table is the 'higher' version. This variation is reminiscent of Canadian raising (cf. 4.6.3), but its distribution is not the same.

Like FACE and GOAT, MOUTH is usually monophthongal (realized as [u]), at least in Scots, e.g. [suθ] 'south', [ku] 'cow' (cf. the orthographic representations *aboot* and *doon* in the Fair Isle extract above).

As for the quality of vowels before /r/ it remains to be mentioned that some Scottish accents, such as middle-class Edinburgh speech have undergone 'the NURSE Merger' (Wells 1982:407). This means that in contrast with accents in the west of Scotland, for example, words like *skirt*, *merge*, and *lurk* all are pronounced with /ɛr/ instead of the three variants shown in Table 4.3.

Finally, the vowels of ScotE and especially the Scots end of the continuum are clearly different from most other accents of English in their distribution over the vocabulary (lexical incidence). Well-known examples are the corresponding words in Scots for *stone, home*, usually spelled *stane, hame* and pronounced /sten/, /hem/ (cf. the spelling *beth* for 'both' in the schoolboy's letter, *braid* for 'broad' in the Macafee text). FOOT and GOOSE, as we have seen, are generally identical in ScotE, but in some local varieties they may be realized in six different ways, depending on the history of the lexical items. The word *boot*, for example, may have the vowel [ø] in the dialect of Glenesk (Wells 1982:397) and a similar vowel quality is found in broad Shetland dialect.

Consonants:
In addition to the retention of /x/ as listed among the salient features, ScotE has kept syllable-initial /hw/ as in *what, which, whisky, overwhelm*, a feature which may some-times be heard in some other varieties of English, such as CanE and AmE. According to Wells (1982:408), 'a case can be made for treating it as a unit phoneme'. A tangible piece of evidence for its phonemic status was experienced by Gunnel Melchers, who was once to be picked up by a Scotsman in a street called *Whinmoor Street*. Since she pronounced it with /w/ he went to *Wynmore Street* instead. In some parts of Shetland, <wh-> is realized as /kw-/, and <qu-> sometimes with hypercorrect /hw/: ['kwɪskɪ] for *whisky*, [hwin] for *queen*. In the north-east of mainland Scotland (Aberdeen, Buchan), <wh->) is realized as /f/, making *what* virtually homophonous with *foot*.

In urban areas, including Lerwick, the small 'capital' of Shetland, the use of glottal stops in medial and final position is increasing rapidly and is socially variable, according to class, age, and gender. In broad Shetland accents there are no dental fricatives, e.g. [tɪnk] for *think*, [der] for *there*, [da] for *the*.

We have already stated that ScotE is rhotic and shown how this has implications for the vowel system. A few words remain to be said about the quality of /r/, however. With regard to the generally embraced stereotype of Scotsmen's trilled r's, we refer you back to 3.2.2. Trilled r's are still heard, but the most common types of /r/ found in Scotland today are an alveolar tap [ɾ] and a postalveolar or retroflex fricative or approximant [ɹ] (Wells 1982:411). Uvular /r/ is not uncommon and can be heard in the speech of the Glaswegian informant on the accompanying CD. Like many other Scottish speakers, he appears to vary the quality of /r/ according to the phonetic environment.

As stated in the list of salient features, /l/ is generally dark, but tends to be clear in the Western Isles and the Highlands, which can probably be attributed to the Gaelic substratum. The same explanation can be given for the strongly aspirated voiceless plosives in these areas; in other parts of Scotland /p t k/ are often unaspirated. Another influence of Gaelic is suggested for the coalescence of /r/ + /s/ into a retroflex sound, a feature otherwise known from Indian English (Wells 1982:628) and Scandinavian EFL.

Prosody:
ScotE differs from RP in the stress pattern of certain words, notably verbs ending in *-ize*, which tend to be stressed on the last syllable.

Information on intonation in ScotE is scarce. According to Chirrey (1999:229), Edinburgh speech patterns are characterized by mid- to low falls, also in questions of all kinds and there is no evidence of HRT. Glasgow speech, on the other hand, is characterized by rising-contour patterns (cf. Brown *et al.* 1980:19).

4.3.3.3 Grammar
The following brief presentation based on Miller 1993 describes colloquial language towards the Scots end of the continuum. As seen from the Fair Isle text quoted in 4.3.2.4, Standard EngE is regularly used in writing. The purpose of Miller's account is, in fact, to inform teachers of English about ScotE grammar, so that they will be better equipped for marking essays and passing judgements in general about children's use of language.

Some of the following characteristics are shared with other varieties of English, especially Northern EngE.

Morphology:
Nonstandard features abound in the past tense and past participle forms of verbs. The forms have sprung from different sources: *sellt* 'sold' and *killt* 'killed' indicate that irregular verbs have become regular. The voiceless ending is a historically based Scots feature as illustrated in the Macafee text above. *Driv* 'drove' and *taen* 'took' are other irregular forms. *Forgot* 'forgotten' (*Should auld acquaintance be forgot?*) was used in earlier forms of Standard English, and *went* for 'gone' was used in Older Scots. Two widely used verbs are *ken* 'know' with *kent* as past tense and past participle, and *gie*

'give' with *gied* as past tense and *gien* as past participle. In Orkney and Shetland *be* is used instead of *have* as the general perfective auxiliary.

Plural forms of nouns such as *wife, leaf, loaf* keep the voiceless consonant, i.e. *wifes, leafs, loafs.* ScotE also retains irregular plurals such as *shune* 'shoes', *een* 'eyes'.

In Orkney and Shetland there is firm retention of two forms of address: informal *du* vs formal (singular) *you*, as brought up by the Shetland informant on the accompanying CD.

Many speakers of Scots have a three-dimensional demonstrative system, similar to that of the north of England, i.e. *this/that/yon* (cf. 4.1.5.2). *Yon* tends to indicate physical as well as emotional distance (expressing dislike or 'otherness'), as in *yon oil companies, yon Southfork* (the Ewing ranch in the soap opera *Dallas*) (recorded in Shetland).

Syntax:
There is unmarked plurality in measure phrases, as exemplified in *50 year*, found in the Macafee text.

With reference to negation, it is characteristic of ScotE in general not to contract *not* with the auxiliary; thus EngE *I won't let you down* would correspond to ScotE *I'll not let you down*. In Scots, negation is expressed by *no* or *not*, as in *She's no leaving* or by the forms *nae* and *n't*, which are always attached to other words, as in *She isnae leaving*.

Scots is 'massively different from Standard English' with regard to modal verbs (Miller 1993:116). It lacks *shall* (replaced by *will* in all contexts, including questions like *Will I pour the coffee?*), *may*, and *ought*. *Need* is exclusively treated as a main verb.

A striking characteristic of Scots is the use of double modals as in *They might could be finishing their work on time*. Such constructions are also found in varieties of AmE (4.5.6.2).

Progressive constructions are used with stative verbs, as in *I wasnae liking it and the lassie I was going wi wasnae liking it* (Miller 1993:121).

Like WelshE, ScotE often has an invariant tag. The ScotE version is *e*, which may be added to positive as well as negative declarative clauses. ScotE, however, also uses the tag *e no*, which is added to positive clauses, i.e. a system like that used in Standard English (*you're liking this, e /no/?*).

In ScotE the definite article is used before nouns denoting institutions and certain periods of time: *the day* 'today', *the morn* 'tomorrow', *at the kirk* 'at church'.

4.3.3.4 Lexicon

As demonstrated even in the brief Macafee text, Scots includes lexical items that will be completely opaque to someone conversant with Standard English only. Such opaque words may stem from different sources, e.g. Old English, as in the case of *rax* Gaelic, or Old Norse. These three, in fact, constitute the most important sources for Scots vocabulary.

Early Scots shared a great deal of its vocabulary with Northern Middle English, including most of its borrowings from Scandinavian. Further examples of words from this source used in Modern Scots are *dreich* 'dry', *gate* 'road', *kirk* 'church', *big* 'build', *lass* 'girl', *lowse* 'loose', *rowan* 'mountain ash'. The Scandinavian element in Orkney and Shetland dialect, which is not an effect of borrowing but due to a substratum, is much more noticeable. Some examples of Shetland dialect words were given in Chapter 1. The Scandinavian-based, traditional vocabulary has tended to remain in the following areas: words clearly relating to the environment and traditional life, such as flora and fauna, weather terminology, and specific tools; colour terms, especially denoting the different colours of sheep; adjectives, mostly negative, describing people's character and behaviour.

The input from Gaelic, beginning at least as early as the twelfth century, has resulted in borrowings such as the widely known and used *cairn* 'a heap of stones', *glen, loch, capercailzie* 'wood-grouse', *tocher* 'dowry'. There are also more recent borrowings, some of which were introduced by Sir Walter Scott: *clan, galore* 'in abundance', *gillie*, especially in the sense of 'a sportsman's attendant', *sporran* 'the leather pouch worn in front of a man's kilt', *whisky*, and *ceilidh* 'an organized evening entertainment'.

As exemplified by *rax*, other elements of the distinctive vocabulary of Scots come from Anglo-Saxon, such as *bannock* 'a round, flat girdle-cake', *but and ben* 'a two-roomed cottage' (also recorded in transported varieties in Canada and New Zealand), *haggis* (the famous dish), *haugh* 'river-meadow land', and *wee* (ME *wei*, a weight).

Another characteristic of Scots vocabulary has to do with borrowing from Latin, which was done independently of English and has resulted in different meanings. *Narrative*, for example, is a legal term in Scots, referring to 'a statement of alleged facts as the basis of a legal action'. On the whole, Scots law has its own, largely Latin-based vocabulary. Many Latin borrowings shared with English differ in form: *dispone* (beside *dispose*), *promove* (besides *promote*).

Considering Scotland's history, especially the so-called Franco-Scottish Alliance (1296–1560), it is not surprising that there are many borrowings from French: *leal* for 'loyal', 'honest', *ashet* 'serving plate', *aumry* 'pantry', Orkney *pidie*, and Shetland *peerie* (cf. the Fair Isle letter) from *petit*. As a result of contacts with craftsmen and traders from the Low Countries, there are also borrowings from Dutch: *cuit* 'ankle', *pinkie* 'the little finger', *golf* (from Du. *kolf*, a club used in a similar game), *scone* (from Middle Du. *schoonbrot* 'fine bread').

For various reasons, most of the Scots words exemplified above are probably quite stable. Some of them, such as the legal terms, are institutionalized, others have come to enjoy symbolic status, and some have become part of General English. There is also popular interest in the dialect vocabulary of Scots, which will help towards preserving a fair selection of the words. Yet it is inevitable that many words inherited from the past will fall into disuse. In rural areas especially, as in most parts of the world, changing lifestyles have caused massive lexical attrition (cf. 4.1.5.3). This is sadly realized by the Orkney writer George Mackay Brown (incidentally, the word *voar* is very much alive in Shetland dialect):

What lovely words have gone into the silence! *Vore*, the springtime, for example. Another is *ice-lowsing*, meaning the thaw – a marvellous word that ... Still, in lonely crofts, there is the *sae-bink*, a stone shelf for water vessels to be set. There is excuse for the vanishing of such a fine word, for now there is little need for the *sae-bink*. (From an article in *The Orcadian*, 27 November 1980)

4.3.4 Further reading

Aitken, A. J. (1984) 'Scots and English in Scotland'. In P. Trudgill (ed.), *Language in the British Isles*. Cambridge: Cambridge University Press, 94–114.
Aitken, A. J. (1985) 'Is Scots a language?' *English Today* 3, 41–45.
Miller, J. (1993) 'The grammar of Scottish English'. In J. and L. Milroy (eds), *Real English*. London: Longman, 99–138.

4.4 IRELAND

... Green English is a grafted tongue, an English foliage on an Irish stem, still nourished by an Irish root. (Loreto Todd, *Green English* (2000:23))

4.4.1 The two countries and their founder populations

Ireland, 'the Emerald Isle' west of Great Britain, has an area of 82,400 sq.km, of which well over four-fifths constitutes the Republic of Ireland (Eire), while the remaining fifth, Northern Ireland (Ulster), is part of the United Kingdom. We will describe Ireland and its varieties of language in one section, as explained in our introduction to this chapter.

Ireland is divided into four provinces, formerly independent kingdoms: Connacht, Munster, Leinster, and Ulster, which in turn are divided into a total of 32 counties. Northern Ireland as a political unit comprises six of Ulster's nine counties.

It is now believed that the Celtic population of Ireland came directly from Gaul, though there may have been early settlers from Britain as well (Thomson 1984:241). The Old Irish name of Ireland was *Ériu* and the Romans, who – like the Anglo-Saxons – never invaded the island, referred to it as *Hibernia*.

Even before the fifth century, the Celts must have been well established; there are early records of their language in a special runic or linear script. There are substantial records of Ireland's history from about the seventh century, written in both Latin and Irish. These languages continued to flourish in spite of the Viking raids from the end of the eighth to the early eleventh century.

As in England, the Vikings did not only come as occasional raiders; many settled in the new country and gradually amalgamated with the indigenous population. The Scandinavian linguistic contribution to Ireland is particularly found in place names, e.g. the element *vig* 'bay', as found in *Wicklow*, and *-ford*, related to *fjord*, as in *Waterford, Wexford*.

The Normans came to Ireland about a century after the Battle of Hastings, not directly from France but from Wales and south-western England. They also left some traces in place-names, such as the elements *-ville* and *cour* 'courtyard'.

The first speakers of English who settled in Ireland were hardly conquerors but appear to have come mostly for religious reasons. The actual colonization from England began in the south-east towards the end of the twelfth century and by the year 1300 two-thirds of Ireland had been conquered. From the very beginning, English law was introduced with the purpose of protecting the colonists and disadvantaging the Irish. Still, these early colonists appear to have amalgamated with the population in much the same way as the Vikings, and there is evidence from the mid-fourteenth century that they had adopted the manners as well as the language of the Irish (Leith 1996:187). By the end of the fifteenth century, only a small area around Dublin, which had been colonized by settlers from Bristol, was strictly under English control. This area is known as 'the Pale' (from *pale* in the sense of 'boundary'; cf. the phrase *beyond the pale*).

During the Tudor and Stuart periods, English control was forcefully reasserted and it was ruled that the English language should be used throughout Ireland. A further complication in the relations was caused by the difference in religious practices after the Reformation in England. Elizabeth I, who saw Irish Catholicism as treachery, especially during the war with Spain, sent troops to Ireland. The Irish were defeated and a new group of colonizers took over their land. Among these were a considerable number of Protestant Scotsmen from the Lowlands, who settled in the north-east, i.e. today's Northern Ireland. The county of Derry was taken over by a group of London merchants; this is why the town of Derry was renamed Londonderry, though the Catholics never called it anything but 'Derry'.

The outcome of the war and the massive colonization in the North caused a major resettlement of the Irish who moved or were forced to move to the poorer, partly barren, west of the country. Naturally, anti-English feelings grew stronger and stronger, and a movement for independence from English rule, also embraced by some Protestants, resulted in an uprising in 1798, the outcome of which was the incorporation of Ireland into the UK (the Act of Union of 1800).

At the time of the Act of Union, it is believed that English was the first language of half the population of Ireland. During the following century, Irish suffered massive abandonment. There were several reasons for this: the famines in the 1840s which led to death as well as large-scale emigration, particularly to North America; the enforcement of universal English-language education; the transfer to English in the Catholic Church.

The movement towards independence kept growing stronger during the nineteenth century; in 1921 the Irish Free State was established, and in 1949 southern Ireland was declared a republic, which meant that 26 of the 32 counties gained independence from the UK.

4.4.2 Ireland as a linguistic area

4.4.2.1 The status of Irish

The Republic of Ireland has two official languages: Irish Gaelic, usually referred to as Irish, and English. Article 4 in the constitution of the Irish Free State states: 'the national language . . . is the Irish language, but the English language shall be equally recognised as an official language . . .'. The revival and maintenance of the Irish language was part and parcel of the independence movement. 'Ireland with its language and without freedom is preferable to Ireland with freedom and without its language' (Eamon De Valera, one of the first leaders of Sinn Féin and Prime Minister of the Irish Republic during several periods). Not surprisingly, the maintenance of Irish in Northern Ireland is very much a political issue (cf. Kallen 1994:188 and http://cain.ulst.ac.uk/issues/language).

Despite all efforts, the number of native Irish speakers has continued to decline. By the end of the millennium there were only a few thousand people left in isolated pockets of Western Ireland, especially in the area known as the *Gaeltacht* 'Irish-speaking district', who still used Irish every day. There are no longer any people who speak only Irish. Yet the 1996 census found that over 30 per cent of the entire population claimed to use Irish on a regular basis. It would appear that this is partly a reflection of a positive attitude or wishful thinking; in other words, most people value the language as a symbol of national or ethnic identity, or as a symbol of cultural distinctiveness.

> In ordinary Irish life, there are places for the Irish language. Almost all of them are either ceremonial, trivial, or exist only in tandem with English. Bus scrolls, street signs, bits and pieces of advertisements, . . . the beginnings and endings of official letters, e.g. the salutation *A chara* [literally 'Oh, friend' but translated as 'My friend' 'Dear Sir'] – then the text of the letter in English – then, at the end, *Mise, le meas* [(I am) (yours) respectfully], and so on. (Edwards 1984:488)

Nevertheless, Irish is available all over Ireland every day through radio and television. The restoration of Irish as a subject as well as the medium of instruction is actively encouraged officially at all levels of education. The University of Galway, for example, is an all-Irish seat of learning.

Irish belongs to the q-Celtic group of Celtic languages (cf. 4.2.2.1), and is thus closely related to Scottish Gaelic. The Irish substratum pervades the English language as spoken in Ireland at all levels of language, most markedly in grammar and discourse.

4.4.2.2 Varieties of English in Ireland

As can be deduced from the account in the previous section, the history of English in Ireland is characterized by a high degree of discontinuity and regional variability. This has resulted in a rich and somewhat confusing terminology denoting minor and major varieties of Irish English (IrE). It is particularly confusing since some of the terms seem to be used synonymously. The following terms are found in the literature: *Yola, Planter English, Anglo-Irish, Ulster Scots* (as discussed in 4.3, it could of course be argued that this is not a variety of English), *Hiberno-English, Irish English.*

Yola (derived from Old English, especially West Saxon *yald* 'old') refers to the old, first form of English spoken in Ireland that survived in pockets, especially in Wexford, until the nineteenth century.

Planter English is sometimes used to denote one of the two main traditions of English in Ireland, the other being Hiberno-English. It refers to language varieties descended from the varieties spoken by the founding populations in the sixteenth and seventeenth centuries and is represented by two varieties, namely Anglo-Irish and Ulster Scots.

Anglo-Irish is descended from the English brought to Ireland by planters, i.e. settlers, from England, modified by contacts with Irish, Ulster Scots, and Hiberno-English. It is socially and regionally variable; a well-known characteristic variety is, for example, the dialect of Kerry in the south-west. Kerrymen are stereotypically viewed as 'different' and subject to so-called 'Kerryman jokes' (the same kind of silly jokes featuring in 'Irish jokes' in other parts of the British Isles). Anglo-Irish is sometimes used as a generic term for 'English as used in Ireland', which is not much appreciated.

Ulster Scots is a variety of Scots/Scottish English spoken mainly in the counties of Antrim, Donegal, and Down, thus not throughout Northern Ireland although its influence is noticeable in the entire region and beyond. As in Scotland, there is a linguistic continuum, relating to social as well as regional factors.

Hiberno-English, in contrast with Planter English, is a range of English spoken by people whose ancestral mother tongue was Irish, i.e. a kind of counterpart to Highland English in Scotland. 'This is a "grafted English", at one and the same time comprehensible to other speakers of English and yet still in communication with the Gaelic language that was the mother tongue of its speakers' ancestors' (Todd 2000:71). It preserves certain Gaelic features at all levels of language; yet, depending on the area, many of its speakers approximate to Anglo-Irish and Ulster Scots. Confusingly, this term, too, is sometimes used as a generic term.

Irish English is a neutral, generic term, simply referring to English as used in Ireland. This is the term we generally use in our descriptive account which, especially in the phonological section, sometimes makes distinctions between *Southern Irish English (SIrE)* and *Northern Irish English (NIrE)*.

4.4.3 Irish English (IrE) – a descriptive account

A 'shortlist' of particularly salient features:

- The LOT, THOUGHT, NORTH, and FORCE vowels are normally unrounded [ɑ, ɑ:].
- /l/ is clear in all positions.
- In SIrE dental stops /t, d/ often replace the fricatives, as in *think*, *thirty*.
- In SIrE post- and intervocalic /t/ is realized as a 'slit fricative' (Wells 1982:429ff.), i.e. a quality almost like [tʃ] or [ts].
- NIrE is most easily distinguished on account of its intonation: 'a rise is the unmarked tone not only for questions but also for statements and commands' (Wells 1982:447). In one of her autobiographical works, the actress Shirley MacLaine describes a meeting with a man from Northern Ireland, who confused her by 'asking questions all the time'.
- The 'hot-news' perfect, indicating a recently performed action, expressed through *after + -ing*, as in *We're after booking our holidays.*

- The nonuse of *yes* and *no*; i.e. the answer to a question such as *Are you thirsty?* will be *I am*.
- *It*-clefting constructions, such as *It's staying in the hotel you are*.

4.4.3.1 Phonology

In the lexical sets below (Table 4.4) as well as the more detailed description to follow, distinctions are often apparent between NIrE and SIrE, which, at least according to phonological criteria, belong to two different 'types' of inner-circle varieties (cf. 3.2.2).

Since neither accent can be classified as 'English-based', it makes sense to provide a contrast with General American as well as Received Pronunciation. The latter accent, according to Wells (1982:418), is 'in no way taken as an unquestioned norm of good pronunciation' in Ireland.

Table 4.4. Irish English lexical sets

NIrE	SIrE	Key word	GA	RP
ɪ	ɪ	KIT	ɪ	ɪ
ɛ	ɛ	DRESS	ɛ	e
a	æ	TRAP	æ	æ
ɒ, ɔ	ɒ	LOT	ɑ	ɒ
ʌ	ʌ	STRUT	ʌ	ʌ
u	ʊ	FOOT	ʊ	ʊ
a	æ, aː	BATH	æ	ɑː
ɔ	ɒ, ɔː	CLOTH	ɔ	ɒ
ʌr	ʌr, ɛr	NURSE	ɜr	ɜː
i	iː	FLEECE	iː	iː
e	eː	FACE	eɪ	eɪ
a	aː	PALM	ɑ	ɑː
ɔ	ɔː	THOUGHT	ɔ	ɔː
o	oː	GOAT	o	əʊ
u	uː	GOOSE	u	uː
aɪ	aɪ	PRICE	aɪ	aɪ
ɔɪ	ɔɪ	CHOICE	ɔɪ	ɔɪ
au	aʊ	MOUTH	aʊ	aʊ
ir	iːr	NEAR	ɪr	ɪə
ɛr	eːr	SQUARE	ɛr	ɛə
ar	aːr	START	ɑr	ɑː
ɔr	ɔːr	NORTH	ɔr	ɔː
or	oːr	FORCE	or	ɔː
ur	uːr	CURE	ʊr	ʊə

The vowel system of SIrE shows close correspondence in quality with the vowel system of Irish.

IrE is firmly rhotic, but unlike some rhotic accents of English, it has a wide range of vowel oppositions in pre-r positions, as seen from NURSE, NEAR, SQUARE, etc. In Dublin speech, NURSE and SQUARE are often merged, as in Scouse (cf. 4.1.5.1), and there is often hypercorrection. The current British Prime Minister is, for example, often referred to as Mr [blɜːr].

As mentioned among the salient features, LOT tends to be unrounded, with a socially variable degree of fronting, sometimes approximating to TRAP. This is illustrated by the following anecdotal evidence from a quiz show:

> In answer to the question 'Which breed of dogs is particularly well known for hunting rats?', a participant immediately came up with *rottweiler* ['ratwaɪlər] instead of the expected *terrier*. (Mícheál Ó Flaithearta, personal communication)

STRUT is often centralized, to the degree of [ə]. In 'popular' Dublin accents FOOT and STRUT are unsplit, as in the north of England.

In parts of the west of Ireland, KIT and DRESS have merged, with a varying degree of closeness. The word *vet*, for example, may be realized as [vɪt] (cf. the motto for the New Zealand presentation in 4.8).

Some FLEECE words, namely those spelt with <ea>, have retained the more 'historical' [eː], e.g. *meat, speak*. Since FACE also has [eː], the following rhyme produced by Alexander Pope in the early eighteenth century would be perfectly possible in Ireland today, thus demonstrating the extremely traditional character of SIrE , a 'Type I' accent (3.2.2):

> Here thou, great ANNA! whom three realms obey,
> Dost sometimes counsel take – and sometimes Tea.

As seen from Table 4.4, BATH and PALM may be identical, but there is a great deal of social and regional variation here. On the whole, 'the opposition /æ–ɑː/ carries a low functional load' (Wells 1982:423), which includes TRAP as well. Most Irishmen, with the exception of 'sophisticated middle-class Dubliners' pronounce both *aunt* and *ant* as /ænt/. A well-known stereotype of SIrE, often represented in fictional dialogue, is the realization of PRICE as [ɔɪ]. In actual fact, there is (recessive) absence of the PRICE–CHOICE opposition, but the quality of the diphthong is extremely variable. KIT and schwa have merged into [ə] in weak checked syllables, making *abbot* rhyme with *rabbit* (Wells 1982:427).

With regard to consonants, the characteristic dental stops were mentioned among the salient features. Thus *tin* and *thin, tree* and *three,* may be homophonous, but there are also hypercorrections, i.e. replacements of stops by fricatives (cf. for example, the written representation of *trust* as *thrust*).

The existence of the salient slit fricative is a substratum effect; all Celtic languages have a kind of 'weakening' of consonants (lenition). An example of this is seen in the

Irish phrase *A Chara*, mentioned in 4.4.2.1, where the vocative *A* causes lenition; *chara* is the lenited form of *cara*.

IrE has clear /l/ and is firmly rhotic. /r/ is usually a postalveolar approximant before stressed vowels, but retroflex inter- and postvocalically.

There is no h dropping and initial [hw] is generally retained. In contrast with other accents of English, but like Irish, IrE has inter- and postvocalic /h/, as in the name *Drogheda* ['drɒhɪdə].

A recessive feature, well known as an Irish stereotype, is the use of [ʃ] and [ʒ] instead of [s] and [z]. In the play *The Irish Masque at Court* (1613), Ben Jonson wrote *faish* for 'face' and *sherve* for 'serve'.

IrE is further characterized by schwa epenthesis, as in *Dublin* ['dʊbəlɪn], *Kathleen* ['kætəliːn]. Like ScotE, IrE has certain word stress patterns that differ from RP (in *-ize* verbs, for example), but there are few categorical differences and a great deal of variability. The intonation of SIrE is RP-like.

A comparison between the lexical sets of NIrE and those of ScotE as seen in 4.3.3.2 tells us that there is striking similarity: there are hardly any phonemic vowel-length distinctions. The Scottish Vowel Length Rule (SVLR) also applies to some extent.

With regard to vowel quality, there is enormous variation in NIrE, conditioned by social class, region, and allegiance as well as style and phonetic environment. This variation is also extremely well researched (cf. for example L. Milroy 1980, J. Milroy 1981, Harris 1984, McCafferty 1999). Here we have to limit ourselves to a few points:

/u/ tends to be virtually unrounded and centralized;
MOUTH words have a characteristic pronunciation, which can be perceived as the PRICE diphthong by outsiders;
In the north (e.g. Coleraine) and Belfast, /ɛ/ and /a/ are often neutralized before or after a velar consonant, making *beg–bag* and *kettle–cattle* homophonous.

The consonants are, on the whole, quite similar to those of SIrE, but the dental sounds are firmly fricative. Although /r/ is generally a retroflex approximant, trilled r's can still be heard in rural areas. /l/ is generally clear, but in Belfast dark /l/ of the ScotE type is often heard.

The characteristic intonation described above can be heard in the recording of the Northern Irish informant on the accompanying CD.

4.4.3.2 Grammar

The following presentation relies heavily on data and analysis from Harris 1993, describing nonstandard grammatical characteristics of IrE usage. Most people in Ireland speak some variety of nonstandard English as their first language. As we have seen, IrE phonology, especially in the south, is very conservative; the same can be said about its grammar.

Like ScotE, IrE has unmarked plurality in nouns indicating measure, time, etc. (*two mile, five year*). Another similarity is the use of 'three-dimensional' deictic systems: *this/that/yon (thon)*.

IrE makes an explicit distinction between singular *you/ye* and plural *youse* (also found in other varieties, such as AusE and AmE). This is exemplified in passing in 3.1.2. Below follows a more telling example, recorded in Belfast for a project led by Lesley Milroy:

> So I said to our Jill and our Mary: 'Youse wash the dishes.' I might as well have said: 'You wash the dishes', for our Jill just got up and put her coat on and went out. (cf. Harris 1993:146)

Another characteristic of IrE is 'nominalization', i.e. giving a word or phrase a noun-like status which it does not generally have, as in *If I had the doing of it again, I'd do it different* ('If I could do it again, I'd do it differently'). This is no doubt related to the Irish substratum; Gaelic is an extremely 'noun-centred' language (Todd 2000:86, 92).

With reference to the very characteristic 'hot-news' perfect, the use of *after* is also found in noun phrases such as *I'm only after my dinner* ('I've just had my dinner'). These constructions are borrowings from Irish.

Another feature relating to the tense system has to do with the description of a situation in the past and persisting into the present, as in *How long have you been here?* Standard English. In IrE, as in Irish but also Germanic languages such as German and Dutch, the present tense is used in this case rather than the perfect, as illustrated in the example quoted in 3.1.2.

'Habitual *be*' is found in IrE, varying in form between *be/be's* (southern) and *do/does be* (northern). There is thus a contrast between *He's sick now* (nonhabitual) with *He be's sick often* (habitual). With verbs other than *be*, the habitual is formed by *do* plus an infinitive. (Harris 1993:162). There are similar constructions in Irish.

Like ScotE, IrE often uses continuous forms of stative verbs (*I was knowing your face*).

A very striking feature is the tendency to represent the logical subject of a sentence by a noun phrase governed by a preposition, as in *The money is with them* 'They have plenty of money' or *There's great humour to him* 'He's very humorous'.

It-clefting, as exemplified in the list of salient features, is a characteristic fronting device in discourse. Another focusing device is the use of sentence tags initiated by *so* as in *It's raining, so it is*.

4.4.3.3 Lexicon

The rich vocabulary of IrE stems from three sources: English, Scots, and Irish. Many of the English metaphors, idioms, and proverbs reflect the semantics of Irish (Todd 2000:88).

Irish words, which should perhaps be referred to as retentions rather than borrowings, are found particularly in the areas of culture, e.g. *banshee* 'fairy woman' and *cairn* 'sacred stone mound', rural life, e.g. *creel* 'basket, *culchie* 'someone from the back of beyond', food, e.g. *bannock* 'homemade bread cake' (also found in ScotE), and social interaction, e.g. *ceili* 'evening visit' and *shannach* 'comfortable gossip'.

Considering the 'discontinuous' history of English in Ireland, it is not surprising that the words of 'planter English' reflect various periods of time. As late as 1990, Todd recorded words in Donegal no longer used in other parts of the English-speaking world, many of which were known and used by Shakespeare and his contemporaries (Todd 2000:61f). 'Retained' words typically include vocabulary denoting people's character and behaviour (cf. Shetland vocabulary as described in 4.3.3.4): *atomy* 'small, insignificant person', *crawthumper* 'person who is overly religious', *mitch* 'play truant'.

A number of words that look like ordinary General English words have different meanings, such as *backward* 'shy', *thick-witted* 'stubborn', *doubt* 'believe' (also found in ScotE). Not surprisingly, NIrE shares a great deal of its lexicon with ScotE and Scots words are experiencing something of a renaissance (cf. the recent *Concise Ulster Dictionary* (Macafee 1996)).

The many dialect words of French origin in IrE are further proof of the link with Scotland, where there is a considerable French element in Scots as well as ScotE.

Some examples of French borrowings: *ashet* 'large plate', *brave* 'fine', *dishabel*s 'night attire'.

In NIrE, according to Todd (1989:341, 347), Catholic speakers tend to prefer words and expressions derived from Irish, whereas Protestants use more Scots-based vocabulary.

4.4.4 Further reading

Harris, J. (1993) 'The grammar of Irish English'. In J. and L. Milroy (eds), *Real English*.
London: Longman, 139–86.
McCafferty, K. (1999) '(London)Derry: between Ulster and local speech – class, ethnicity and language change'. In P. Foulkes and G. Docherty (eds), *Urban Voices*.
London: Arnold, 246–64.
Todd, L. (2000) *Green English. Ireland's influence on the English language*. Dublin: The O'Brien Press.

4.5 THE USA

During the administration of President Jimmy Carter, a Georgian with a local Georgian accent, a popular American television program had a character representing a state department official, who spoke conspicuously like a Georgian. When a New Yorker next to him called attention to his Georgian accent, he replied, 'We don't have an accent any more. You do.' (quoted from Suzanne Romaine, *Language in Society* (1994))

4.5.1 An introductory note

The USA occupies a special position among the inner-circle countries in that it has by far the greatest number of first-language users of English. Like EngE, American English (AmE) is also a 'reference variety' and increasingly used as a model in teaching English as a foreign language throughout the world. Its impact on other varieties of English, including EngE, is undisputed (cf. 3.2 for some examples and Chapters 6 and 7 for further discussion).

In view of the worldwide impact of AmE, it may seem paradoxical that English is not legally declared the official language of the USA. As in the UK (cf. 4.1.1), its status is simply taken for granted; it is a *de facto* if not *de jure* official language (cf.McArthur 1998:38). About 20 years ago, however, the first steps were taken towards making English the official language in the form of a proposal for a constitutional amendment. This proposal was not accepted by the Senate, but since then, two major organizations, US English and English First have been continuing the efforts. No decision has been taken as yet and there are also a number of groups opposing what they call the English Only movement (cf. Tottie 2002:240 and www.englishfirst.org).

In this section we focus on AmE as a variety in its own right, which means, in particular, that we do not view it so much against EngE as describe internal variation. We refer you to 3.2 and 4.6 for discussions and examples of British–American differences and to Tottie (2002) for an elaborate account.

In view of its role as a 'reference variety', we do not highlight salient features for AmE, but include a discussion of the definition of 'standard', which is somewhat more problematic than in the case of Standard EngE/RP, at least with regard to phonology (cf. our motto for this section).

4.5.2 The country and its people

Area: 9,629,091 sq.km
Population: 282 million (of which about 240 million use English as their first language)
Capital: Washington, DC

Fig. 4.3. The USA

About 80 per cent of the US population live in metropolitan areas. A telling proof of the thrust of domestic migration westwards is the geographical median for the population which is now near St Louis, Missouri, but was near Philadelphia 200 years ago.

When Europeans began colonizing North America in the late fifteenth century, the continent had already been inhabited by humans for more than 10,000 years. It is estimated that the Native Americans numbered about four million at the time of the arrival of Columbus. In AmE, the linguistic heritage of the indigenous population is reflected in masses of place names, e.g. *Kalamazoo* 'boiling pot', *Mississippi* 'the father of the waters', *Tennessee* 'winding river', and a number of lexical borrowings, many of which are now not only part of Standard AmE but also of General English, such as *moccasin, hickory*.

Before turning to the coming of the English, we would like to draw your attention to some other important early settlements in North America, which have left considerable traces in language and culture:

- In the early seventeenth century, the Dutch West India Company set up an important trading post along the Hudson River. In 1660 there were about 10,000 inhabitants and a real colony had been set up, called *Nieuw Nederland*. Its capital was *Nieuw Amsterdam*, which later came to be named *New York*. The Dutch colony did not survive into the next century, but left its mark on place- names in New York City and all over New York state, such as *Brooklyn* (named after the Dutch city of *Breukelen*), *Wall Street* (from Du. *wal*, referring to the palisades erected against Indian raiders), *Harlem*. Lexical borrowings are also plentiful, e.g. *stoop* 'small porch' and *cookie*.
- The late seventeenth century saw the emergence of a French colony in Louisiana, with its thriving capital, New Orleans. The end of Louisiana as a French colony came in 1803 when it was bought by the US, but the English presence in the area 'came far too late to erase the heavy French influence, which only now is beginning to fade from New Orleans speech' (Wolfram and Schilling Estes 1998:102). The French element in Louisiana was later reinforced by the immigration of Acadians from Canada (cf. the term *Cajun*). There is also a variety known as Louisiana Creole, which is largely French-based.
- In the late seventeenth century, the Quaker colonization of Pennsylvania began. It soon attracted large groups of Germans who also came for religious reasons. A variety of German, known as *Pennsylvania Dutch*, is still spoken in inland Pennsylvania (cf. the famous feature film *Witness*).

The English came to North America in the late sixteenth century. The first permanent settlement was in Virginia, which became a colony in 1609. The best known early settlement is probably that of the 'Pilgrim Fathers', Puritans opposing the teaching propagated by the Church of England. In 1620 they sailed on the *Mayflower* from Plymouth (in England's West Country) and gave the same name to their place of arrival in Massachusetts.

During the following century, 13 British colonies were founded, all along the east coast. Before the Boston Tea Party leading to the War of Independence, the colonies did not form a union but in 1776, they met in Philadelphia for the *Declaration of Independence*. In 1783, independence was acknowledged.

During the first half of the nineteenth century the USA – although still not politically 'united' in today's sense – expanded westwards, and by 1848 comprised roughly the area corresponding to the contiguous states today.

From the 1830s, massive immigration from Europe took place, beginning with Irish, Scots, and German settlers, but later including virtually all nations. Many immigrant groups tended to concentrate in particular areas, such as Scandinavians in Minnesota and Wisconsin. Although the nineteenth and twentieth century immigration happened rather late in the history of the English language, it has resulted in noticeable substratum effects, such as the alleged influence of Italian speech on New York City English (cf. Trudgill 1995:45ff.).

Since the 1970s, the majority of immigrants have come from Asia and from South and Central America. Statistics from 2001 show that 12.5 per cent of the US population were of 'Hispanic' origin (Tottie 2002:51).

Virtually all parts of the British Isles as well as all walks of life are represented in the English-speaking founder population. In reconstructing the origins and dialects of the Pilgrim Fathers, Wakelin (1986) found that among only three married couples of this little group the following areas were represented: Yorkshire, Lancashire, the Isle of Man, Somerset, Gloucestershire, London.

4.5.3 Regional and social variation in language – an overview

In the USA, as in Canada, it is in the east that we find the richest regional diversity in language. This is clearly related to the time depth of the settlement history; as we have seen, the first colonies were all situated in this part of the country. The mid- and far west, on the other hand, was not settled by English speakers until the nineteenth century. The westward migration had a 'band-like' character, i.e. the inhabitants of each colony moved more or less straight in a westerly direction. This explains why dialect boundaries in the USA tend to run horizontally. There is, for example a *grea[s]y/grea[z]y* line, north of which the medial consonant is voiceless, and a *pail/bucket* line, where the first word typifies northern speech. In line with the above, the boundaries tend to break up in the west, however.

It is noteworthy that today's most distinctive dialects of AmE had already been established by the late eighteenth century. Many of the dialects can be further subdivided (for details, cf. Wolfram and Schilling Estes 1998:102ff., Tottie 2002:210, and http://us.english.uga.edu). Some detailed information about regional characteristics is included below. The main dialect areas are:

The North

▪ New England, with Boston as its centre, at least formerly a very prestigious variety, which still shows the greatest affinity with EngE, e.g. in being nonrhotic.

■ New York, comprising Upstate New York with the Dutch-influenced (especially with reference to vocabulary) Hudson Valley area as well as New York City, which could, in fact, also be listed as a dialect region in its own right.

■ an area extending westwards from upstate New York to the Pacific.

The Midland

There is less agreement as to what constitutes this region; the following reflects a traditionally based division.

■ the Philadelphia area (the Delaware Valley)

■ the Pittsburgh area (the Upper Ohio Valley)

■ part of the inland areas of Virginia, North and South Carolina, and Georgia

■ a large area across Tennessee and western Arkansas, then spreading further incorporating virtually the whole of the western USA. In more popular, or folk-linguistic classifications, the accents in this category are considered to be southern, however (cf. Niedzielski and Preston 2000).

The South

■ the coastal and some inland areas of Delaware, Maryland, Virginia, North and South Carolina, Georgia, the 'Gulf States', i.e. Florida, Alabama, Mississippi, Louisiana, and (eastern) Texas.

Before turning to a description of some recent work on AmE varieties, exclusively based on phonological criteria, we would like to comment on the popular belief that in some relic areas of the USA, notably in the Appalachians, people still 'speak like Shakespeare'. Although it is certainly true that a) AmE in general has undergone less innovation than spoken EngE and b) that a great many traditional dialect features are still used in certain remote areas, the whole concept of surviving Elizabethan varieties is a linguistic myth. Yet it is not without significance, since it has played a part in marking identity and taking pride in local dialect (Montgomery 1998).

Increasingly, dialect surveys tend to be based on phonological systems rather than isolated lexical items such as *pail* vs *bucket* or unsystematic phonetic details. This new type of survey is very much connected with the work of William Labov, who is particularly interested in vowel systems (cf. Labov 1994). In agreement with the preceding dialect divisions, he determined that there were three major dialect areas in the USA: Southern, Midland (comprising more than half of the nation and typically having the LOT/THOUGHT Merger) and Northern (or rather 'Northern Cities', chain shift in the vowel system). According to Labov, the regions are diverging rather than converging. Recently he has suggested that four main dialect areas may be distinguished: North, Midland, South, and West (cf. Wolfram and Schilling Estes 1998: 120ff. and www.ling.upenn.edu/phonoatlas/home.gtml for more detailed information about the chain shift and Labov's description of current dialect diversity in North America). A brief account of the chain shifts is also given in 4.5.6.1 below.

The USA, like the UK, is characterized by a high degree of social stratification. Through the pioneering work conducted by Labov and his research group in

Philadelphia since the 1960s, a great deal is now known about the relationship between social class and the use of linguistic, often regionally based, features, about mechanisms of language change, and about the role of other factors such as gender and ethnicity. We now turn to a brief account of two important ethnic varieties in American English, regarded as 'varieties in their own right'.

4.5.4 Two ethnic varieties

4.5.4.1 African American Vernacular English (AAVE).

This variety, which used to be referred to as Black (Vernacular) English can be characterized as a social as well as regional variety which in popular usage is often referred to as *Ebonics*. This is a political rather than a linguistic term; it was introduced in the 1970s to highlight the African origin of the variety and became widely known during a heated debate in the mid-1990s on the legitimacy of the variety in a school setting (cf. Tottie 2002:239 for a report on the 'Oakland debate').

As the name suggests, AAVE is used by the black population of the USA, but not by all and to a varying degree; in other words, there is continuous variation according to social class, style, and region. Characteristic age differences also emerge in that young speakers tend to use more AAVE features than older speakers for the purpose of marking identity.

During the last few decades, an enormous amount of research has been devoted to AAVE; yet there is no definitive agreement as to its origin. The three most common theories are: 1) it is a creole language, a native-speaker variety descended from a pidgin; 2) it is a dialect of English based on the varieties the slaves learnt from their masters, which explains its many Southern features; 3) it is derived from West African languages (cf. the definition of *Ebonics* above). Trudgill (1995:59f) identifies AAVE as 'a separate ethnic-group variety which identifies its speakers as black rather than white' and sees no problem in combining 1) and 2) above in speculating about the origin of the variety. (For further information on AAVE cf. Mufwene *et al.* 1998).

Without further comment, we have chosen the following brief extract from Alice Walker's *The Color Purple* to illustrate some characteristic features of AAVE, many of which are also found in other nonstandard varieties of English.

> He come home with a girl from round Gray. She be my age but they married. He be on her all the time. She walk round like she don't know what hit her. I think she thought she love him. But he got so many of us. All needing somethin.

> My little sister Nettie is got a boyfriend in the same shape almost as Pa. His wife died. She was kilt by her boyfriend coming home from church. He got only three children though. He seen Nettie in church and now every Sunday evening here come Mr. .... I tell Nettie to keep at her books. It be more then a notion taking care of children ain't even yourn. And look what happen to Ma.

4.5.4.2 Chicano English

This variety is spoken by descendants of Hispanics from Mexico (the word *Chicano* is derived from *Mexicano*). In contrast with other names of varieties arisen from

Spanish-English contacts, such as 'Tex-Mex', 'Spanglish' and 'englañol', it is well defined (cf. also the account of Puerto Rico in 5.6.2). It should be regarded as a systematic form of speech acquired from childhood; its speakers are not only people who know both English and Spanish but also those who know no Spanish at all but are members of a Hispanic community of Mexican origin (e.g. in east Los Angeles). Speakers of Chicano English are known to codeswitch a great deal, shifting to a more standard variety when speaking to non-Chicanos.

Unlike AAVE, its characteristic features are virtually restricted to phonology; its syntax and morphology approximate to Standard English. Among its characteristics are: /ʃ/–/tʃ/ neutralization to the effect that /ʃ/ is used exclusively; general devoicing of /z/; devoicing of /v/ in final position; dental stops instead of fricatives. (For an exhaustive treatment of Chicano English, cf. Penfield and Ornstein-Galicia 1985.)

4.5.5 Standard American English/General American – a 'reference variety'

The codification of American English begun by Noah Webster in 1789 was mentioned in 3.2.1. In 1828 he published *An American Dictionary of the English Language*, the American counterpart to Johnson's dictionary. Webster's dictionary, which is larger than Johnson's by about a third, not only lists lexical items but also gives advice as to usage, suggests new, 'American' spellings, such as *fiber, defense, color*, and gives guidance as to pronunciation.

The codified American Standard variety is maintained and updated through the publication of dictionaries such as the *American Heritage Dictionary*. The *Longman Pronunciation Dictionary* (Wells 2000) is very reliable for AmE as well as EngE 'standard pronunciations'. Yet, as our motto suggests, the concept of standard in the USA is not so easily defined, especially with regard to pronunciation, but also to vocabulary:

> Classifications of standardness will . . . be somewhat flexible with respect to the regional variety being judged. Thus, the *r*-less pronunciations which characterize Eastern New England or Southeastern American pronunciation (as in *cah* for *car* or *beah* for *bear*) may be judged as standard English, as will the *r*-ful pronunciations that characterize certain other dialects. And people may be judged as standard English speakers whether they *go to the beach*, *go to the shore*, or *go to the ocean* for a summer vacation. . . . there are regional standards which are recognized within the broad and informal notion of standard American English . . . For the most part, Americans do not assign strong positive, or prestige, value to any particular native American English dialect. (Wolfram and Schilling Estes 1998:11f)

The term General American used throughout this book, referring to American accents without a great deal of regional colouring, is seldom used by Americans – linguists included – who prefer 'Network English/Standard/' . In comparing RP and 'Network English', Lesley Milroy (1999:174) points out that these accents are 'horses of a very different colour'. Whereas Network English is a majority accent, whose speakers describe themselves and are described by others as having no accent, 'RP is saliently marked for class and in no sense is nor ever has been a mainstream accent'.

4.5.6 American English (AmE) – a descriptive account with special reference to regional variation in phonology

4.5.6.1 Phonology

We begin by showing a selection of lexical sets from Wells 1982 (Table 4.5) demonstrating regional variation; GA is contrasted with accents representing New England, New York City, and the south. The third major dialect area, i.e. Midland, is not represented, since it is largely identical to General American. The data is taken from Wells (1982), but we omit a great deal of variation due to phonetic environment. To complete the table, we have added sets representing pre-<r> vowels in the 'South' column; note that the quality of these is related to variable rhoticity.

Table 4.5. US lexical sets

The South	New England	New York City	Key word	GA
æ, æɪ	æ	æ, æə, ɛə	TRAP	æ
ɑ	ɒ	ɑ, ɑə	LOT	ɑ
æ, æɪ	a, æ	æə, ɛə	BATH	æ
ɔ	ɒ	ɔə	CLOTH	ɔ
ɑ	a	ɑə	PALM	ɑ
ɔ	ɒ	ɔə	THOUGHT	ɔ
oʊ	o	oʊ	GOAT	o
u, ɪu	u	u, ɪu	GOOSE	u
aɪ – a(ː) – aɛ	aɪ	ɑɪ	PRICE	aɪ
æʊ	aʊ	aʊ	MOUTH	aʊ
ɪə – ɛə – ɪɚ	iə	ɪə(r)	NEAR	ɪr
æɪ – ær	æə	ɛə(r)	SQUARE	ɛr
ɑː – ɑr	a	ɑə(r) ɑr	START	ɑr
ɔː – ɔːr	ɒ	ɔə(r)	NORTH	ɔr
oə – oʊ – oʊr	oə	ɔə(r)	FORCE	or
oə – ʊə – oʊ – oʊr	uə	ʊə(r)	CURE	ʊr

A limited commentary on the sets and some other features, including consonants:

New York City: Note particularly the variable rhoticity, the variability along the open-close dimension in TRAP and BATH, the CLOTH–THOUGHT merger, the quality of NURSE and the realizations of the dental fricatives as affricates or stops.

Traditionally, New York City has been a nonrhotic accent, but is now variably so.

Non-prevocalic /r/ has become a socially significant variable, carefully investigated by Labov in his famous *The Social Stratification of English in New York City* (Labov 1966). The results show that rhoticity is a prestige marker but also that there is great variability according to age and style. Nonrhotic New York City accents characteristically have linking and intrusive /r/, and sometimes add /r/ at the end of any word ending in a vowel.

A well-known, somewhat stereotypical New York City feature is the CHOICE-like quality of NURSE, as in the popular representation of *thirty-third* as *toity-toid*. Although this feature is said to be recessive, it can still be heard, at least in stage performances, e.g. in *West Side Story*. There are also hypercorrections as in *earl* for *oil*.

The quality of TRAP and BATH was also investigated by Labov, who recorded a spectrum of variants, from fairly open (more prestigious) to very close [ɪːə]; this is what Trudgill (1995:46) has in mind when he talks about the 'beard-like' quality of *bad* ascribed to the Italian substratum. Varying degree of closeness in CLOTH and THOUGHT, on the other hand, is not seen as socially significant. This variability, conducive to change is now seen as part of the major vowel shift known as 'the northern cities chain shift'.

New England: Traditionally, this area shares many of its characteristic features with EngE, but the impact of General American is increasing. We have already (4.5.3) mentioned the nonrhoticity found particularly in the Boston area. As in New York City, linking as well as intrusive /r/ occurs, also in 'end positions' such as Cuba ['kjubər] (as once pronounced by John Kennedy, a famous Bostonian).

The south: As indicated in 4.5.3, the linguistic south comprises a very large area, and the uniformity of its speech must not be exaggerated. Nevertheless, it is possible to list some particularly salient features that will apply to most areas, such as the tendency towards particularly marked differences in length between stressed and unstressed syllables, caricatured in *Urp* for *Europe*, *fern* for *foreign*, *Prezdet* for *President* (*The Jimmy Carter Dictionary*). This is popularly known as 'the southern drawl'. A contributing factor in the perception of the drawl is the fact that many vowels tend to have diphthongal off-glides, making, for example, *egg* rhyme with *vague* (cf. Wells 1982:535).

Another striking feature is the PRICE monophthong, given as an alternative in Table 4.4. In representing a southern accent the English writer Kingsley Amis wrote *Ah, Apollo jars* for *I apologize* (quoted from Wells 1982:529).

As seen from Table 4.4, TRAP and BATH may be realized as diphthongs, which is the case in certain regions and to some extent dependent on the following consonant. This is caricatured in Jimmy Carter's Georgian accent as *glade* for *glad*.

In many southern dialects, KIT and DRESS tend to merge before nasal sounds, making e.g. *pin* and *pen* homophonous (usually realized as [pɪn]).

Nonrhoticity is found in the south as well as New England. Some areas, such as the early settlements in Tidewater Virginia are r-ful (Wolfram and Schilling Estes

1998:97) as are certain mountain areas. From a social point of view, nonrhoticity, interestingly, is associated with two quite distinct social groups, namely upper-class white people and black people (cf. Wells 1982:542). It is worth pointing out that nonrhoticity is not connected with low prestige as it can be in New York City. Southern accents tend not to have 'r-liasion', i.e. neither linking nor intrusive /r/. Some lower-class speakers and AAVE speakers do not pronounce intervocalic /r/, as in *Carolina*, which is unique in World Englishes.

AAVE shares most of the characteristic features of the south but typically also tends to have cluster reduction as in [tʃal] 'child' and labiodental fricatives or dental stops instead of dental fricatives in words such as *mouth, brother*.

A brief presentation of the ongoing dramatic major shifts in American vowel systems as studied by Labov and his research group and documented at (www.ling.upenn.edu/phonoatlas/home.gtml):

The northern cities shift, which is based on recordings from Chicago, Detroit, Buffalo, Rochester, and Syracuse) begins with the raising and fronting of TRAP, followed by the fronting of LOT (which moves into the position that TRAP used to have). THOUGHT, STRUT, and DRESS then follow suit, i.e. taking the positions of LOT, THOUGHT, and STRUT, respectively. KIT is lowered and centralized.

The southern shift is more complicated and the temporal sequences are not as well established. In his description, Labov begins by describing the monophthongization of PRICE (cf. the lexical sets above). This has probably brought about the lowering of FACE, which in turn has triggered a similar movement of FLEECE. The most dramatic part of the southern shift is perhaps the remarkable fronting of GOOSE and THOUGHT.

4.5.6.2 Grammar

Regional, nonstandard AmE grammar shares most of the features described in the corresponding EngE section, such as unmarked plurality, multiple negation, and a simplified verb agreement system. In the short extract from *The Color Purple* above, illustrating AAVE, some of these features are exemplified, as is also 'copula deletion' and 'invariant be'. Note also the nonstandard pronominal form *yourn*.

The characteristic historically based 'a-prefixing' verb forms indicating continuous action are still used in Appalachian English, e.g. *He was a-holding three dogs*. Here we also find double modals as in *I might could go* (a feature of ScotE, too, as described in 4.3.3.3). Another regional feature, typically found in parts of Pennsylvania and Ohio (and also in ScotE) is the preference for constructions like *My hair needs combed* instead of *needs combing*.

As in IrE, varieties of AmE have special second person plural forms, such as *yous(e)*. In the south, *you all* or *y'all* is the most frequent form, *you'uns* is found in the Pittsburgh area, and in informal English generally expressions like *you guys, you people* are used.

A well-known feature of regional AmE is so-called 'positive *anymore*', as in *They watch a lot of videos anymore*, meaning 'nowadays', 'currently' (Wolfram and Schilling Estes 1998:142). This usage is typically found in the Midland area.

4.5.6.3 Lexicon

In 3.2.1.2 a number of examples were given illustrating characteristics of AmE vocabulary, especially as contrasted with EngE. Here we will restrict ourselves to making a few comments on regional and nonstandard lexical variation. There is no point in producing some kind of random listing.

Regional AmE vocabulary is extremely well documented in the monumental *Dictionary of American Regional English (DARE)*. Items to be included in the dictionary were elicited by means of a questionnaire in which 41 different categories of lexical difference are outlined, such as food, animals, and furniture but also physical states and emotions.

According to Wolfram and Schilling Estes (1998:60ff.), 'the number of dialectally sensitive words runs well into the thousands'. Based on their own research experiences, they suggest some sets of lexical items reflecting cross-dialectal vocabulary differences and illustrating broadening, narrowing, and lexical innovation. These are some of their examples:

faucet/spigot/tap 'a device with a valve for regulating the flow of a liquid';
Snap beans/string beans/green beans 'a type of vegetable with a stringy fiber on the pods';
Earth worm/angleworm/fishing worm/night crawler 'a type of worm used in fishing'.

A great deal of dialect research in the USA has been devoted to lexical mapping, whereby isoglosses such as the *pail/bucket* line were determined. An excellent work of this kind is Carver 1987, using 800 lexical items from *DARE*. Although linguists often claim that lexical differences are not very useful indicators of dialect areas, Carver's findings support not only boundaries established in cultural geography but also phonological distribution patterns.

4.5.7 Further reading

Schneider, E. W. (ed.) (1996) *Focus on the USA*. Varieties of English Around the World G 16. Amsterdam: Benjamins.
Tottie, G. (2002) *An Introduction to American English*. Oxford: Blackwell.
Wolfram, W. and Schilling-Estes N. (1998) *American English*. Oxford: Blackwell.

4.6 CANADA

Oot and aboot

4.6.1 The country and its settlement history

Area:	9,976,000 sq.km
Population:	29.5 million (of which well over 60 per cent have English as their first language and almost 25 per cent French)
Capital:	Ottawa

Fig. 4.4. Canada

With its almost 10 million square kilometres, Canada is the second largest country in the world. Its population is unevenly distributed: more than half of its inhabitants live in a relatively small area near the Great Lakes and the St Lawrence River, i.e. in the southern parts of Ontario and Quebec. Canadian society is highly urbanized: three-quarters of the population live in cities.

The name Canada is derived from the indigenous Iroquois Indian word *kanata* 'village', 'settlement'. It was taken up in the sixteenth century by the first French explorers.

When British exploration and settlement on a large scale began somewhat later, conflicts naturally arose between British and French interests. In 1763 the French were forced to cede all their North American colonies to Britain with the exception of the small islands of Saint-Pierre and Miquelon south-west of Newfoundland, which still belong to France. French colonists were expelled from Acadia/Nova Scotia and many moved to French Louisiana in what is now the USA (where the word *Acadien* was anglicized to *Cajun*), but in Quebec they remained and continued to use the French language, legal system, etc.

Although there were some earlier settlements, e.g. in Newfoundland, the English-speaking 'founder population' of Canada can mainly be related to two significant 'waves' of immigration in the eighteenth and nineteenth centuries:

■ The base of Canadian English is derived from a large group of pro-British 'loyalists' who left the USA for Canada after the War of Independence. To begin with, they came from coastal New England and settled on the Canadian coast, but later some of these incomers moved into Ontario and Quebec. Other groups came from Pennsylvania, New Jersey, New York, and Vermont, settling in areas around the Great Lakes.

■ In the early nineteenth century, in connection with the 1812–14 war with the USA, large groups of immigrants (more than doubling the population) were – for political reasons – recruited from Britain and Ireland 'to dilute the broad base of American ancestry' (Chambers 1998:x). Another massive input from English-speaking countries, especially Scotland and Ireland, came in the 1850s.

From the mid-nineteenth century to the late 1970s, general immigration on a large scale was encouraged by the Canadian Government. Canada has, in fact, been one of the world's main immigrant-receiving societies and has an official policy of 'multi-culturalism' based on the ideology that the best way of catering for the demographic diversity is to view it as a 'mosaic' rather than a 'melting-pot'. In other words, people of diverse origins and communities are free to preserve and enhance their cultural heritage while participating as equal partners in Canadian society.

4.6.2 Canada as a linguistic area

Before turning to a detailed description of this variety, we give a brief overview of some demographically- and culturally-based aspects of the language situation in Canada, including some that are not exclusively related to Canadian English (CanE).

4.6.2.1 Multilingualism, with special reference to French-English bilingualism
The Canadian government's support of multiculturalism naturally includes a celebration and promotion of multilingualism, i.e. 'the ability to speak, at some level, more than one language'. This policy is clearly implemented in the media and in education, especially in 'immersion schools', where the second language is the medium of instruction in all subjects and encouraged in free periods as well.

At the federal level, Canada has two official languages: English, which is the mother tongue of about 63 per cent of the population (the 'anglophones'), and French, with about 25 per cent native speakers (the 'francophones'). This means that the two languages enjoy equal status in all federal departments, judicial bodies, and adminis-trative agencies. At the provincial level, on the other hand, only three provinces are officially bilingual: Quebec (since 1867), Manitoba (since 1870), and New Brunswick (since 1982). This is not to say that other provinces are opposed to the idea of 'insti-tutional bilingualism' (the obligation and capacity of state institutions to operate in two languages). At the grass-roots level, Canadian bilingualism is characterized by fluctuation rather than stability (Chambers 1991:95ff.).

4.6.2.2 Conflicting norms and standards in anglophone Canada
In his presentation of Canadian phonology, Wells (1982:496) accounts for examples of hypercorrection not heard anywhere else in the English-speaking world: words such as *moon, noon, too* are pronounced with /-ju/, i.e. mistakenly adhering to a perceived British norm without yod dropping. This is clearly symptomatic of the conflicting

British and American norms and standards that characterize CanE, not only with regard to phonology but also spelling, vocabulary, and, to some extent, grammar.

As a result of different settlement histories, there are regional differences: the Prairie provinces, for example, are clearly more American than Ontario, which is reflected, among other things, in spelling preferences among schoolchildren (Ireland 1979). The word *colour*, for example, was spelt with *-our* by more than 85 per cent of Ireland's informants in Ontario, but only by 30 per cent of those in Alberta. 'These double standards are the linguistic legacy of the first two immigrations in our history' (Chambers 1998:264).

A less obvious, but equally important reason for the existence of double, even conflicting, standards is of an attitudinal rather than regional character. Until fairly recently, it has been fashionable to imitate British, or rather EngE, speech as well as manners. The hypercorrect pronunciation of *moon* highlights this fashion. However, according to Chambers (1998:264), 'the Anglo-Canadian gentlefolk have become relics, along with the Union Jack, the British Commonwealth, and "God Save the Queen"'.

In part, the marked pro-British preferences had to do with anti-American attitudes. A widely used interdisciplinary academic textbook in 'Canadian studies' courses has the telling title *A Passion for Identity*. In particular, this passion has sprung from a need for establishing an identity clearly distinct from the USA.

The importance of the need for a marked Canadian identity *vis-à-vis* the southern neighbour is discussed in the article 'The Demise of the Canadianism *Chesterfield*' (Chambers 1994). It is suggested that the 'demise' of this word (as used in a generic sense) together with another well-known Canadianism, the so-called 'Canadian raising' in words such as *knife* and *house* (cf. below), is clearly related to more relaxed attitudes to the USA, especially after the free trade agreements in the 1980s.

The monumental *Canadian Oxford Dictionary* (1998) reflects current variability in CanE, which, according to Chambers (1998:269) 'admits more pronunciation and vocabulary variants than other English varieties' (this claim obviously refers to standard varieties only).

4.6.2.3 Regional diversity

As in the USA, the vast expanses in the west are indeed fairly homogeneous, whereas the eastern provinces where English first arrived, are remarkably rich in dialects. The most distinctive region ethnographically as well as linguistically is Newfoundland. An important reason for its distinctiveness is that it simply has the longest history of the English-speaking communities. Other reasons are its special living conditions and ways of life, the sizeable groups of early English-speaking immigrants from linguistically distinctive areas such as Devon, Cornwall, Scotland, and Ireland, and the fact that it did not join the Canadian federation until 1949.

It is no coincidence that another island-based speech community, namely Prince Edward Island, is also regionally distinctive (cf. the *Dictionary of Prince Edward*

Island English (Pratt 1988)). There are many interesting enclave varieties, such as the well-known German-influenced dialect of Lunenburg, Nova Scotia (cf. 4.6.3.2), and those founded by Scottish and Irish settlers in other Atlantic provinces and the Ottawa River Valley. In other areas, rural dialects reflect input from settlements representing various language groups: Ukrainian, Italian, Dutch, Scandinavian, and, of course, French. These are largely unstudied, but the current Dialect Topography project is remedying this shortcoming quite rapidly and results are continuously shown on the website of the Department of Linguistics, University of Toronto (www.chass.utoronto.ca/~chambers/).

4.6.3 Canadian English – a descriptive account

A shortlist of particularly salient features:

- Canadian raising, a feature found in the lexical sets PRICE and MOUTH, so called because the starting-point of the diphthongs /aʊ/ and /aɪ/ is raised, i.e. closer, than in the reference accents when followed by voiceless consonants, as in *out, house, knife, night*, but consequently not in *loud, houses, knives, ride*, etc. The motto for the section on Canada in this book is a stereotypical American representation of Canadian raising. Although the stereotype demonstrates awareness of a characteristic feature, its representation is not very satisfactory; in phonetic transcription the diphthongs are generally rendered as [əɪ] and [ʌʊ].
  On the website www.yorku.ca/twainweb/troberts/raising.html instructive examples can be listened to.
- the use of the tag *eh* – another well-known Canadian stereotype; in fact, there is even a linguistic textbook called *Canajan, Eh?* (Orkin 1997). Although this tag is not uncommon in many other varieties, such as, for example, ScotE, it is more frequent and has an extended function as a discourse marker in CanE. Examples of this feature can also be heard on the website mentioned above.
- the occurrence of EngE-type lexical-incidental pronunciations such as *shone* (with a short vowel), *corollary, capillary* with the stress on the first syllable; in most cases, however, there is regionally, socially, and individually based variation between EngE-type and AmE-type realizations.
- the unique use of certain lexical items, often 'recycled' English words and French borrowings. Compare for example, the distinction between *prime minister* (federal chief minister) and *premier* (provincial chief minister), the use of *province* and *provincial* referring to the major political divisions of the country, and the use of *riding* in the modern sense of 'constituency'.

4.6.3.1 Spelling

Until recently there have been no fixed spelling conventions for CanE to be, for example, recommended by editors, but with the publication of the *Canadian Oxford Dictionary,* based on some 20 million words of Canadian text, a form of codification has indeed taken place.

A quick check on some lexical items representing well-known differences in British and American spelling conventions reveals the following:

- *-our* vs *-or*

  The British form is given as the first alternative, i.e. it has been found to be most commonly used, e.g. *colour* (also *color*). The headword entry for *color* is followed by 'var. of *colour*'. All *-our* words seem to follow this pattern: *behaviour, favour, humour, neighbour*, etc.

- *-re* vs *-er*

  Here, too, the British form is generally given as the first alternative: *centre, theatre, meagre, metre*, and *-er* forms are, like *-or* ones, listed as acceptable variants, without further specification. The headword entry *calibre*, on the other hand, is followed by: (esp. US *caliber*).

- *-ise (-yse)* vs *-ize (-yze)*

  Here the American form is always given as the first alternative, with the exception of *advertise* which has no acceptable variant. *-ise* forms are given as variants but usually labelled 'esp. Brit'. Admittedly, this American/British distinction is hardly valid anymore; a look at a recent corpus-based British dictionary such as the *Collins Cobuild* reveals that a number of verbs such as *realize, criticize* are given as main headword entries followed by a note that *-ise* spellings are also used in Britain; *analyse*, on the other hand is the first form, whereas *analyze* is said to be American.

Spelling is not a major issue in the description of world Englishes, but in the case of CanE, it may function as a marker of identity and shifting attitudes (cf. the regional diversity described in 4.6.2.2). This is clearly a linguistic level which is characterized by extremely high general awareness, as illustrated in the following plea from a *Globe and Mail* columnist after reading a style book for Canadian Press, making *-or* spellings the rule:

> This may be a trifling matter. But language is a keystone of culture, and a culture is distinguished by many subtle shadings of sounds, looks and behaviour. I say, with uncontrite and *u*-ful fervour, let's keep vigour and ardour (etc.) in our English! (Cochrane 1992)

4.6.3.2 Phonology

As we have already seen from the *moon* example, CanE phonology, like spelling, shows signs of vacillations between British and American norms. It should be pointed out, however, that this divided usage or 'conflict' is almost exclusively restricted to lexical incidence, although in some cases, such as yod dropping, sizeable groups of words follow the same pattern. As for phonetic realization, phonotactic distribution and phonemic systems, on the other hand, CanE is in almost total agreement with GA.

Let us now consider the lexical sets, comparing CanE and Newfoundland, its most 'deviant' accent, to GA as well as RP (Table 4.6).

Table 4.6. Canadian lexical sets

CanE	Newfoundland	Key word	GA	RP
ɪ	ɪ	KIT	ɪ	ɪ
ɛ	ɛ, ɪ	DRESS	ɛ	e
æ	æ	TRAP	æ	æ
ɑ	ɑ	LOT	ɑ	ɒ
ʌ	ɔ̈	STRUT	ʌ	ʌ
ʊ	ʊ	FOOT	ʊ	ʊ
æ	æː	BATH	æ	ɑː
ɑ	ɑː	CLOTH	ɔ	ɒ
ɜr	ɜr	NURSE	ɜr	ɜː
i	iː	FLEECE	iː	iː
eɪ	ɛː, ɛɪ	FACE	eɪ	eɪ
ɑ	æ, ɑː	PALM	ɑ	ɑː
ɑ	ɑː	THOUGHT	ɔ	ɔː
o	ʌʊ	GOAT	o	əʊ
u	uː	GOOSE	u	uː
aɪ, əɪ	əi	PRICE	aɪ	aɪ
ɔɪ	əi	CHOICE	ɔɪ	ɔɪ
ɑʊ, ʌʊ	əu	MOUTH	aʊ	aʊ
ɪr	ɛr	NEAR	ɪr	ɪə
ɛr	ɛr	SQUARE	ɛr	ɛə
ɑr	ær	START	ɑr	ɑː
or	ɔ̈r	NORTH	ɔr	ɔː
or	ɔ̈r	FORCE	or	ɔː
ʊr	ɔ̈r	CURE	ʊr	ʊə

PRICE and MOUTH typically show variation, being candidates for Canadian raising. A great number of Canadians, especially in parts of the Atlantic provinces, do not produce this feature, but if used, it constitutes a very interesting linguistic variable in the study of social variation and change in CanE. It would appear, as already hinted at, that raising, at least in the /aʊ/ diphthong, is recessive. Whereas sociolinguistic studies in the late 1970s still demonstrate a great deal of allophonic variation, more recent research suggests remarkable nationwide convergence (Chambers 1995:64ff.). The general picture is that the sound change is towards the standard American phonetic realization and that it is led by young women.

The term 'Canadian raising' indicates, obviously, that the phenomenon is the result of a raising process. There is, however, no general agreement on this score. Britain (1992:30) has emphasized that in analyses of ongoing linguistic change the focus should not exclusively be on the end result of the change but also on what the change has developed from. The fact that wider diphthongs occurred in front of voiced consonants before they occurred in front of voiceless consonants is phonetically plausible and, in fact, attested from a number of other varieties of English such as those spoken in St Helena, Tristan da Cunha, and the Falkland Islands. In all these areas, there has – as in Canada – been considerable dialect mixing. A case in point is also Scots/Scottish English where *tight* is realized as [tɔɪt] and *tied* as [taɪd]. The distributional rules are not the same, however (cf. 4.3.3.2).

A few points will be made about some other aspects of the vowel system; notably, virtually all the following comments have to do with open back vowels.

Most Canadian accents have a single merged vowel phoneme for the sets THOUGHT, CLOTH, LOT, PALM, and START. The quality of the vowel is open, back, and variably – but never more than lightly – rounded.

A well-known feature, used as one of the criteria for distinguishing varieties of English from each other by Trudgill and Hannah (1994:6; cf. also 3.2.2 above), is in fact the THOUGHT–LOT merger, i.e. there is neither length nor quality distinction in word pairs such as *cot–caught, rot–wrought, stock–stalk, collar–caller.*

An interesting recent sociolinguistic study (Clarke *et al.* 1995) shows that back vowels in CanE, i.e. [u ʊ o ɑ] are presently undergoing a shift to the effect that they are fronted. Language-external factors appear to be highly relevant in the interpretation of the results; teenage high school students, especially young women, are the trendsetters, who seem to participate in certain patterns of vowel shifting that are found in urban California as well. It is suggested that the prestige of the new vocalic features are reinforced by association with the speech of many (particularly female) national newscasters in both the USA and Canada.

In Nova Scotian speech different pronunciations may be heard in PALM and LOT words, with the first set having more fronted vowels. Newfoundland speech, as always, is the most 'deviant' (cf. the notations in Table 4.6 above). Note, for example, that in parts of the province the short vowel system is reduced to five rather than six, since *bit* and *bet* tend to be merged as [bɪt] (KIT and DRESS merger), whereas [ɛ] is found in NEAR and SQUARE words such as *beer, bare, bare* (Wells 1982:500) and [ɔ̈] in NORTH, FORCE, and CURE (at least in broad accents). The realization of the STRUT vowel demonstrates affinity with Irish English; it is back, rounded, and centralized [ɔ̈]. PRICE and VOICE are often merged as [əɪ].

The Canadian consonant system is virtually identical with that of GA, including the existence of certain recessive features, such as /hw-/ pronunciations in *wh-* words. For a recent study, cf. the Dialect Topography website, mentioned in 4.6.2.3.

Lunenburg in Nova Scotia is the only mainland white Canadian community to be nonrhotic, except when pronouncing words where /r/ occurs after [ɜː] (Trudgill 2000:197). Whereas the nonrhoticity can be connected with the early loyalists from New England, settling here in the eighteenth century, other features in the accent point to input not only from German but also from Irish and Scottish English.

In broad Newfoundland accents, especially in Irish settlement areas, dental plosives are used instead of fricatives as in *that* (cf. the poem below). In some accents, labiodental fricatives are used instead, as in Cockney or Estuary English, e.g. [bæːf] for *bath*. Substratum effects of Irish and Scottish settlements are shown in the quality of postvocalic /l/, which is generally clear in Irish areas but dark in Scottish areas and elsewhere (Paddock 1982:88). Finally, h dropping is widely used in broad accents, as also exemplified in the following beginning of a poem by Harold Paddock:

'Ow I knows I'm A Newf
(a pome fer Ray Guy)

Because of my laingwich:
   h'In my case
   h'I comes from dat Far Greatest Bay
   And can't 'andle h'aitches,
   And 'aves dis h'irresistible h'urge
   To write h'onreadable pomes.

CanE prosody does not appear to be distinctive in any way. As in some other varieties, high rising terminals have been widely used during the last 10 years.

> When Canadians argue about British versus American pronunciation, the phonology is not discussed but taken for granted; the questions at issue are just those of lexical incidence. Does *schedule*, they ask, begin with /ʃ/ or with /sk/? Does (or should) *leisure* rhyme with *seizure* or with *pleasure*? (Wells 1982:491)

The following brief presentation of lexical-incidental issues in CanE is based on data from the *Canadian Oxford Dictionary* and some findings of the Dialect Topography project (cf. above).

A general trend already emerging in the 1972 nationwide Survey of Canadian English, based on data from schoolchildren and their parents, is towards an increase in the use of the American variants at the expense of the British. Thus e.g. *lever* with /e/, yod dropping in *news*, *either* with /iː/ were all favoured by the younger age group. On the whole, the *Canadian Oxford Dictionary* gives further evidence of the general trend, albeit with certain conflicting instances, especially with regard to yod dropping. Admittedly, present-day RP allows variation, too; yod-dropped forms of *suit* and *super*, for example, are the winners according to Wells (2000).

A special case is that of *genuine*, with the alternative pronunciations /-ɪn/ and /-aɪn/. Incidentally, Wells (2000) marks the second alternative off as 'incorrect' for both British and American English. Awareness of this pronunciation is interestingly reflected in the following poem written in 1837 by an English traveller:

> To the Ladies of the City of Toronto
> Our ladies are the best kind
> Of all others the most fine;
> In their manners and their minds,
> Most refined and *genuine*.
>   (cf. McConnell 1979:30)

Interestingly, the Canadian dictionary also accounts for a few 'fudged' pronunciations, such as *tomato* with /æ/, given as the only alternative after /eɪ/.

4.6.3.3 Grammar

There are few truly distinctive features in CanE grammar; if any, they tend to be found in morphology rather than syntax or relate to discourse and the lexicon. Sentence-initial *as well* is claimed to be uniquely Canadian, as in *As well, I include my CV*. Some British-type structures linger on, such as *Has the milkman been yet?* rather than *... been here ...* (Trudgill and Hannah 1994:77) and the tendency to say *Have you got ...?* rather than *Do you have ...?*, but the American structures are by no means uncommon. It would seem that – from a language proficiency point of view – there is no need for a specific grammar of Canadian Standard English; yet ongoing research based on the large text corpora now available will probably reveal other cases where CanE occupies an intermediate position.

Morphological characteristics include certain forms in the strong verb system, of which some have been subject to sociolinguistic studies. In the Dialect Topography project, an apparent-time study demonstrates a rapid increase in the past tense forms *dove* and *snuck*, as also found in AmE, instead of *dived* and *sneaked*. A stable British form, on the other hand, is found in the past tense of *shine*, always realized as /ʃɑn/.

The frequent use of the tag *eh?* was included among the salient features. Its specific function as a discourse marker in CanE has to do with ascertaining the comprehension, continued interest, agreement, etc., of the person or persons addressed (*it's way out in the suburbs, eh, so I can't get there by bike*); in other words, it has an important conversational and narrative function.

Nonstandard – especially traditional-dialect – grammar typically reflects settlement history: the 'hot-news' perfect as in *I'm after doin' it*, which is a Hiberno-English construction (4.4.2.2), is found in the Ottawa River Valley and in Newfoundland. Another aspectual feature found in Newfoundland English, which has its roots in England's West Country, is the use of habitual unstressed *da* 'do' (and *did*), as in *I da wear a heavy shirt all year round* (Paddock 1982:77). *Yiz* or *youse*, i.e. plural forms of the second person pronoun, which are common in Hiberno-English, are also found in Newfoundland English, as are constructions like *it's sorry you will be* for 'you will be sorry'.

4.6.3.4 Lexicon

As indicated by the *Chesterfield* example, there is a general trend towards AmE vocabulary, but a quick search for British vs American priorities in the *Canadian*

Oxford Dictionary resulted in a somewhat mixed pattern. Unlike spelling and pronunciation preferences, it is not quite clear which variant is the most frequent in the dictionary database. The following British terms were definitely given as 'normal' in CanE: *bonnet* and *tap* (given as head entries with cross-references from *hood* and *faucet*), *autumn* ('also called *fall*'), *fortnight, queue, shop* (*line* and *store* are labelled N.Amer). *Gasolene*, on the other hand, is the head entry with a cross-reference from *petrol*. As for the well-known pairs *subway–underground, sidewalk–pavement, spanner–wrench, candy–sweet*, it is not made quite clear where CanE stands. Finally, a person dispensing medicine is called neither *druggist* nor *chemist* but *pharmacist*.

The above is only one aspect of CanE vocabulary, which is also characterized by a great deal of innovation, partly due to the need for new words for new surroundings, and, naturally, borrowing as a result of long-standing and intense contact with other varieties of language. The following exemplifies some lexical categories:

Extension of meaning is found in names for 'similar-looking' plants and types of vegetation: *crocus* 'a type of prairie anemone', *bush* 'the back country' (cf. AusE), and in a number of 'revived' words, as exemplified among the salient features.

Ice hockey (or *hockey* in CanE) terms represent Canadianisms which have been adopted in General English: *boarding, blue line, icing*, whereas others are true foreignisms, encapsulating Canadian life: *Quebec heater* 'a type of heating stove', *bombardier* 'a characteristic winter vehicle', metaphors such as *corduroy road* (a road made by putting down logs, making a bumpy surface like that of ribbed corduroy cloth) and *(frost) boil* (an eruption in a road produced by frost).

With reference to borrowing, French has been an important donor language, but only before the mid-nineteenth century, reflecting the exploration and settlement history: *voyageur, bateau, concession* 'grant of land', *prairie, rapids, chute, bayou* 'lumbering area', *depot*. Some words in this category are now more or less restricted to place name elements: *sault, dalles, grande, bois, butte*. Many place names are the result of misinterpretations of French words, i.e. folk etymology, such as *Cape Despair* (from *Le Cap d'Espoir*). Similarly, a winter vehicle known as a *carry-all* is an English interpretation of *cariole*. A great many French loanwords are restricted to certain regions: *anse* 'cove' as in *L'Anse aux Meadowes* in Newfoundland, *frazil* (flaky ice-crystals formed in turbulent water), above all used in the east, and *poudre* (fine, drifting snow) used in the north.

The linguistically and politically important French-based words *francophone* and *anglophone* are fairly recent. These words are indeed Canadianisms, as are some related words, such as the opposites *francophobe* and *francophile*.

Borrowings from Indian languages include: *pemmican* (a meat dish), *saskatoon* (a shrub with edible berries), thousands of place names, including the name of the nation, as already mentioned, and *Toronto*, whose etymology is disputed but sometimes given as 'meeting-place'. Yet, according to McConnell (1979:81), surprisingly few Indian words have entered CanE. Even fewer come from Inuit languages; some well-known examples are *anorak, kayak*, and *mukluk* (a kind of shoe); the first two are of course now used in General English.

4.6.4 Further reading

Bailey, R. W. (1982) 'The English language in Canada'. In R.W. Bailey and M. Görlach (eds), *English as a World Language*. Ann Arbor: The University of Michigan Press, 134–76.

Clarke, S. (ed.) (1993) *Focus on Canada*. Varieties of English Around the World. General Series Vol. 11. Amsterdam: Benjamins.

McConnell, R. E. (1979) *Our Own Voice. Canadian English and How it is Studied*. Toronto: Gage Educational Publishing Ltd.

4.7 AUSTRALIA

> ... I've not found it so easy to pass it ['correct', RP-like pronunciation] on to the grandchildren. They sound much more Australian than I think we would like them to be. (Joan Hawker, Australian informant for the BBC series *The Story of English*)

> John Clark, native speaker of Australian English (Professor John Clark, introducing himself on the accompanying CD to this book)

4.7.1 The country and its people

Area: 7,686,850 sq.km
Population: about 20 million (of whom more than two million do not have English as their first language)
Capital: Canberra

Fig. 4.5. Australia

Australia is a federation of the states of New South Wales, Victoria, Queensland, South Australia, Western Australia, Tasmania, and Northern Territory.

Before the first Europeans (the Dutch) went there at the beginning of the seventeenth century, there had been speculations about an unknown southern land, *Terra Australis Incognita*, situated somewhere further south than Asia and Africa.

The Aboriginal people in Australia belong to different tribes, and at one time spoke about 200 different languages, related to each other but not to any other language family. Today, the Aborigines constitute no more than one per cent of the country's population and their languages have suffered and are suffering massive death, with 90 per cent of the present languages moribund (Crystal 2000:87).

Continuing the history of the British settlement of Australia from where we left it in Chapter 2, it is worth pointing out that not until the 1840s did free settlers outnumber those with convict origins (Eagleson 1983:415). The 1850s saw an enormous population growth due to the 'goldrushes'. The convicts and other early settlers in Australia came from various parts of Great Britain, but above all from the south-east region of England. Another sizeable group consisted of almost 2000 Irish political prisoners who were transported between 1789 and 1805.

As the prisoners got their 'ticket of leave', they began spreading out into the country, looking for suitable land for sheep farming in particular. Towards the end of the nineteenth century when Australia had more than three million inhabitants, it was very rural with more than 70 per cent of the population living in the countryside. Today, a century later, the situation is different, with well over 80 per cent living in cities.

Before 1950, immigration to Australia was dominated by British and Irish settlers, although there were also some well-known settlements by Germans in the Barossa Valley and Italians in Queensland. More recent immigration has been extremely varied, representing most European as well as Asian countries.

4.7.2 English in Australia – an overview

In contrast with some other countries described in this chapter, English was the only significant language from the outset of colonization. Nowhere else is the characterization of English as a 'killer language' more adequate; the death of Aboriginal languages as outlined above is directly or indirectly caused by the presence of English. The founder population in the eighteenth and nineteenth centuries was almost exclusively English-speaking. Today, Australian English (AusE) can certainly be described as a variety in its own right, if not a third reference variety. AusE is, for example, increasingly used in EFL teaching, especially in East and South-East Asia. Like other major varieties of English, it is also codified in major dictionaries (cf. in particular the 1997 edition of the *Macquarie Dictionary* and consult its website www.macquariedictionary.com.au).

4.7.2.1 A historical perspective – changing attitudes

Considering the structure of the first English-speaking population of Australia, it is hardly surprising that early observations on language down under often comment on the connection with prison life, roughness, vulgarity, etc.

In fact, a special variety called *flash language* 'the cant or jargon of thieves' developed, consisting of slang vocabulary used to assert group solidarity. Some of these words have survived as cultural 'keywords' in Australia (cf. 4.7.3.4. for some examples). Paradoxically, the word *flash* has now come to be used about 'deviating' speakers in Aboriginal communities, using the language of educated whites.

Early observers of AusE usually commented – often with a critical undertone – on the predominance of Cockney-like speech. By contrast, others – writing at the same time – seemed to praise the pure speech heard in the new colony. Opinions clearly vary among the early observers as to what characterizes 'pure' English; it could mean 'nonregional', as well as 'not American', or 'not Cockney'.

The alleged similarity between AusE and Cockney is not just a myth or a biased stereotype; as we will see, especially in the description of AusE phonology, the varieties share a number of features. Yet the still widely held view that Cockney and AusE are virtually the same is absurd. For one thing, both varieties, like all languages, have been subject to change. The accents can easily be distinguished (cf. Wells 1982:594), let alone other levels of language, especially lexical features.

AusE today is indeed a variety in its own right, as signalled by the second motto of this section. The first motto, recorded some 20 years ago, reflects lingering expressions of allegiance to EngE, especially RP, but today the high regard for this accent seems to be virtually gone.

Like most varieties of English, including EngE, AusE is currently subject to influence from AmE, e.g. with regard to word stress, as in *harass* with the stress on the second syllable. Another American-like phonological feature is the voicing of intervocalic /t/, but its origin in Australian speech is not absolutely clear. As exemplified in 4.7.3.1, there is a degree of Americanization in spelling, but – not surprisingly – it is above all the lexicon that has been influenced. This is demonstrated in detail in Burridge and Mulder (1998:283ff.), who also point to the 'double competence' of Australians, which is often apparent in 'global' word quizzes, where Australians tend to beat American as well as British competitors since they master two varieties.

4.7.2.2 Regional variation

In 3.1.1 we mentioned that regional linguistic variation is comparatively limited in Australian English, which may seem strange considering the vastness of the country.

'From Perth to Sydney is over 3000 kilometres, yet their accents are practically indistinguishable.' (Wells 1982: 593). However, according to the most recent textbook on AusE (Burridge and Mulder 1998), it is likely – since regional diversity is partly a function of time – that physical and social distance will eventually have the effect of increasing regional differences.

It is actually possible to exemplify regional differences in vocabulary: a type of sausage is known as *polony* or *saveloy* in most areas, but in Adelaide it is *fritz* and in Brisbane and Sydney *devon*. There is, probably, also some phonological variation, which is currently investigated in a project at Monash University. Among the features studied are L vocalization, which is a new feature in AusE, and variation in BATH. It appears, for example, that Melbourne speakers use a vowel whose quality approximates to northern EngE. In the Barossa Valley, the German substratum is the source of some characteristics, such as the use of *bring/come/take with* (cf. German *mitbringen/mitkommen/mitnehmen*) and final devoicing ('Auslautverhärtung').

4.7.2.3 Social variation

The best-known and most comprehensive investigation of AusE accents was conducted by Mitchell and Delbridge around 1960 (reported in their 1965 monograph). It can be described as the first large-scale sociolinguistic survey ever, preceding even Labov's early work on Martha's Vineyard by a few years. It is true that the range of the informants was narrow: they were all schoolchildren of the same age, but large numbers were recorded and the results show clear social stratification, relating to gender, type of school, family background, and place of residence (town or country).

The vowels represented in the following words, read by all informants, were found to be particularly socially significant*: beet, boot, say, so, high, how.* On the basis of the overall results, Mitchell and Delbridge distinguished among three main varieties of AusE: Broad, General, and Cultivated. The third category, sometimes referred to as 'acrolect', shows the greatest affinity with RP. The distribution of informants over the three categories was as follows: Broad 34 per cent, General 55 per cent, Cultivated 11 per cent. Mitchell and Delbridge emphasize that the figures should not be taken too literally; we are dealing with a continuum and the percentages should be viewed as suggestive of relative tendencies. On the accompanying CD, you can hear the six test words used by Mitchell and Delbridge, realized in three versions and a brief comment on them made by an Australian phonetician. For a detailed description of their phonetic realization, cf. 4.7.3.2.

4.7.2.4 Aboriginal English

The most important and probably also best researched ethnic variety of AusE is Aboriginal English. It is not easily defined, since it covers 'the full range from broken and Pidgin English, through a creole to nonstandard to a complete mastery of standard English' (Eagleson 1983:432), in other words, it is used both as a first and as a second language.

Towards the 'English' end of the continuum, Aboriginal English is characterized by a retroflex articulatory setting (a substratum effect) and some nonstandard grammatical features reminiscent of AAVE, such as copula deletion (*he half-caste*), unmarked plurality (*how many huncle you got?*) and *bin* as a marker of past tense (*that man bin come inside bar*). These examples are from northern Australia (Eagleson 1983:433).

Aborigines living in urban settings, who have generally lost their indigenous languages, speak varieties even closer to the 'English end'. Their language is usually a nonstandard variety of English sharing features that are found worldwide: multiple negation, differences in verb agreement, nonstandard forms of irregular verbs. Note that Standard English is generally not considered a prestige variety within the

Aboriginal community, as signalled by the use of the term *flash language* mentioned above (4.7.2.1).

4.7.3 Australian English (AusE) – a descriptive account

A 'shortlist' of particularly salient features:

- the front [aː] in PALM and START (a feature shared with NZE)
- the wide, 'Cockney-like' diphthongs in FLEECE, FACE, PRICE, GOOSE, GOAT, and MOUTH
- the close (but not as close as in NZE) front vowels, especially DRESS
- the use of two extremely productive noun suffixes: *-ie* and *-o* (*wharfie* 'docker', *smoko* 'a stop for a rest and a smoke')
- the special use of *she* as a generic pronoun: *she's jake* 'it's fine'
- a highly characteristic vocabulary, e.g. *sheila* 'girl', *tucker* 'food', *billabong* 'a waterhole formed by a broken meander of a river', *drongo* 'idiot', *yacker* 'work'.

4.7.3.1 Spelling

The spelling of AusE, as laid down in the *Macquarie Dictionary*, for example, basically follows the British tradition. Making some searches from the Macquarie website (cf. the beginning of 4.7.2) we were surprised to find both *colour* and *color* but only *labour*. Yet, according to Burridge and Mulder (1998:92ff.), 'the Australian Labor Party has spelt its name without a *u* since early this century'. Corpus-based studies of AusE show that ratios between *-or* and *-our* vary considerably, depending on the word. On the other hand, verbs like *realize*, *sympathise*, tend to stick 100 per cent to the spelling used in the second word.

4.7.3.2 Phonology

Below, you will find our presentation of the lexical sets (Table 4.7). Since the three accents of AusE described by Mitchell and Delbridge (cf. 4.7.2.3) are basically distinguished by the six vowels/diphthongs listed among the salient features, we only show a complete table for these particular sets, using a narrow transcription. A complete list is given for General Australian, adapting data from Wells (1982).

In characterizing the Australian vowel system, Wells (1982:595) aptly remarks: 'Phonologically, all Australian English is very close to RP, phonetically, it is not.' In other words: the phonemic inventory, the number, and distribution of distinctive units is identical, but the quality of virtually all vowels is different (cf. for example the front rather than back vowel in PALM and START).

The transcription of the six distinctive lexical sets should give a good idea of their actual realization. It is, for example, obvious that 'Cultivated' approximates to RP in having 'unshifted' diphthongs. 'Broad' differs from General not only in having wider, more radically shifted diphthongs, but also in diphthong length (Wells 1982:597). In addition, Broad MOUTH often begins with a nasal vowel, exemplifying the Australian 'twang'. Note that in Broad and General as distinct from Cultivated and RP, PRICE and MOUTH have very different starting points.

Table 4.7. Australian lexical sets

Broad AusE	General AusE	Cultivated AusE	Key word	RP
	ɪ		KIT	ɪ
	e		DRESS	e
	æ		TRAP	æ
	ɒ		LOT	ɒ
	ʌ		STRUT	ʌ
	ʊ		FOOT	ʊ
	aː		BATH	ɑː
	ɒ		CLOTH	ɒ
	ɜː		NURSE	ɜː
əːɪ	+i	ii	FLEECE	iː
ʌːɪ, aːɪ	ʌɪ	ɛɪ	FACE	eɪ
	aː		PALM	ɑː
	ɔː		THOUGHT	ɔː
ʌːʊ,aːʉ	ʌʉ	öʊ	GOAT	əʊ
əːʉ	ʊʉ	ʊu	GOOSE	uː
ɒːɪ	ɒɪ	aɪ	PRICE	aɪ
	ɔɪ		CHOICE	ɔɪ
ɛːʊ	æʊ	aʊ	MOUTH	aʊ
	ɪə, iːə, iː		NEAR	ɪə
	eə		SQUARE	ɛə
	aː		START	ɑː
	ɔː		NORTH	ɔː
	ɔː		FORCE	ɔː
	ʊə – ɔː – uːə – uː		CURE	ʊə

As mentioned among the salient features, the front short vowels tend to be a great deal closer than in RP and, indeed, than would appear from Table 4.7. The Australian speaker on the CD, for example, pronounces *ten* virtually like [tɪn].

In a number of BATH words, especially those where the vowel is followed by a nasal plus another consonant, such as *dance, plant*, the TRAP vowel is often heard. This could be due to American influence, but may also be related to a dialect background in England (cf. 4.7.2.2).

It would appear that there is a general fronting tendency in AusE vowels, affecting NURSE as well; this vowel can be rather more front as well as closer than the symbol in the table indicates.

As seen from the table, there is a tendency for the centring diphthongs to be monophthongal, although AusE is firmly nonrhotic.

Although schwa is replacing /ɪ/ in RP in a number of unstressed affixes such as the adjectival ending *-ate*, it is much more dominant in AusE, regularly used in inflectional endings such as *-ed, -es* ['wɒntəd], ['bɒksəz] (the second transcription could refer to *boxes* as well as *boxers*).

The nonrhoticity of AusE has already been mentioned, as has the tendency towards intervocalic T Voicing (4.7.2.1). H dropping may occur as well as hypercorrect forms, as evidenced in one of the examples of Aboriginal English (4.7.2.4).

The HRT intonation pattern is very common in AusE and were observed as early as the 1960s by Mitchell and Delbridge, who called it 'the interview tune' and character-ized it as 'abnormal'. More recently, it has been carefully investigated in Sydney by Horvath (1985), who found that it was predominantly used by teenagers, females, lower working class, and either Greeks or 'Anglos'. The most common function of HRT, according to Horvath, is to request the heightened participation of the listener.

4.7.3.3 Grammar

Among the salient features we mentioned a morphological characteristic, i.e. the striking productivity of *-ie* (sometimes a process of clipping and expanding (Cramley 2001:95) but also representing other types of affixation) and *-o* suffixes. Another type of clipping is also common, as in *beaut* for 'beauty' or 'beautiful', *uni* for 'university', *Oz* for 'Australia', *roo* for 'kangaroo'.

Corpus-based studies of AusE grammar as compared to other varieties show tendencies rather than categorical differences. Hundt (1998a), studying subjunctives in BrE, AmE, AusE, and NZE, found that the southern hemisphere varieties were virtually the same, and that they occupied an intermediate position in relation to the two reference varieties.

As in AmE, collective nouns, such as *committee, government*, nearly always take singular verb forms in AusE, in contrast with Standard EngE, where the perception of the collective noun as a 'monolith' or as a group of individuals determines the choice of verb form.

4.7.3.4 Lexicon

As we have seen, Aboriginal languages have not had an impact on AusE phonology or grammar, with the possible exception of the word formation pattern known as reduplication, as exemplified in the term *never-never* for the desert regions. For various reasons, lexical borrowing has not been extensive either: there was not a great deal of close contact; the Aborigines spoke many different languages; they were essentially nomads and had very different ways of life. A number of place names have been adopted, however, such as *Wagga Wagga* and *Wollongong*. Since the Australian landscape, flora, and fauna were so markedly different from anything the early settlers had experienced, it is not surprising that they borrowed a number of words denoting animals, plants, etc: *kangaroo, wallaby, koala, kookaburra, dingo, budgerigar, coolibah, billabong*. In all, the *Australian National Dictionary* (1988) records some 400 borrowings from Aboriginal languages.

The flash language, originating among the prisoners and their keepers, has contributed many words that have come to symbolize Australian life, such as the heteronyms *new chum* 'a novice', originally a new fellow prisoner, *old hand*, originally referring to an ex-convict, *swag*, now in the sense 'large quantity' but originally referring to a thief's loot (cf. also *swagman* as used in *Waltzing Matilda*, referring to a tramp).

The convicts may have had the gift of the gab, but owing to their mostly urban background, they had brought no adequate vocabulary for the 'pastoral' life they began to lead when they left the prisons. This explains the somewhat military, technical, and rather 'bleached' vocabulary for rural activities and certain topographical features in AusE, exemplified by the following lexical items: *station* for 'stock farm', *squatter* 'occupier of public land without a title', *oak* for an Australian tree that does not belong to the Quercus family, *paddock* for 'meadow', *river* and *creek* denoting all categories of running water replacing a number of terms in English dialects.

A special type of idiom demonstrating the input from the London area is the extensive use of rhyming slang (cf. 4.1.5.3) in AusE: *Dawn Fraser – razor, Joe Blake – snake, Captain Cook – a look, willy wag – swag.*

Considering the impact of AmE, AusE appears to be somewhat more 'American' than NZE with regard to certain food terminology as investigated by Burridge and Mulder (1998:283). Whereas New Zealanders used *eggplant* as well as *aubergine*, Australians exclusively used the American term. The same pattern applied to *snow pea/sugar pea* and *zucchini/courgette*. In other cases both AusE and NZE used the British as well as the American term, sometimes adding a third form, e.g. *patty tin* (BrE), *muffin tin* (AmE), and *patty pan* (found in AusE).

4.7.4 Further reading

Burridge, K. and J. Mulder (1998) *English in Australia and New Zealand.* Melbourne: Oxford University Press.

Turner, G. W. (1994) 'English in Australia'. In R. Burchfield (ed.), *The Cambridge History of the English Language V.* Cambridge: Cambridge University Press, 277–327.

4.8 NEW ZEALAND/AOTEAROA

Sux suck sheep wint to the vit

4.8.1 The country and its settlement history

Area: 268,000 sq.km
Population: 3.8 million (of which 95 per cent speak English as their first language)
Capital: Wellington

It is proper to refer to the country whose language is described in this section by two names: *New Zealand*, originally called *Nieuw Zeeland*, after the province of Zeeland in the Netherlands, by the Dutch explorers in the seventeenth century, and *Aotearoa*, 'land of the long white cloud' named by the Maori settlers, perhaps on first sighting

Fig. 4.6. New Zealand

the islands more than a thousand years ago. In the 1980s, the term *Aotearoa New Zealand* was coined as a symbolic name to represent the joint Maori and Pakeha (people of predominantly European descent) components of New Zealand culture and society. For convenience, however, the country will usually be referred to as New Zealand in the following presentation.

The Maori were first recorded in European history by the Dutchman Abel Tasman who reached the west coast of the South Island in 1642. It was not until 120 years later that attempts were made at making territorial claims by European explorers, and it was only in 1840 that the Union Jack was hoisted and most of the Maori chiefs were induced to accept Queen Victoria's guardianship.

New Zealand was granted self-government in 1852, and a full parliamentary system was set up in 1856. The following decades were characterized by a great deal of turbulence, especially the conflict between the white settlers and the Maori, especially in the North Island, which ended in 1872 and resulted in substantial loss of land and general humiliation on the part of the Maori.

As indicated in the introductory paragraph, things have improved in present-day Aotearoa. In 1987 the Maori Language Act was passed, giving official status to Maori co-equally with English, and establishing a Maori Language Commission. Although the language has gained increasing official recognition, it is endangered and has been 'brought to the edge of extinction as a language of everyday interaction' (Bell and Holmes 1990:153).

The Maori today constitute about 14 per cent of the population. Another three per cent are twentieth-century immigrants from South Pacific islands. There are also sizeable groups of immigrants from various European countries as well as Chinese and Indian minorities.

Three main 'types' of English-speaking immigrants can be distinguished (cf. Bauer 1994:383ff.):

- In the period 1840 to well into the 1880s, groups of immigrants from various distinctive parts of the British Isles (London, the West Country, Scotland) came to New Zealand, often for religious/ideological reasons. The place names in the south-eastern part of the South Island, for example, bear witness to the dominating Scottish settlements, e.g. Dunedin and Invercargill.
- In the early 1860s, Australians dominated a wave of immigrants who came because of the discovery of gold on the west coast of the South Island.
- In the 1870s, 'assisted' (subsidized) immigration, took place on a large scale, dominated by immigrants from southern England.

Since then, immigration has continued to be an important factor in the growth of New Zealand's population, e.g. from various European countries after the Second World War. Yet, towards the end of the nineteenth century there were more New Zealand-born Europeans in New Zealand than immigrants, and from this time onwards it can be assumed that the development of the English language in New Zealand reflects New Zealand rather than British or Australian trends.

In contrast with Canada, South Africa, and even Australia, New Zealand can be described as an unusually monolingual country. Only Pacific Island Polynesians who settled in New Zealand from the 1950s and some very recent immigrant groups, especially from Asia, use their native languages extensively outside the home domain (Bell and Kuiper 2000:13).

New Zealand is not characterized by strongly stratified social classes as found in the UK and USA. Although the gap between the rich and the poor has been somewhat widened during the 1990s, New Zealand can still be described as an egalitarian society, with neither a land-owning upper class aristocracy nor an industrial proletariat (Bell and Kuiper 2000:13).

Judging by NZ sociolinguistic research (e.g. Bell 2000, Britain 1992, Stubbe and Holmes 2000) the most significant social parameter is ethnicity, in particular with reference to Maori vs Pakeha English. There is also a strong correlation between ethnicity and class in that Maori are over-represented in lower socio-economic groups (Bell 2000:224).

4.8.2 The emergence of New Zealand English (NZE)

Comments on a distinctive variety of New Zealand speech date back to the turn of the last century. In line with observations on language use in schools in most Anglophone countries, anything perceived as deviating from Standard EngE/RP was viewed as impure and corrupt.

School inspectors in New Zealand were particularly keen to pick on realizations of the four closing diphthongs /eɪ/, /aɪ/, /əʊ/, /aʊ/, which were perceived as wider than the RP-like norm: '... the word is *house* not *heouse*', '... they will call *lady lidy* ...'. The 'impure' pronunciation was generally ascribed to laziness and slovenliness, and compared to lower-class speech in England. Other characteristic features of NZE which are known to date back to this early period, such as the raised quality of front vowels (cf. the *Shitland* example quoted in Chapter 3), are never mentioned in the school inspectors' reports. They were probably not seen as socially significant in the same way. In fact, they may not even have been perceived; for some reason changes in short-vowel quality tend to stay below awareness for a long time after initiation.

In recent years, great strides have been made towards tracing the emergence of NZE by the ONZE (Origins of New Zealand English) project, (for detailed informative material, cf. www.ling.canterbury.ac.nz/ONZE). Among other things, data from the project indicate that some of the oldest informants already had close realizations of /e/ and /æ/ and had merged NEAR and SQUARE (see further below). A general characteristic of the early stages of the formation of NZE is the high degree of variability (Gordon and Trudgill 1999).

In a lexical study on the dialectal origins of NZE, Bauer (2000) found that a high proportion of the earliest British dialect words have come in via AusE, but over the twentieth century the number of dialect words 'travelling direct' to New Zealand has increased.

In contrast with the sizeable component of regional dialect words from all over the British Isles, as documented by Bauer, NZE phonology exhibits a striking likeness to accents in south-eastern England, as indeed to the Australian English accent.

The origins of Maori Vernacular English (cf. Bell 2000:222) are simply described as 'the transference of features from the Maori language by the first generations of Maori who learned English as a second language'. To some extent, these features have been maintained and transmitted across the intervening generations. The maintenance, even revival, of some Maori features can also be related to consciousness-raising and marking of identity.

4.8.3 New Zealand English – a descriptive account

A 'shortlist' of particularly salient features:

- the centralized quality of the KIT vowel: [ə] rather than [ɪ]. This is what the spelling 'sux suck' in the motto, an Australian stereotypical perception of NZE, suggests. This is, indeed, the most salient feature in distinguishing between an AusE and a NZE accent. The rest of the motto indicates that the DRESS vowel is also perceived as different from AusE, i.e. extremely close.
- the merging of the diphthongs in NEAR and SQUARE, i.e. words like *beer* and *bear* are homophonous.
- the front [aː] in BATH, PALM, and START.
- the rounding and fronting of the NURSE vowel; in some broader accents it is also raised and realized as [øː], as in German *Möwe*.
- the Maori element in the lexicon, increasingly used in everyday conversation.

4.8.3.1 Spelling

NZE spelling, as codified in *DNZE*, follows British conventions. Alternative spellings are only given for certain nonstandard entries and Maori words, e.g. early forms of the word *Maori* itself: *Mahrie, Máodi, Mowrie . . .*

4.8.3.2 Phonology

With the exception of the NEAR/SQUARE (variable) merger mentioned among the salient features, the phonemic inventory of NZE remains identical with that of RP. It is in the phonetic realization that we find the differences, but they are indeed considerable, at least among the vowels.

Until fairly recently, RP enjoyed very high prestige in New Zealand. As late as a few decades ago, parents often made their children take elocution classes given by a teacher from England, as reported by one of our New Zealand informants. However, changing attitudes to the 'mother country' and increased awareness of national identity as in so many other regions throughout the world, have largely done away with the view of RP as a norm. 'Anyway we're not British' is the telling title of a thesis recently submitted at Wellington University (Vine 1995). Yet in some domains, such as television commercials, where it is often used for advertising quality products, RP 'remains a "classy" acrolect' (Bayard 2000:322). Attitudes to American accents are positive, but have not resulted in major influence on NZE phonology; if any, it is restricted to lexical incidence and is largely identical with changes observed in RP, such as *schedule* with initial [sk] and *research* with the stress on the first syllable. Because of this, the NZE version of Wells' lexical sets below (Table 4.8) is only contrasted with RP.

With a few exceptions, the symbols used for NZE phonology, quoted from Wells (1982:609), look deceptively similar to those used for RP. Further qualification is called for, especially with regard to the short front vowels, which are closer in NZE than in AusE and very much closer than in RP. A kind of chain shift appears to have taken place: TRAP is realized as [ɛ] rather than [æ] and DRESS is often closer than [e], which means that it approximates to [ɪ].

There is some controversy concerning the origins and development of these vowels (cf. Woods 2000:98ff.). Whereas some linguists argue that their quality represents innovation and change, the ONZE group has demonstrated that the vowels were in a relatively close position in the input dialect (there is, for example, evidence of a very close TRAP vowel in traditional Cockney). Yet the fact that they have become closer over time, i.e. that we are indeed dealing with a kind of shift, is now largely undisputed. The central quality of KIT has long been held to be due to input from Scottish English, but recently Gordon (1994) has shown that in stressed position it represents an innovation in NZE.

To non-New Zealanders the quality of these vowels is not only striking but extremely confusing, and there is an abundance of anecdotal evidence of cross-dialectal miscomprehension. Gordon and Deverson (1998:37) relate the following story:

Table 4.8. New Zealand lexical sets

NZE	Key word	RP
ə	KIT	ɪ
e	DRESS	e
æ	TRAP	æ
ɒ	LOT	ɒ
ʌ	STRUT	ʌ
ʊ	FOOT	ʊ
aː	BATH	ɑː
ɒ	CLOTH	ɒ
ɜː	NURSE	ɜː
iː	FLEECE	iː
ʌɪ	FACE	eɪ
aː	PALM	ɑː
ɔː	THOUGHT	ɔː
ʌʊ	GOAT	əʊ
uː	GOOSE	uː
ɑɪ	PRICE	aɪ
ɔɪ	CHOICE	ɔɪ
æʊ	MOUTH	aʊ
iə, iːə – iː, eə	NEAR	ɪə
eə	SQUARE	ɛə
aː	START	ɑː
ɔː	NORTH	ɔː
ɔː	FORCE	ɔː
ʊə, uːə – uː, ɔː	CURE	ʊə

When Ivan Illich the educationalist came to New Zealand he rang a friend and the phone was answered by his friend's young daughter. When he asked to speak to her father he thought she replied, 'He's dead'. After his momentary shock he realized that she was saying, 'Here's Dad'.

As in present-day RP and Estuary English, /ɪ/ in final position, e.g. in *happy*, is realised as [i], even [iː].

The diphthongs in FACE, PRICE, GOAT, and MOUTH are variable, especially along a social continuum. In comparison with RP they are generally wider, although less so than in AusE.

The quality of the merged diphthong of NEAR and SQUARE is variable, approximating either to /iə/ or to /eə/, as the following story, reported by Elizabeth Gordon, illustrates:

> Once when my family was having a meal my son began to recount a story he had heard at school about a knight who had been engaged in a fight. During the fight the knight's spear was broken. My son then said, 'He went back to the castle to get his spear spear'. My niece who was with us at the time said, 'No, that's not how you say it – you should say, "He went back to the castle to get his spare spare"'. (Gordon and Deverson 1998:44)

The BATH vowel, i.e. the set distinguished in RP and GA as /ɑː/ vs /æ/, is generally [aː] in NZE, except in the 'Scottish' area on the South Island. American-like realizations are increasing among younger speakers and in certain domains such as radio and television.

The Scottish area is also characterized by rhoticity ('the Southland burr'). Even young speakers retain the /r/, but only after the NURSE vowel, as in *bird, girl* – not in *beer, horse*, etc. Interestingly, though, an astonishing number of ONZE informants from all over New Zealand are rhotic. This is one of several findings from the project that have provided increased knowledge about the phonology of nineteenth-century EngE.

Another Scottish-like feature heard in New Zealand in the realization of <wh-> as [hw], i.e. making a distinction between words such as *wine* and *whine*, *wail* and *whale* (cf. also AmE and CanE phonology). This distinction used to be encouraged in elocution classes.

In contrast with RP, /l/ is always dark in present-day NZE. As in Cockney and Estuary English, it may be vocalized at the end of a word or before a consonant, as in *pull, children*. A characteristic of NZE is also that /l/ influences the preceding vowel, in particular /ʌ/, so that the stressed vowel in a word like *vulture* is realized as [ɒ].

On the suprasegmental level a striking feature of NZE is the frequent use of high rising terminals (HRTs) (cf. 3.2.2). This feature was not listed among the top salient ones, because it is reported from a number of other varieties.

There is, in fact, a possibility that HRT originated in NZ. There is scattered evidence of HRT in some ONZE data from the late 1940s (Gordon and Trudgill 1999), but it was really first noted in the early 1960s in the speech of Maori schoolchildren. Since then, HRTs have been widely studied and found to be 'clearly a characteristic of the young, of women, and of Maori' (Warren and Britain 2000:155). A recent detailed sociolinguistic study (Britain 1992) suggests that the feature may have been initiated by Maori speakers. One of its main functions is to emphasize speaker–hearer solidarity and it was found to be most used 'by those members of New Zealand society for whom the affective meaning of conversation is an important cultural characteristic, namely Pakeha women and Maori' (Britain 1992:98). In fact, Maori speakers could be expected to use a higher proportion of addressee-oriented devices overall than Pakeha. In analysing narrative structure, Stubbe and Holmes (2000:257) found that there is, 'a more general tendency in Maori interactions to leave meanings relatively inexplicit' and that from a Pakeha perspective, 'ideas often appear to be introduced in fairly sketchy fashion'. Indeed, the use of HRT seems to fit very well into this general pattern.

4.8.3.3 Grammar

'NZE is different from other national varieties of English in terms of preferences for certain variants rather than categorically different grammatical rules'. These words introduce the publisher's presentation of Marianne Hundt's *New Zealand English Grammar: Fact or Fiction? A Corpus-based Study in Morphosyntactic Variation* (Hundt 1998b). NZE constitutes a typical mix of variants available in General English and it cannot be described as definitely British or American.

Comparing NZE with AusE, Hundt finds that 'the two are virtually indistinguishable when it comes to grammar'.

Some of the preferences/characteristics of NZE grammar are:

- *-ves* plurals rather than *-fs* in words such as *hoof, roof, wharf*
- increasing use of unmarked plurality in words of Maori origin (cf. for example the word *Maori* itself and *iwi* 'tribe, tribes' (*the two local iwi*), but the plural of *Kiwi* is *Kiwis*
- the use of the indicative in mandative sentences, as in *I recommend that this meeting passes a motion tonight commissioning me to travel to Wellington* (Hundt 1998a:166).

Nonstandard features include the use of plural *yous(e)*, especially frequently used in representations of the language of Maori speakers of English, and, as in AusE, *she* as a nonreferring pronoun (*she'll be jake*, expressing confidence in a happy outcome, reassurance, agreement, etc).

4.8.3.4 Lexicon

One of the salient features of NZE must be the impact of Maori on its lexicon. There is, however, much more of interest in NZE vocabulary than this markedly foreign element. *The Dictionary of New Zealand English (DNZE)* contains some 6000 main headword entries, providing a historical record of New Zealand words and phrases from their earliest use to the present day. It is true that some 700 entries are shared with AusE, but the dictionary's format – well over 900 large, three-column pages in small print – do not include General English lexical items, at least not if they carry the same meaning. Under the headword *cow*, for example, we find various senses relating to 'an extended use of Brit. Slang *cow* a derog. term for a woman', for example in phrases such as *a cow of, cows of*, with the intriguing example *These tricky cows of horses*.

Yet the bulk of the vocabulary used by New Zealanders is definitely shared with other inner-circle varieties, especially Standard EngE. Next to the Maori language, American English is probably the most obvious source of new lexical items in NZE. It is not clear whether people actually know whether the origins of the words they use are British or American, or whether they consciously favour one or the other. A recent study (Vine 1995) reports that New Zealanders often assign different meanings to British/American word pairs.

One of the most interesting aspects of NZE, as richly documented in *DNZE*, is the alteration of form and extension of meaning affecting general English words. A well-known example is the clipped form *bach* 'a holiday house', probably derived from *bachelorize* 'to live alone'. As in AusE, *-y/-ie* is an extremely productive suffix in creating familiar forms of the names of common objects, creatures, and people: *cardie* 'cardigan', *fleecie* 'fleece-picker', *humpie* 'humpback whale', *lippy* 'lipstick', *rellie* 'relative', *sammy* 'sandwich'. A characteristic example of conversion is the use of *farewell* as a verb: *The Child Care Centre is holding a party brunch to farewell Maggie Haggerty.*

A great many words relating to NZ society, topography, flora, and fauna have developed additional and new meanings: *elder* 'a person of recognized authority in a Maori community', *creek* 'small river' rather than 'inlet' (cf. variation in AmE described in 4.5), *bush* 'rainforest' (in the South Island sometimes 'a clump of native trees'). Countless names of plants and animals, such as *birch, beech, magpie, robin, bream,* refer to different, but similar-looking, species in the new environment.

A great deal of the material presented in *DNZE* also demonstrates that this is an extremely innovative variety of English. Distinctively NZ lexical items have been created from a wide range of domains and many are related to present-day, everyday life, not exclusively restricted to NZ: *mob* 'a herd (flock) of cattle (sheep)', *watersider* 'docker', *glide time* 'flexible work hours', *stair-dancer* 'thief in multistorey buildings', *half-pie* 'unsatisfactory' (cf. Holmes 1998:38). The last word is probably a hybrid in that the second element is derived from Maori *pai* 'good'.

Among its 6000 headwords, *DNZE* includes 700 Maori words. Early borrowings from Maori have been described as 'receiver-oriented', 'Pakeha-driven', whereas recent ones are 'donor-oriented', 'Maori-driven'. The Maori borrowings relate to a variety of domains: flora and fauna, obviously, but increasingly also to social and cultural concepts: *kia ora* 'hello', 'goodbye', 'good health', *kohanga reo* 'language nest', providing preschool children with immersion in Maori language and culture, *hangi* 'a traditional earth oven and the meal cooked in it', *haka* 'dance with chant', *taonga* 'treasure, valuables', *hui* 'meeting', *powhiri* 'welcome ceremony', *kuia* 'old or senior woman', *whakapapa* 'family tree', and the particularly emotive word *papakainga* 'homeground', 'the area where one's original kinship group came from and lived'.

4.8.4 Further reading

Bell, A. and J. Holmes (eds) (1990) *New Zealand Ways of Speaking English.* Clevedon: Multilingual Matters.

Bell, A. and K. Kuiper (eds) (2000) *New Zealand English.* VEAW General Series 25. Amsterdam: Benjamins.

Gordon, E. and T. Deverson (1998) *New Zealand English and English in New Zealand.* Auckland: New House Publishers.

4.9 SOUTH AFRICA

No English word conveys the exact meaning of the word 'veld', nor indeed can England be said to have the thing meant. (The Revd J. P. Legg in *Cape Illustrated Magazine*, 1891, quoted from Silva (1998)).

4.9.1 Introduction

Since English in South Africa is not predominantly used by first-language speakers, the full presentation of the country as a linguistic area will be found in Chapter 5. Here we merely supply a linguistic description of the first-language variety.

English came to South Africa around 1800, roughly at the same time as it arrived in Australia. The first real settlement took place in the eastern Cape in 1820 as a result of the British government's attempts to recruit prospective immigrants. The early settlers came from various parts of the British Isles, yet predominantly from southern England, and were mainly of working-class or lower middle-class backgrounds. In the 1850s a new wave of immigrants, mostly from the Midlands, Yorkshire, and Lancashire and of middle- and upper-middle class origin, arrived and settled in Natal on the eastern seaboard. Major settlements later in the nineteenth century were particularly related to the diamond and gold mines.

As a result of the rather different regional and above all social structures of the early settlements, two South African varieties of English emerged: in Natal, which maintained closer ties to Britain, Standard EngE was emulated as the prestige model, whereas 'Cape English', which was characterized by Cockney-like features, carried low prestige. As in other southern-hemisphere varieties of 'transported English', RP was the model until long after the Second World War, but has now been replaced by 'respectable SAfE', largely based on the Natal accent.

SAfE differs from other transported varieties such as AusE, NZE, CanE, and AmE in always having existed in a complex multilingual and multicultural environment (Silva 1998:70). Hence the influence from other languages is more marked, especially in the lexicon, and it is more difficult to 'isolate' the first-language variety from English as used by competent L2 speakers. It should also be pointed out that first-language users of present-day SAfE represent a range of different societal and regional groups, e.g. 'coloured' speakers in Cape Town, white speakers of East Cape origin, Indian speakers (mainly in Natal), white speakers with a 'Natal' accent, and white members of the Transvaal working class (Branford 1994:472).

As a variety in its own right, South African English (SAfE) has been codified in several dictionaries, most recently in *A Dictionary of South African English on Historical Principles*, published by Oxford University Press in 1996. This dictionary represents all ethnic varieties of English in the country but gives information on the provenance of regional or 'group' vocabulary for words that may not be widely familiar to South Africans (Silva 1998:82).

4.9.2 South African English (SAfE) – a descriptive account

A 'shortlist' of particularly salient features:

- ■ [ɑː] in BATH, PALM, and START, i.e. like RP but unlike AusE and NZE
- ■ allophonic variation in KIT (the 'KIT SPLIT'): [ɪ] adjacent to velar consonants, after /h/, word-initially, usually before /ʃ/, and sometimes before affricates, i.e. in words such as *king, dig, hitch, fish*; [ə] in other environments, i.e. in words such as *fit, thin, risk, still*
- ■ unaspirated /p, t, k/, probably due to a substratum effect from Afrikaans
- ■ extensive borrowing in the lexicon from African languages as well as Afrikaans, as exemplified in the motto above.

4.9.2.1 A note on spelling

SAfE, as codified in the Oxford dictionary mentioned above, follows British conventions. Borrowed lexical items from Afrikaans and African languages are usually not anglicized in any way: *ag* (roughly equivalent to German *ach*), *braai* 'barbecue', *veld(t)* 'open grassland', *lekker* 'nice', *tokoloshe* 'malevolent spirit'.

4.9.2.2 Phonology

As usual, the lexical sets are based on Wells (1982) (Table 4.9). They can be described as representing 'respectable SAfE' as mentioned above (4.9.1).

In our list of salient features we referred to the KIT split as a case of allophonic variation, which seems to be the prevalent view today (cf. Lass 1987:304). According to Wells (1982:612ff.), however, it is possible to argue for the existence of two different phonemes, namely /ɪ/ and /ə/, at least in broad accents, in which words like *kit* and *bit* do not even rhyme.

As in AusE and NZE, the quality of DRESS and TRAP is quite close and clearly diverging from RP which is undergoing a shift in the opposite direction (cf. 4.1.5.1). The starting point of SQUARE is [e] and it is often realized as a monophthong. PRICE has also undergone a similar development, i.e. reducing the second element. In some speakers virtually all diphthongs are characterized by weakening of the second element whereas others have diphthong shifts similar to AusE.

As described among the salient features, START, BATH, and PALM are characterized by a very back quality. In broad accents, the vowel is even slightly rounded [ɒː]. As in AusE and NZE, NURSE tends to be closer and fronter than in RP, and also weakly rounded [øː]. GOOSE is often central [ʉː] as in 'modern' RP.

SAfE is firmly nonrhotic to the degree of not even having linking or intrusive /r/ as observed in a great number of its speakers. Prevocalic /r/ is a fricative, tap, or trill (the last-mentioned quality is probably an effect of the Afrikaans substratum). /l/ is generally clear but nevertheless seems to have a lowering effect on a preceding DRESS or GOAT.

The lack of aspiration, as described among the salient features, is variable but not stigmatized (Wells 1982:618). Afrikaans-based lexical items, such as *ag*, often exemplify the voiceless fricative [x], which has become a feature of SAfE, although it does not enjoy phonemic status.

Table 4.9. Native-speaker South African lexical sets

SAfE	Key word	RP
ɪ; ə	KIT	ɪ
e	DRESS	e
æ	TRAP	æ
ɒ	LOT	ɒ
ʌ	STRUT	ʌ
ʊ	FOOT	ʊ
ɑː	BATH	ɑː
ɒ	CLOTH	ɒ
ɜː	NURSE	ɜː
iː	FLEECE	iː
əɪ	FACE	eɪ
ɑː	PALM	ɑː
ɔː	THOUGHT	ɔː
əʊ	GOAT	əʊ
uː	GOOSE	uː
aɪ	PRICE	aɪ
ɔɪ	CHOICE	ɔɪ
aʊ	MOUTH	aʊ
ɪə	NEAR	ɪə
eə	SQUARE	ɛə
ɑː	START	ɑː
ɔː	NORTH	ɔː
ɔː	FORCE	ɔː
ʊə	CURE	ʊə

4.9.2.3 Grammar

The morphology and syntax of formal SAfE can hardly be distinguished from Standard EngE or General English. In informal speech, the following characteristics are often found:

- 'Non-negative' *no* as sentence-initiator, as in the following conversation (quoted from Branford 1994:489):

    Can you deliver it? No, sure, we'll send it this afternoon.

    Afrikaans has a parallel construction (cf. also the sentence-initiator *ag*, mentioned in 4.9.2.1, a borrowing from Afrikaans).
- As a reinforcing marker of the progressive aspect, *busy* is used with certain verbs

where it does not have its normal sense of 'activity', as in *He was busy lying in bed.*

▪ *Is it?* is used as a kind of 'all-purpose response', as in *He's left for St Helena. Is it?*

4.9.2.4 Lexicon

In the following brief description of SAfE vocabulary, we take a theme-related approach, since many aspects of South African life, culture, and environment are encoded in the vocabulary (Branford 1994:445). We also try to relate part of the lexicon to the typology laid out in 3.2.1, though not spelling it out in all cases.

Landscapes: most of the basic topographical vocabulary, such as *veld* [velt, felt], 'open country', 'broad high grassland', mentioned in the motto and often used as a national symbol, was established in SAfE as early as the first half of the nineteenth century and the bulk of this vocabulary is of Dutch/Afrikaans origin. Other words in this category include *backveld* 'back country', *drift* 'ford', *rand* 'ridge', *platteland* 'inland countryside'. Among the words listed here, *veld* tends to be the only one included in general dictionaries such as the *Encarta World English Dictionary*, but they should probably all be classified as local form foreignisms with exclusively local referents.

Settlement: *dorp* 'small town', *location* originally 'an area of land granted for settlement', but later 'segregated urban area for blacks', *township*, replacing *location* in its later sense, *shacklands*, also denoting areas set aside for the black population. *Location* and *township* represent the categories 'partial tautonym + heteronym', whereas *shacklands* is probably just a tautonym.

Flora and fauna: there are many examples of borrowings from Dutch/Afrikaans denoting similar-looking, but often unrelated species: *boekenhout* 'beech', *tiger* 'leopard'; these can both be seen as examples of partial tautonyms, although only one as seen from an English perspective. Other words are loan translations or Dutch coinages: *stinkwood* 'a hardwood tree', *fynbos* 'delicate bush', denoting a special vegetation type found in the coastal areas of the Cape, which has now become a key environmental term.

A study of 100 randomly selected names in this category showed that 80 per cent were of Dutch/Afrikaans or English origin and only 11 per cent were from indigenous languages (Branford 1994:450).

Words denoting people: owing to the ethnic diversity in South Africa and the dramatic social and political changes, this is a very rich and complicated category, which has been the subject of a great deal of recent research (Branford 1994:451ff., Silva 1998, Smit 1998). One example is the notorious *kaffir*, characterized as offensive and a misnomer as early as the beginning of the nineteenth century, but living on in nonstandard spoken language. Its more neutral counterpart is simply *native*. *Bantu*, as a human noun, is also controversial; it has become very much associated with apartheid, since – during the 1950s – it replaced *native* in legislation.

As the name of a language, however, it has remained neutral. The well-known *boer*, derived from the Dutch word for 'farmer', has become a multifaceted word; Branford recognizes at least seven different meanings, ranging from 'Dutch-speaking farmer' to 'the South African government' (at least before 1994). *'Coloured'* has long been used in the sense of 'South African of mixed descent', distinguished from 'black' as well as 'white'. Its status is now somewhat questionable, as usually indicated by the use of single quotes around the word.

Kinship, relationships, politics: there are a number of early borrowings from Dutch/Afrikaans: *oom* 'uncle', 'respectful third-person address', *oupa* 'grandpa', *baas* 'master', *trek* in the sense of 'emigrate' (originally 'pull'). This word has many senses and derivatives and has become 'a powerful symbol of national endeavour. Both as noun and verb, it is one of the most widely used South African words in the English-speaking world' (Branford 1994:464). Yet, sadly, the best-known word in this category is probably *apartheid* 'separateness', first recorded in 1929 and used in the sense of 'segregation' from 1947.

4.9.3 Further reading

Branford, W. (1994) 'English in South Africa'. In R. Burchfield (ed.), *The Cambridge History of the English Language V.* Cambridge: Cambridge University Press, 430–96.
Silva, P. (1998) 'South African English: oppressor or liberator?' In H. Lindquist *et al.* (eds), *The Major Varieties of English, Acta Wexionensia Humaniora No.1.* Växjö: Växjö University, 69–77.

4.10 LIBERIA

Liberia, Liberian, from Latin *liber* free (as founded as a settlement for freed Black slaves from the US) (OED)

The Republic of Liberia is situated on the Atlantic coast of West Africa (cf. Fig. 5.3). Liberia was founded in 1822 as a settlement for freed slaves from the USA, and was proclaimed independent in 1847. The link with America is clearly symbolized in the Liberian flag, which has red and white stripes as well as one white star against a blue background. Liberia deserves its own section in this chapter because English is its only official language and also used as a first language by part of its population. Most of the first-language speakers of English in Liberia are descendants of nineteenth century black American settlers, who were encouraged and helped by a group of philanthropical societies to leave the USA for what was conceived as their own home-land. These descendants, known as *Americo-Liberians* (*Mericos* or *Congos* in more popular usage), have established English in the area.

Several varieties of Liberian English can be distinguished along a social continuum, but *Liberian Settler English*, which is clearly related to AAVE in the USA, is the true first-language variety, which will be briefly described here. We will refer to the variety as LSE.

Phonology: in comparison with other African English varieties, LSE has a rich vowel system, e.g. with qualitative contrasts between KIT and FLEECE as well as between FOOT and GOOSE. Another difference is the realization of the final vowel in words such as *happy*, where LSE has [ɛ] but other varieties have [i]. A characteristic also found in AAVE is the tendency to delete final consonants, especially /t/, /d/ and any fricative, e.g [blʌ] *blood*, [grahapa] *grasshopper*, [klo] *clothes* (Wells 1982:635). Consonantal reduction is also found in words such as *catch* [kɛʃ] and *reach* [riʃ], in which the affricate has been simplified to a fricative. As in AAVE, stops replace the dental fricatives in initial position, but Cockney-like [f] and [v] are used in final position: [dæ] *that*, [briv] *breathe*. LSE is nonrhotic with frequent loss of /r/ also intervocalically as in AAVE and some accents in the American South. According to Wells (1982:636), *care* and *carry* may be homophones, realized as [kɛː]. Final /l/ is lost or vocalized. A conservative feature of LSE is the retention of initial [hw], also found in American accents. Another link with AmE is the tapped realization of intervocalic /t/.

Grammar: LSE generally shows great affinity with AAVE, e.g. in the use of nonstandard forms in the verb phrase: *I do see boy all de time* (habitual), *I ain see him*, verbal *-s* used with first and second person pronouns (cf. Poplack and Tagliamonte 2002), *he done come* 'he has come'. 'In Liberia the use of *done* carries affective force as a "badge" of Settler identity. It is used only by Settlers, and it is identified by Settler and non-Settler alike as being a distinctively Settler feature' (Singler 1987:89).

Lexicon: LSE vocabulary includes reduplicated forms such as *bugabug* 'termite' and retains older meanings, such as *favour* in the sense of 'resemble'. *Outside child* 'a child acknowledged although born outside marriage' is an example of a localism.

As representing traditional language in an early AAVE exclave, LSE has attracted increasing attention, since it provides important evidence in the debate on the history of AAVE (cf. recent work by Poplack and Tagliamonte).

4.10.1 Further reading

Singler, J. (1991) 'Liberian Settler English and the ex-slave recordings: a comparative study'. In G. Bailey *et al.* (eds), *The Emergence of Black English: Text and Commentary*. Amsterdam and Philadelphia: Benjamins, 249–74.

4.11 THE CARIBBEAN

In recent years a BBC Television producer asked me what African languages I spoke, and if I spoke them when I'm with other West Indians. (Caryl Phillips, *The European Tribe* (1987))

There are three main island groups in the Caribbean: the Greater and Lesser Antilles and the Bahamas. In addition, some adjacent areas in Central and South America are culturally and historically connected with the West Indies. Bermuda is situated to the north of the Caribbean proper but belongs linguistically with the English-speaking West Indies (Wells 1982:561).

Fig. 4.7. The Caribbean showing some islands mentioned in the text

The name *Caribbean* is derived from *Carib*, denoting the indigenous Amerindian people once inhabiting the area and known to Columbus; it was in his time that some of their words were borrowed into European languages, e.g. *canoe* and *tobacco*. Of the Caribs themselves there is hardly a trace, however; they had literally vanished only a few decades after the advent of the European conquerors.

Contrary to what the BBC producer figuring in the motto seemed to believe there are no speakers of African languages in the West Indies but a great number of first-language English speakers. This is not the case on all of the islands, however (cf. further 5.6.2).

English is an official language in Jamaica and the Cayman Islands, the Virgin Islands, Anguilla, St Kitts and Nevis, Montserrat, Antigua, Dominica, St Lucia, St Vincent, Barbados, Grenada, Trinidad and Tobago, the Bahamas, and Bermuda. In many of these island speech communities there is a language continuum, with Standard English at one end and a basilectal English-based creole at the other, i.e. a 'postcreole continuum', but in St Lucia, Dominica and Grenada the creole is French-based.

Caribbean English at the creole end of the continuum is probably derived from the pidgin forms of communication used first between the slaves and the sailors during the time of the notorious 'Atlantic triangle' (Europe → West Africa → the Caribbean and the American coast → Europe) and later between the slaves and the landowners (3.3).

The study of English-based creoles, not least in the Caribbean, has played an important part in sociolinguistics during several decades and there is an ongoing debate on their origin and relatedness. It is beyond the scope of our book to do justice to this research and rather than try to present it in a simplistic fashion we refer the interested reader to major recent publications such as Mufwene (2001). We define the terms *pidgin* and *creole* very traditionally as 'a mixed and reduced, often transient form of language used in contact situations' and 'a mother-tongue variety derived from a pidgin', i.e. 'the acquisition of native speakers by a language' (phrase attributed to G. Sankoff). In the West Indies, creoles are of long standing, well established as early as the end of the seventeenth century. Locally, they are usually referred to as *patois (patwa)*.

The Caribbean islands have rather different settlement histories and this is of course reflected in the language situation. We have already mentioned the prevalence of languages other than English in many areas, but there is also characteristic variation in English itself, e.g. in phonology, as shown in the lexical sets below, representing three different speech communities: Jamaica, Trinidad, and the Bahamas.

Jamaica is the largest island with the largest English-speaking population, has its own tertiary education at the University of the West Indies and has considerable cultural influence worldwide. Its language is documented in the *Dictionary of Jamaican English*, which has been instrumental in the development of fictional writing in Jamaica and the Caribbean at large. The Jamaican postcreole continuum covers the full range from basilect to acrolect and is well researched. To illustrate the contrast between basilect and acrolect, we quote some examples from DeCamp (1971:355): *pikni, nyam, nana* (basilect) correspond to *child, eat, granny* (acrolect); initial /t,d/ (basilect) sometimes correspond to dental fricatives in the acrolect; *no ben* (basilect) corresponds to *didn't* (acrolect). For historical reasons, Jamaican English, like most Caribbean English varieties, has been more British- than American-oriented, which means that the acrolect approximates to Standard EngE/RP. Yet recent years have seen 'the functional dethronement' of Standard English as the exclusive language of public–formal domains and there is a shift towards a local variety as the new standard, which has been described as 'a projection of a native linguistic identity'.

Trinidad, by contrast, has been English-speaking for less than two centuries. The first colonizers were Spanish and in the early nineteenth century French was the predominant language, owing to the increased presence of French-speaking planters and their slaves. On the whole, Trinidad has a very mixed population, with immigrant groups from other parts of the West Indies, Asia, and Portugal (certain phonological mergers can probably be ascribed to French, Spanish, or Indian influence). Today, English is the mother tongue of most Trinidadians, however. Despite the difference in founder population, Trinidadian creole has many similarities with Jamaican (Sebba 1997:248), but is clearly different in its nonrhoticity. This may have to do with the lateness of English settlements in Trinidad, i.e. when non-prevocalic *r* had been lost in urban speech in the south-east of England, but nonrhoticity is also found in some very early English settlements in the Caribbean, e.g. St Kitts (Wells 1982:578).

The Bahamas, a large and scattered group of islands south-east of Florida and north of Cuba, were virtually uninhabited when the first English settlers arrived in the mid-seventeenth century. They were religious dissidents and came from Bermuda as well as direct from England. Towards the end of the following century, the Bahamas became a haven for American loyalists, who also brought their slaves. Most of the loyalists came from the American south, New York, and New England, which explains the general nonrhoticity of Bahamian English (Trudgill 2002:35).

In presenting some phonological features of these three varieties of Caribbean English, we rely chiefly on Wells (1982) (Table 4.10). The italicized *x* in the representation of Wells' lexical sets stands for 'socially variable', i.e. along the postcreole continuum. When such variation is indicated, it begins from the basilectal end.

Phonology:

Table 4.10. Caribbean lexical sets

Jamaica	Trinidad	Bahamas	Key word	RP
ɪ	ɪ	ɪ	KIT	ɪ
ɛ	ɛ	ɛ	DRESS	e
a	a	a	TRAP	æ
a *x* ɒ	ɒ	ɑ	LOT	ɒ
ʌ	ɒ *x* ʌ	ʌ	STRUT	ʌ
ʊ	ʊ	ʊ	FOOT	ʊ
aː	a *x* ɑ	aː	BATH	ɑ
aː *x* ɔː	ɔ *x* ɒ	ɒː	CLOTH	ɒ
ʌ *x* ʌr *x* ɜːr	ɒ *x* ɜ	əi	NURSE	ɜː
iː	i	iː	FLEECE	iː
eː [iɛ *x* eː]	e	eː	FACE	eɪ
aː	a *x* ɑ	aː, ɑː	PALM	ɑː
aː *x* ɔː	ɒ *x* ɔ	ɑː	THOUGHT	ɔː
oː [uɔ *x* oː]	o	oː	GOAT	əʊ
uː	u	uː	GOOSE	uː
aɪ	aɪ	ʌɪ	PRICE	aɪ
aɪ *x* ɔɪ	ɔɪ	əi	CHOICE	ɔɪ
ɔʊ	ɔʊ	aʊ	MOUTH	aʊ
eːr [iɛɹ *x* eːɹ]	eə	ea	NEAR	ɪə
eːr [iɛɹ *x* eːɹ]	eə	ea	SQUARE	ɛə
aː (r)	a *x* ɑ	aː	START	ɑː
aː (r) *x* ɔː (r)	ɒ *x* ɔ	oa	NORTH	ɔː
oːr	ɒ *x* ɔ	oa	FORCE	ɔː
oːr	ɒ *x* ɔ	oa	CURE	ʊə

As can be deduced from the table, the vowel systems are generally simpler than in RP, with several mergers, especially involving TRAP, LOT, BATH, CLOTH, PALM, and THOUGHT. The presence of rhoticity in Jamaica explains some of the differences in the vowel systems. In weak syllables, final and preconsonantal historical /r/ is lost, however (cf. Wells 1982:577 for a detailed account of the complex rhoticity situation in Jamaica).

The quality of STRUT is generally back and rounded, especially in Trinidad and the Bahamas. In nonacrolectal Trinidadian it may merge with several other sets, as seen from the table. In nonacrolectal Bahamian English, NURSE and CHOICE have merged into a diphthong with a central starting point.

Th stopping, i.e. the use of [t,d] instead of [θ, ð] as exemplified in the general account of the Jamaican continuum above, is characteristic of most nonacrolectal Caribbean accents. The use of dental fricatives is viewed as a prestige marker, which is demonstrated by hypercorrections such as [fʊθ] for *foot*. Another general characteristic is the reduction of consonant clusters, especially in final position. Initial clusters beginning with /s/ tend to be reduced in the basilect, as in [kratʃ] for *scratch*.

As in traditional Cockney, there is *v–w* confusion, mostly to the effect that initial *v-* is realized as [w]. This is especially the case in the Bahamas, where – also as a result of the NURSE–CHOICE merger – *voice*, *worse*, and *verse* may be homophonous.

H dropping is found in Jamaica, especially in Kingston, its capital, and to some extent in the Bahamas. A characteristic of Jamaican creole is also the use of the 'glides' [j] and [w] after stops before vowels, as in [kjat] for *cat*, [bwaɪ] for *boy*.

Finally, a general feature of Caribbean English is its syllable-timed rhythm (cf. 3.2.2), possibly – but not exclusively – attributable to an African substratum. This has resulted in word stress patterns different from RP or GA, e.g. final stress in verbs ending in *-ize*, and also in nonreduction of vowels in unstressed position.

The following brief presentation of grammatical and lexical features refers to Caribbean English in general.

Grammar: Caribbean acrolectal syntax approximates to General English, as can be seen in the difference between basilect and acrolect exemplified in the description of Jamaica above. An illustrative example of the full-range Jamaican continuum is given by Sebba (1997:211): realizations of the phrase *I am eating* 'from top to bottom' run: /aɪ æmiːtm/, /a ɪz iːtm/, /a iitm/, /mi iːtm/, /mi a iːt/, /mi a nyam/. The examples towards the basilectal end show the characteristic marking of tense and aspect by a particle. There are also habitual markers, taking various forms, such as *doz, da, iz, z* (Holm 1994:375ff.). A marker of completed action is *don*, placed before or after the verb in Jamaican creole, and there is also an 'irrealiz' marker, *go*, indicating that the action of the following verb is not (yet) a part of reality. Plural forms of nouns are also indicated by particles, placed before or after the noun, e.g. *di man dem*. The following example from Trinidad exemplifies the lack of a genitive marker: *mi fada kuzn hows* 'my father's cousin's house'. In some varieties, two forms of address are retained: *yu* vs /wʌnʌ/ (Barbados), *yu* vs *all-yu* (Trinidad).

Lexicon: Most of the Caribbean creole vocabulary demonstrates clearly that English is the 'lexifier' language, and the portion of African-derived words has been estimated at less than five per cent (Holm 1994:357). Still, African languages have probably affected the lexicon in the common use of reduplication as a word formation device: *poto-poto* 'slimy', *batta-batta* 'to beat repeatedly', *big-big* 'huge', *picky-picky* 'choosy'.

Creole word-formation, in general, is very free and innovative, as exemplified by *jokifying* (Crystal 1995:345) and *broughtupcy* 'the state of being well brought up' (Holm 1994:361).

In contrast with phonology and syntax, Caribbean vocabulary is characterized by striking regional variation. A comparative study of Jamaica, Trinidad, and the Bahamas showed that only about 20 per cent of the non-General English vocabulary was shared (Crystal 1995:345).

4.11.1 Further reading

Holm, J. (1994) 'English in the Caribbean'. In R. Burchfield (ed.), *The Cambridge History of the English Language V*. Cambridge: Cambridge University Press, 328–81.

The outer circle

5.1 SOCIAL AND POLITICAL ISSUES SURROUNDING USE OF ENGLISH IN THE OUTER CIRCLE

5.1.1 The survival of English

As we mentioned in Chapter 2, English was introduced in outer circle countries because they were colonized – mainly by military force – by English-speaking countries. So it would not be surprising if the independent postcolonial states had rejected its use. And indeed when they became independent in the period 1947–1965, many ex-colonies accepted the argument for a local official language put forward by the President of India K. R. Narayanan on 14 September 1999, the fiftieth anniversary of the adoption of Hindi as national language in India:

> Ours is a democratic country in which the people and their welfare are supreme. In such a situation it becomes necessary that official work is carried out in a language spoken by the common people. Maybe Mahatma Gandhi had the same thing in his mind when he said, '... The first and the greatest social service we can render is to revert to our vernaculars, to restore Hindi to its natural place as the national language and to carry out provincial proceedings in our respective vernaculars and national proceedings in Hindi.' Today while the official language of the Union is Hindi in Devanagri script, the multilingual character of India has been maintained.

Some countries carried this kind of policy through. In Malaysia, for example, government policy since 1969 (Gill 2002) has replaced English with Malay throughout the administration and education systems and made Malay (more precisely its codified form 'Bahasa Malaysia') the national language. This was part of a general reform of the country which consciously favoured the indigenous ethnic groups, primarily Malays, and thus disfavoured the non-Malay-speaking Chinese and Indian groups, who had previously been economically more powerful. Clearly it met some resistance from those who were less fluent in Malay than in English, but it was implemented anyway. (English remains dominant in the business sector, where non-Malays remain powerful.)

However, Malaysia is the exception. As a consequence of population movements under colonialism, and of boundaries drawn to suit European interests rather than local conditions, many of the postcolonial states were multinational, or multilingual, but in most it was not politically feasible to select one local language for official purposes. Arguments often put forward for the maintenance of English are its neutrality in conflicts between rival national languages, its established position (the fact that educational materials, government documents, etc., already exist in English) and its association with science, education, and development. The established position is of course a valid argument. The notion of English as a vehicle for modernity and modernization may be valid, but it incorporates an aspect of 'liberal' ideology (3.4.1) which is not uncontested. This is the view that poorer countries are essentially behind richer ones in a linear process of 'development' and need 'modernization' to catch up. An alternative 'radical' position argues that poor countries are poor because rich ones are rich, and they are kept in a dependent state by more or less conscious policies of rich countries. Here the continued use of English is seen as a tool for maintaining the dominance of the USA (and Britain) and hence as a hindrance to achieving true independence and welfare.

5.1.2 The language pyramid

Fig. 5.1. The language pyramid

The 'pyramid' above (Fig. 5.1) illustrates a very common situation in postcolonial territories. There are three 'layers' of competing languages. At the top is English. Then there is one or several 'national' languages which have nationalist value and are spoken by a majority or dominant group (Bahasa Malaysia and Hindi in the examples above) or are lingua francas, that is languages used by non-native speakers to communicate with one another. Then there are the languages of minority groups. The ruling classes typically are educated in English and use it for many purposes, often paying mere lip service to extended use of the national language(s). A large group use the national languages for most purposes and sometimes seek to impose them on all citizens, at least as the medium of instruction. Minority groups may prefer English to the national languages because of its ethnic 'neutrality', in the sense that because English is not the language of any group, no ethnic group has an advantage if it is used. In the Malaysian case, of course, there was a deliberate policy of advantaging the previously disadvantaged Malay speakers.

In any case, the majority of proposals to replace English as a language of administration and higher education (and often nearly all education) have failed. In India and other multinational states this can be ascribed to the 'neutrality' of the language but it is less clear why English remains predominant among the elite in largely monolingual states like Botswana (Southern Africa) or states with a local lingua franca, like Swahili in Tanzania and Kenya. One may suspect that continuation of English maintains the advantage of the elite who know the language (Phillipson

1992), but it must be considered that in Africa independence brought a massive increase in educational provision for the majority, and it was doubtless thought more important to bring some education to most of the population than to spend resources on developing new media for that education.

Thus many postcolonial states continue to use English for a variety of functions (just as others continue the use of French or Portuguese). But as we have seen (3.4.4.2), in most cases it is only a minority of citizens that master the language. This leads to unequal access to power and justice. Schmied (1991) for example, reports that parliament in Botswana is conducted in English although all members can speak Setswana and not all are proficient in English; in Malawi there was an English-language test for MPs and in Ghana (as in many other countries) proficiency in English is a prerequisite for political activity.[1] In many African countries, moreover, law courts are conducted in English, so the accused will often only understand proceedings via an interpreter, who may not be proficient both in the particular dialect of an African language spoken by the accused and in English. Nevertheless the use of English is not seriously challenged at the grass roots in most cases, and its role as 'modern' and practical is accepted.

5.2 SOME COMMON FEATURES OF THE 'NEW ENGLISHES'

The varieties of English spoken in outer circle countries have been called 'New Englishes', but the term is controversial. Singh (1998) and Mufwene (2000) argue that it is meaningless, in so far as no linguistic characteristic is common to all and only 'New Englishes' and all varieties are recreated by children from a mixed pool of features, so all are 'new' in every generation. These points are certainly true, and it is important to avoid suggesting that the new (mainly non-native) varieties are inferior to the old (mainly native) ones. It is also certainly true that the 'new/old' dichotomy is only one of many that could be established: rhotic vs nonrhotic, British spelling vs American spelling, autonomous vs substrate, etc. Nevertheless the Englishes of India, Nigeria, and Singapore and many other outer-circle countries do share a number of superficial linguistic characteristics which, taken together, make it convenient to describe them as a group separately from American, British, Australian, New Zealand, etc. varieties (Platt, Weber and Ho 1984). The explanation for some of these shared features is that the outer-circle varieties mostly have a substratum (3.3) which is very different from English; for others it is that the varieties are mainly acquired by formal learning at school. The varieties conventionally regarded as resulting from decreolization in the Caribbean (4.11) may occupy a middle position, sharing some, but not all of the features to be listed below (Platt *et al.* 1984).

---

1 One might contrast the European Parliament, in which all participants have (in 2002) the right to speak in their country's official language and hear proceedings interpreted into it. The cost in technical equipment and interpreting is beyond the current capacity of most outer circle countries, and even so the guarantee only extends to official languages, not mother tongues: indigenous minority languages like Sami/Lappish, Catalan, or Welsh are excluded, let alone immigrant minority languages like Turkish, Punjabi, or Arabic.

5.2.1 Some sociolinguistic features

Outer-circle varieties are usually spoken as part of a multilingual repertoire which may include two or three other languages spoken in different circumstances: English at work, one local language at home, another with one's peer group, for example. Hence outer-circle varieties are frequently not as well-developed in some registers as others. One can imagine that Indian English baby language or even love language is less frequently used than scientific or administrative Indian English, for example.

Furthermore, because of this multilingualism, the outer circle and postcreole varieties are characterized by internal variation of proficiency. In an inner-circle region like Yorkshire there will be a wide variation among speakers (and within a speaker for different situations) from strongly local speech features to completely standard or nonlocal ones. Some members of the community will have difficulty in expressing themselves in formal or written Standard English. But most (excepting recent immigrants, for example) will have full proficiency in some kind of English. Outer-circle speakers will not only vary in the degree to which their English (in a given situation) has local features, but also in their proficiency in English at all. In some situations those with low proficiency in English may be much more proficient in pidgin or creole; in others the dominant language will be a local one. In any case, there are learner errors as well as varietal features. Where pidgin English is widely used for communication among less educated speakers with different mother tongues, or as an informal register, the pidgin will be the basilect (3.4.2.4) and it will have a reasonable-sized vocabulary and range of functions; where another language performs these functions, the 'basilect' is the English of low-proficiency learners, characterized by limited vocabulary and efficiency as a means of communication.

5.2.2 Phonology

5.2.2.1 Segments

Some phonological features are common to most of the languages of the world – for example, front unrounded vowels, /n/, /m/, /t/, /d/, /b/. Others are found in fewer languages (and are often learnt relatively later by children learning their first language): front rounded vowels like French *u* and German *ü*, and English /θ/ and /ð/. Crudely and nontechnically, the first type of features can be called *unmarked*, the second *marked*. Sounds and distinctions in English which are unmarked are likely to be found in substrate languages and so to be represented in outer-circle varieties. Sounds and distinctions which are marked will probably not be found in substrate languages and so may not be represented in outer-circle varieties, particularly if they do not distinguish many words or are very difficult to learn.

In general the inner-circle vowel systems, with 20–24 different phonemes, are complex in relation to those of most languages. Consequently substrates tend to result in simplified systems. For example, the distinction between short lax /ɪ/ and long tense

/iː/ is rather infrequent in the world's languages and is typically missing in outer-circle varieties. Long monophthongs like /eː/ and /oː/ are more frequent than diphthongs like /eɪ/ and /oʊ/ (/əʊ/) in languages in general, and therefore also in the substrate languages. Consequently /eː/ and /oː/ are frequent realizations of the diphthongs in FACE and GOAT, in the outer-circle varieties as well as in Caribbean (and Scottish, etc.) English.

Many outer-circle varieties, (like the Caribbean postcreoles, AAVE, and the substrate variety Irish English) do not have 'marked' /θ/ and /ð/, often replacing them with dental or alveolar stops of some kind. English also has more and longer consonant clusters at the ends of words like *hosts* and *filmed* than many other languages and so these are simplified in many varieties.

One should note that an alternative explanation of shared differences from inner-circle norms would lay more emphasis on the internal logic of English making some distinctions dispensable (cf. Peng and Ann 2000). Thus /ð/ very rarely distinguishes words from one another and substitution with /d/ causes little communicative difficulty (even inner-circle speakers who say /ð/ often write *da* for *the* in SMS text messages).

The rhoticity of varieties of English from the outer circle seems to vary from speaker to speaker and authorities often disagree about whether a particular variety, such as Indian English, is rhotic. We interpret this as meaning that the rhoticity of a particular variety or idiolect derives from the interplay of up to five factors:

- The substrate language structure. If, like Chinese and many African languages, it does not allow sequences like VrC or Vr#., this will weigh against rhoticity. If, like Indian languages, Tagalog/Filipino, and Malay, it does allow them, this will favour rhoticity.
- How the language is acquired. School learning will tend to produce spelling pronunciation.
- Source. Obviously varieties introduced by speakers from England will tend to be nonrhotic, those introduced by Americans (and Scots, etc.) will tend to be rhotic.
- Model. The way teachers pronounce (influenced of course by the above three factors) will be very influential, as will models in the local mass media.
- Endonormativity (3.4.2.2). If the local attitude is highly endonormative, speakers will want to speak in the local way conditioned by the above four factors; to the extent that it is exonormative, they may be influenced by the dominant American pattern on television and films, and become more rhotic.

5.2.2.2 Suprasegmentals

Although it is not clear whether there is a convincing acoustic basis for the claim, some languages appear to be stress-timed (3.2.2), like British or American English, with very roughly equal periods (perceptually) between stressed syllables, irrespective of the number of unstressed syllables between them. If we say 'a NICE aDAPTable MAN' in a stress-timed variety the time between the peak of /naɪs/ and the peak of /dæpt/ is about the same as the time between /dæpt/ and /mæn/ even though there is one syllable in the first period and there are two in the second. Moreover the stressed syllables are much longer than the unstressed ones. Germanic languages – English, German, Dutch, Scandinavian – are stress-timed but the majority of other languages are syllable-timed,[2] that is each syllable takes up roughly (perceptually) the same amount of time. The period between /dæpt/ and /mæn/ in a syllable-timed variety would be noticeably longer than that between /naɪs/ and /dæpt/. Such languages are perceived by speakers of stress-timed languages as 'staccato' or 'machine-gun-like'. Most of the substrate languages for outer-circle varieties are syllable-timed, as is Caribbean Creole, so that the corresponding varieties of English are less strongly stress-timed than most inner-circle varieties.[3] An effect of stress-timing is that unstressed syllables are reduced in length and their vowels are often reduced to /ə/ or /ɪ/, or to syllabic /l/, /r/, /n/ (/ə ˈnaɪs əˈdæptəbl ˈmæn/). In a syllable-timed variety unstressed vowels may retain the 'full' pronunciation suggested by the spelling: /ˈnaɪs æˈdæpteɪbel ˈmæn/.[4]

Since stress and intonation are closely related, the intonation systems of outer-circle varieties are usually very different from those of inner-circle ones, but they are usually fairly different from one another as well, as the substrates have different systems.

5.2.3 Syntax

The outer-circle varieties differ fairly systematically from inner-circle ones in a number of syntactic characteristics. One general one is a greater tolerance in relation to the status of local variants. Where inner-circle varieties have different syntactic usage, they are often mutually exclusive: one is British, one is American, and the non-local construction is perceived as alien by both sides.[5] In outer-circle varieties, however, both local usages and metropolitan standard usages may co-occur without speakers regarding either as alien. Furthermore British-based outer-circle varieties are increasingly influenced by US English. Bamgbose (1995) mentions this as a phenomenon that began in the 1980s in Nigeria as American printed and electronic material became more and more available. This means that British, American, and local usages may co-exist.

---

2 Platt *et al.* (1984) cite authorities for the main substrate languages with some doubts about India. They cite Bansal saying that Indian English is 'neither syllable-timed not stress-timed' and Ohala saying that 'Hindi stress is far weaker than English'. However Nihalani, Tongue, and Hosali say 'All the Indian languages have syllable-timed rhythm'.

3 Caribbean varieties may be (rather) syllable-timed, and some varieties of New Zealand English, especially those spoken by Maori people, are said to be becoming more so.

4 Many speakers will have learnt English first at school, where the written language may be emphasized, so avoidance of reduction may also be due to pronouncing words as they are spelt.

5 This is an oversimplification: Americans will tend to perceive a British usage as alien, but because British speakers are inundated with written and spoken AmEng, they will often perceive non-stereotyped American usages as equally acceptable, much in the way described for outer-circle varieties. However the number of differing syntactic usages is very small.

As with phonology, the outer-circle varieties often have features in common because they tend to eliminate features which are typical of inner-circle English but not of other languages (or which are inherently dispensable in English). For example, British/US Standard English[6] has an unusually complicated system of tag questions – phrases like *don't you, aren't you, should he, will he* in the following examples.

You like fish, don't you?	You don't like fish, do you?
You're having fish, aren't you?	You're not having fish, are you?
He should eat more fish, shouldn't he?	He shouldn't eat so much fish, should he?
He'll come, won't he?	He won't come, will he?
etc.	

In most languages, including the main substrates all these phrases can be translated by one or two short phrases irrespective of whether the sentence to which the tag is attached is positive or negative and irrespective of the auxiliary or subject in the main verb. (German *nicht (wahr)? oder?,* French *n'est-ce pas?,* Thai *caj maj?* Hindi-Urdu *na?* West African Pidgin *no bin so?*). Consequently, many varieties of outer-circle English also use a single phrase or a few variants for this function:[7] Examples are listed in Table 5.1 below:

Table 5.1. Question tags used in outer-circle varieties

Tag	Countries used, according to Platt *et al.* (1984) and Schmied (1991)
no?	India, Sri Lanka
isn't it?	India, Sri Lanka, Singapore/Malaysia, East and West Africa
not so?	East and West Africa
is it?	Singapore/Malaysia

The details of usage are different in each variety, but the principle of using one or two invariant phrases instead of the complex and variable system of inner-circle English is constant. Similar, but different simplifications occur for confirmation questions:

A: He's lost his job.

B :   Has he? (US, UK) *Is it?* (South African English, all varieties, Indian English, etc.)

5.2.4 Lexis

Another example of elimination of a complex and unusual system found in inner-circle English concerns a set of words which are singular but refer to plural or

---

6 Even though invariant *innit* is spreading in and around London, particularly among those of non-Anglo descent.

7 And in some inner-circle varieties of English, such as Welsh (*is it?*), and native-speaker outer-circle ones like White South African (*nè*) which also have a simpler form in the substrate.

collective concepts: words like *software, luggage, furniture, cutlery, crockery, faculty* ('the teachers at a university as a whole'), *staff* ('the workers in an organization as a whole'), *alphabet* ('the set of letters as a whole'), *toast*, etc. Inner-circle varieties typically have singular count nouns referring to individual items *(program, suitcase, chair, knife, plate*, etc.) but these are too specific and alongside them there are general phrases with *piece, item* or another classifier *(piece/item of luggage/software/furniture, member of staff*, etc.). This is a rather complex system and the relation between the 'plural' sense and the singular form is not transparent. Outer-circle varieties tend to simplify the system and make these words ordinary singulars with a general sense, so that one can speak *of a software, some softwares, a staff of the school, some staffs,* or *an alphabet* (= 'a letter of the alphabet'). Platt *et al.* (1984) note that singular noncount words which refer to genuinely uncountable substances like *mud* or abstractions like *hope* are not converted in this way, making it more a rationalization than a simplification.

Sometimes specific items thought to be typical of a particular variety are actually more widespread. Thus Adegbija (1989) took *trouble shooter* 'one who stirs up trouble' (by contrast with Brit/US 'one who solves problems') to be a Nigerian feature, while Nihalani *et al.* (1979) record it as an Indian one. Similarly *fill a form (*rather than *fill out/in*) has been reported as typical of both Nigeria and Kenya. The latter is probably just a 'natural' simplification, but it would be interesting to know whether 'causer' is merely a 'natural' reinterpretation of *shooter,* or if there is some common source here. Some items quoted as local are so widespread that it would seem rational to treat their outer-circle meaning as the General English one, with the British/US version a localism. Thus *hawker* (older British 'door-to-door salesperson') means 'stationary street food salesperson' in Ghana and South Africa, and also in South East Asia, and *stay* means 'live/dwell fairly permanently' in South Africa, Uganda and Nigeria, Scotland, Singapore/Malaysia, and Guam. *Bungalow* means 'upmarket tropical house' in Asia and East and West Africa so the meanings 'barrack' in South Africa and 'one-storey house' in Britain look like localisms.

5.2.5 Pragmatics

Some aspects of pragmatics are linguistic. In many languages the equivalent of *yes* means 'what you said is true' and *no* means 'what you said is false'. So in West Africa one may get interactions like

A: You're not tired, are you/is it?
B: Yes. ['it is correct that I am not tired']

Other aspects are determined by culture rather than language. For example, cultural change in Western countries has meant that forms of address have changed rapidly in the last 50 years, but this cultural change has not necessarily taken place in other societies. Consequently it is not uncommon for outer-circle varieties to use more formal or hierarchical types of address. On the other hand, intimacy and solidarity are often established by the use of kinship terms (*brother, sister, auntie, uncle*) instead of terms like *mate, dear, honey,* etc., and this often reflects substrate usage as well as perhaps cultural difference.

This distinction between culture and language is hard to maintain, however. Situations seen as distinct by one variety may be merged in another, and this may be cultural or simply linguistic. In many parts of Africa people say 'sorry' both where people in Britain and America might say 'bad luck', that is, when something bad happens to the addressee, and where they say 'sorry', that is where the speaker has caused something bad for the addressee. On the other hand, in West Africa there is a specific greeting to one who is working: *well done*, which has no specific equivalent in inner-circle English. Thus West African English recognizes a distinction not made by inner-circle English (but made, for example in Danish *God arbejdslust*).

5.2.6 Paralanguage

Paralanguage – gesture, facial expression, etc., proxemics – is largely culturally determined. Many Indians and Sri Lankans shake their heads for *yes* and nod for *no*, for example, whether speaking English or another language. The only generalization would be that the paralanguage systems of outer-circle varieties are usually very different from those of inner-circle ones, being based in different cultures.

5.2.7 Further reading

Comparisons of outer-circle varieties are made in Platt *et al.* (1984), and Schmied (1989). Crystal (1995) provides lively background and discussion. An up-to-date, highly original, approach is found in Mufwene (2001).

5.3 SOUTH ASIA: INDIA, PAKISTAN, BANGLADESH, SRI LANKA, ETC.

... it is impossible for us, with our limited means, to attempt to educate the body of the people. We must at present do our best to form a class who may be interpreters between us and the millions whom we govern; a class of persons, Indian in blood and colour, but English in taste, in opinions, in morals, and in intellect. To that class we may leave it to refine the vernacular dialects of the country, to enrich those dialects with terms of science borrowed from the Western nomenclature, and to render them by degrees fit vehicles for conveying knowledge to the great mass of the population. (Thomas Babington Macaulay *Minute on Education* 1835)

The defeatism of wearing the chains of English – which is more foreign to us in its essence than Chinese and even French – have to be thrown out of our mentality. Ansar Hussain Khan (*The Rediscovery of India: A New Subcontinent*, Hyderabad, Orient Longman Ltd. (1995))

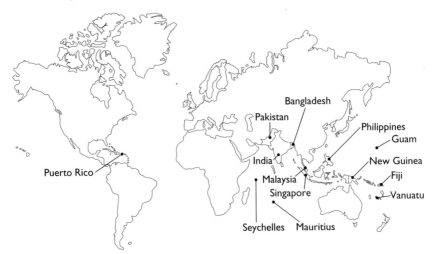

Fig. 5.2. Countries mentioned in 5.3, 5.5, and 5.6

5.3.1 The countries and the history of the introduction of English

Table 5.2. South Asian countries and their proportion of English speakers

Country	Area (000 sq. km)	Population (1995)	Capital	Mother-tongue English	Functional command of English
India	3166	935.7m	New Delhi	0.32m	37m (*c*.4 per cent)
Bangladesh	144	120m	Dhaka	–	3.1m (*c*.2.5 per cent)
Pakistan	804	140.5m	Islamabad	–	16m (*c*.13 per cent)
Sri Lanka	66	18.1m	Colombo	0.01m	1.85m (*c*.10 per cent)
Nepal	141	20.1m	Katmandhu	–	5.9m (*c*.30 per cent)

Reference figures

Barbados	0.430	0.265m
Ireland	69	3.8m
UK	245	59.5m
USA	9,363	282.0m

Sources: *The Times World Atlas*, Crystal (1995)

5.3.1.1 The languages of South Asia

Many hundreds of languages are spoken in South Asia, many by very small numbers. The dominant positions are held by Indo-Aryan languages related to Hindi/Urdu in the north, Dravidian languages such as Tamil in the south, and English as the ex-colonial language in most areas. The main Indian languages have been written as long as or longer than European ones. Old Indo-Aryan literature dates from 500 BC, Tamil from the time of Christ. Many other languages have 1000 or more years of literary history.

Hindi-Urdu, as a typical Indo-Aryan language, has many features familiar from European languages – noun gender, various declensions of nouns inflected for subject and nonsubject cases, and singular and plural, verbs inflected for tense and person, etc. The Dravidian languages are agglutinative and thus also have complex affix systems indicating tense, case, prepositions, etc. Both Indo-Aryan and Dravidian languages have rich consonantal systems, with aspirated and unaspirated stops, both voiced and voiceless, and characteristic retroflex dentals.

5.3.1.2 History

In the second millennium BC Indo-Aryan languages spread over much of Northern India, and classical Hindu literature and religious texts are written in one of these – Sanskrit, a language related to Latin and Greek and of a similar age and status. It is plausible that Dravidian languages were spoken in Northern India before the spread of Indo-Aryan.

India was united politically by the Buddhist emperor Asoka in 270 BC but Buddhism was later replaced by a revived Hinduism except in the north (Nepal, Bhutan) and extreme south (Sri Lanka). In the thirteenth century Islam was brought to India and Muslim (Persian-speaking) Mogul emperors controlled much of the country from the fifteenth to the nineteenth centuries. Thus when Portuguese traders arrived in the sixteenth century, Persian was the language of the court, Sanskrit that of Hindu literary and religious writing, and Arabic that of Islamic theologians, although most people of course spoke their own vernaculars, Indo-Aryan, Dravidian, or others.

In the course of the eighteenth century the British East India Company, based in Kalikut (Calcutta) in Bengal, achieved a dominant position and took more and more power from the Mogul emperor. As it gradually assumed responsibility for civil government and education, the company government was torn between 'orientalists' who favoured education in local languages and 'westernizers', who favoured English-language education. Indians themselves were divided as in other similar situations, with some seeing English as the key to Western knowledge, and others wanting to maintain the local classical languages Persian, Sanskrit, and Arabic. The westernizers won the argument. The revealing quotation from Macaulay that is the motto of this section encapsulates the case for the westernizers – and the reason that some people are sceptical of the use of English today.

By the time of Macaulay's *Minute* English had become necessary for career success, and so education in English was taken up quite widely. Increasing English-language education throughout the nineteenth and twentieth centuries led to the establishment of English as the common language of the elite.

The first half of the twentieth century was dominated by the struggle for freedom from Britain which culminated in independence in 1947 and unfortunately in the partition of the country, in which millions of people who had lived in areas of mixed religious population were driven out, Muslims (many of them Urdu-speaking) to Pakistan and what was later Bangladesh, then East Pakistan, Hindus to India.

5.3.1.3 The current situation

A small group of South Asians (100,000 or so) have English as their mother tongue and ethnic identity. They are the 'Anglo-Indians' – descendants of mixed marriages many generations ago.

For other South Asians, proficiency in English varies widely and the education system is the main source of input. South Asians typically live in fairly large and relatively linguistically homogeneous areas comparable to European states, so there is little need for a pidgin or basilect (but Mehrotra (2000) shows that something of the kind does exist).

Krishnaswamy and Burde (1998) list five domains for English in India: bureaucracy, education, print-media communication and advertising, intellectual and literary writing, and social interaction. English continues alongside Hindi and local languages in national administration and in quasi-state bodies like medical councils, and the higher courts. Banks in the south often use English alongside the local language even though legislation requires them to train staff in Hindi and use that language with nonlocals. State schools theoretically operate a 'three-language policy' so that children learn the local language, or at least that of their state, Hindi (or in Hindi-speaking states another Indian language), and English. However, this has been diluted so that Hindi and English may be alternative second languages in some schools, and at the same time private and state-supported English-medium schools of varying quality take more and more children. Although each state has thriving local-language newspapers, English-language papers are widely read. English books take up a large part of the more prestigious end of the market. In 1989 a third of all books published in India and a fifth of all periodicals were in English. Of course national television and radio and the vast output of films from 'Bollywood' in Bombay/Mumbai and other centres are exclusively in Indian languages, but Krishnaswamy and Burde (1998:42) say 'English is now on the MTV and STAR TV network and is increasingly becoming the carrier of pop-culture'.

Finally, a proportion of South Asians use spoken English in daily life. Most commonly there is code-mixing of English words and phrases into local languages; travellers may use English outside their own states; formal conferences and discussions may be held in English; and people use English to show off or as a mark of their age or position.

Rahman (1997) describes the three-way conflict in Pakistani education between English, Urdu, and the regional languages, a conflict which is characteristic of the whole subcontinent. In Pakistan, it appears, Urdu is the normal medium of school instruction except in Sindh where in rural areas there is instruction in Sindhi. However the elite has always ensured the existence of a few high-status schools using English as a medium and they want to retain these and retain English as the medium of higher education. The Islamic 'Urdu proto-elite' (many of them descendants of people expelled from India at partition) would like to see Urdu as the medium of all education. The regionalists and 'ethno-nationalists' want to increase the proportion of education delivered in local languages, particularly Sindhi, and consequently oppose

the extension of Urdu as a medium. The result is a stalemate in which English retains
its position, and in fact expands in the school system.

5.3.2 South Asian English – a descriptive account

5.3.2.1 A shortlist of particularly salient features

- retroflex stops for /d/ and /t/: these are the stereotype feature of the variety
- syllable timing, and relatively lightly marked word stress
- intonation characterized by rather short intonation units (so that the placement of
  sentence stress may seem uninformative)
- a characteristic vocabulary borrowed from substrate languages: to *gehrao* is to
  prevent someone from leaving his office as a protest, a *lakh* is a hundred
  thousand, a *crore* is 10 million
- stylistic features which may strike inner-circle readers as mixture of level.

South Asian English is predominantly spelt in the British style.

5.3.2.2 Phonology

The phonology of South Asian English depends on the substratum and on the degree
of accommodation to RP (or nowadays GA): speakers of different South Asian
languages will have different accents, and consequently, as in Britain and the USA,
many speakers have strongly regional accents which are hard for outsiders to understand.

Nihalani *et al.* (1979) provide a dictionary which aims to codify Indian English
pronunciation, giving examples as shown in Table 5.3.

Table 5.3. Proposed codified phonology for South Asian English

Spelling	IndE	RP	GA	Spelling	IndE	RP	GA
pleasure	plɛʃər	pleʒə	plɛʒər	turn	tərn	tɜːn	tɜrn
those	d̪oːz	ðəʊz	ðoz	ton	tən	tʌn	tʌn
thing	t̪ɪŋ	θɪŋ	θɪŋ				

The vowel system is variable, as shown in Table 5.4, but acrolectal speakers make
most of the distinctions characteristic of RP, although they merge LOT and CAUGHT
and distinguish NORTH from FORCE.

Indian English is usually said to be rhotic, but many speakers do not pronounce all
non-prevocalic /r/s. /r/ is often a tap (as in Scottish, for example), sometimes
retroflexed. The most striking feature of most South Asian English is the retroflex
alveolars /t/, /d/ /ʂ//z̩/ /l/ which correspond to alveolar /t/, /d/, etc. in other varieties.
Correspondingly, the dental fricatives may be pronounced as dental stops, as in Irish
English. The voiceless stops /p/, /t/, /k/ may be unaspirated. Postalveolars (/tʃ, dʒ, ʃ,
ʒ/) may be pronounced with contact between the blade of the tongue and the roof of
the mouth (rather than its tip as in other varieties). There may be merger of /ʃ, ʒ/ as
/ʃ/. Differing mother tongues of course lead to different consonant systems. In some

Table 5.4. South Asian lexical sets

Nihalani *et al.*	Wells	Key word	GA	RP	Jamaica (Wells)
ɪ	ɪ	KIT	ɪ	ɪ	ɪ/i
ɛ	ɛ	DRESS	ɛ	e	ɛ
æ	æ	TRAP	æ	æ	a
ɒ	ɒ	LOT	ɑ	ɒ	a ɒ
ə	ʌ ə	STRUT	ʌ	ʌ	ʌ
ʊ	ʊ	FOOT	ʊ	ʊ	ʊ
aː	a, æ	BATH	æ	ɑː	aː
ɒ	ɒ, ɔ	CLOTH	ɔ	ɒ	ɔː aː
ər	ər, ʌr	NURSE	ɜr	ɜː	ɜː(r)
iː	i	FLEECE	i	iː	iː
eː	e	FACE	eɪ	eɪ	ʌɪ
aː	a	PALM	ɑ	ɑː	aː
ɒ	ɔ	THOUGHT	ɔ	ɔː	ɔː aː
oː	oː	GOAT	o	əʊ	oː
uː	u	GOOSE	u	uː	uː
aɪ	aɪ	PRICE	aɪ	aɪ	aɪ
ɒɪ	ɔɪ	CHOICE	ɔɪ	ɔɪ	aɪ ɔɪ
aʊ	aʊ	MOUTH	aʊ	aʊ	ɔʊ
ɪər	ɪər	NEAR	ɪr	ɪə	eːr
eər	eər	SQUARE	er	eə	eːr
aːr	ɑr	START	ɑr	ɑː	aːr
ɒr	ɒr, ɔr	NORTH	ɔr	ɔː	aːr
or	or	FORCE	or	ɔː	oːr
ʊər	ʊər	CURE	ʊr	ʊə	oːr
ɪ	ɪ, i	happY	ə	ə	ɪ
ər	ər	lettER	ər	ə	a, ʌr, ə
ə	a, ə	commA	ə	ə	a, ʌr, ə

varieties /v/ and /w/ fall together or clusters may be simplified by inserting an initial vowel as in *sport,* for example.

South Asian English has a number of characteristic prosodic features, but these are not very well described. Word stress is probably not distinctive and varies widely among individuals (Wilshire 2002). It may also vary with the placement of stress in the speaker's mother tongue (Platt *et al.* 1984) and is said to be a major impediment to understanding among South Asians from different parts of the subcontinent. Bansal (1990) gives examples like /nɛˈsɛsəri/ *necessary* /ɛtˈmɒsfɪə/. Sentence stress and the intonation system apparently bear less weight of meaning than their RP/GA equivalents. There may be final rises where other varieties have falls. The pitch range of South Asian English may be rather wider than that of RP/GA, and the functions of volume change may be different, so that RP/GA speakers may appear cold to South Asians, while South Asians may appear excited or angry to RP/GA speakers.

5.3.2.3 Grammar

As with other outer-circle varieties, published written usage shows relatively more syntactic differences from British and American standard than they have from each other. It is not easy to tell which of these are to be treated as varietal features and which as differences in standards of subediting, particularly as greater tolerance or inclusiveness may be a varietal feature of some outer-circle varieties. This means that we can find written varieties which are very close grammatically to British usage, some that differ noticeably, and some that differ so much that they are nonstandard. It is reasonable to regard the language of the 'quality' Indian newspapers *The Times of India* and *The Hindu* as representative of 'standardizing' Indian English.

This seems to show some genuine differences of usage from other standards. For example, in British and American varieties the most common complementation pattern for the verb *pelt* is illustrated by *they pelted the Minister with rotten eggs*, with the information focus on what was thrown. In Standard Indian English usage the most common pattern is illustrated by *They pelted stones at the Minister,* where *pelt* has the same complementation pattern as *throw,* and information focus seems to be on the target. Moreover, virtually all uses of the verb *pelt* in *The Hindu* and *The Times of India* refer to the pelting of stones, so that the collocations of *pelt* are actually different in IndE: *pelt* collocates with *stones* as reliably as *rancid* does with *butter.* Consequently *stones* does not carry very much information and is not appropriately put in focus position. Consequently *They pelted stones at him* is not merely a simplification but actually a more appropriate construction, given the collocations of *pelt* in Indian English.

South Asian English is fairly well documented by Nihalani *et al.* (1979), who give a rich selection of Indian usages, but without indications of how general they are or how much they appear in the standard of, for example, *The Times of India.* They mention many of the 'New English' syntactic features listed in 5.2. A typical one is the distribution of particles and prepositions after verbs. In South Asian English one can *fill up a vacancy, start with the lesson, show up the main point,* or *shirk away one's responsibilities*, where British or American speakers would do without the particle/preposition. On the other hand one can *side someone,* or *grapple a problem,* where other varieties require *with.*

South Asian English often uses the progressive where other varieties use a simple form, for example with stative verbs, so that *I am knowing* is possible. This can be regarded as neutralization of the stative/dynamic contrast and is perhaps parallel to the neutralization of the count/noncount distinction that produces *luggages.*

A final example of syntactic difference that could be mentioned is the neutralization of the distinction found in many other varieties between *a bottle of beer* 'a bottle full of beer, a certain quantity of beer' and *a beer bottle* 'a type of bottle'. This leads to usages like *fish tins* 'tins containing fish' and *chalk piece* 'piece of chalk'. These fit into a general pattern of local noun + noun constructions which includes more abstract compounds like *pindrop silence* and *dagger look* from *You could hear a pin drop* and *to look daggers at someone*.

5.3.2.4 Lexis

Many of the characteristic lexical items of South Asian English are borrowed foreignisms referring to local cultural features. In political contexts one might come across *lathi*, 'type of baton' or *gherao* 'besiege someone in his/her office as a form of protest'. In discussion of Indian costume there will be many foreignisms as in this quotation from an article in *The Hindu* (25 December 1997) which we refer to again later.

> Rarely does one find a young Tamil boy in mundu or a young girl in pavadai in New Delhi or Mumbai. Jeans and T- shirts form the outdoor wear while at home it is the lungi for the boys and jeans again for the girls. For a consideration, the girls may change over to salwar-kameez and the boys to formal pants but the mundu and pavadai are definitely out.

In such a text the foreignisms are perhaps not items borrowed into South Asian English, but code mixing which relies on the reader being bilingual and familiar with the words from another language.

Other foreignisms, however, use English elements (including General English borrowings from South Asian languages): *military hotel/Brahmin hotel* 'non-vegetarian/vegetarian hotel'; *finger-ring* as opposed to *nose-ring*; *collector* 'type of senior district official'.

Local words which lexicalize general concepts not lexicalized in other varieties include borrowed forms like *crore* '10 million' and *lakh/lac* '100,000'. Others use English elements. *Furlong* '220 yards' has been retained as a frequent measure although it has become archaic in other varieties. New formations include *co-daughter-in-law, co-brother* ' husband's brother's wife', 'wife's sister's husband' (which may somehow reflect the local culture), *shoe-bite* 'blister caused by ill-fitting shoe'. There is a compounding element which lexicalizes 'illegal remover of fairly large items', combining 'thief' and 'kidnapper': *lifter,* as in *baby-lifter, bicycle-lifter, cattle-lifter, car-lifter, child-lifter, taxi-lifter* (Kennedy 1993).

Most tautonyms are English words adapted with a different meaning. In South Asian English they include: *bogey* 'railway carriage', *cracker* 'firework', *fire* 'be angry with', *cut* 'slaughter an animal', *copy-book* 'notebook'. In some tautonym pairs South Asian English shares a form with US English but differs from British English, perhaps because of separate inheritance: *cot* 'light bed for an adult' and *dresser* 'dressing table' (British 'bed for small child' and 'cupboard with open shelves above'). South Asian English may also (according to Nihalani *et al.* 1979) retain the older forms *bioscope* and *talkies* for *cinema/movies/movie house*. Other possible examples of separate inheritance or retention are *dickey* 'trunk/boot of a car' and the Pakistani term *gay girl* 'prostitute' (Kennedy 1993) – earlier British English used *gay* in this sense. Tautonyms can arise from borrowing as well. Kennedy (1993) mentions a Pakistani English form *looter* 'bank robber/robber of bus passengers', which she derives from Hindi/Urdu *lutera.*

Some heteronyms are borrowings from local languages: *goonda* 'hooligan', *dacoit* 'bandit', *channa* 'chick peas', *pucca/pucka* 'genuine/good quality'. Others derive from English roots: *eveninger* 'evening newspaper' (in Pakistan), *schoolgoer* 'school-child', *cooling glasses* 'sunglasses', *finger chips* 'US French fries/UK chips', *carcade* 'motorcade'. There are many heteronymic idioms: *an egg, double-fry* 'a fried egg, flipped over'; *collar him out* 'throw him out;' *I have a soft corner for him* '... a soft spot ...'. Some of these are loan translations like *stop eating my head* 'stop getting at me' from Hindi.

There is also a heteronymic compounding element – the borrowed form *wallah* (3.2.4.1) which forms nouns meaning 'person associated with' and so is equivalent to suffixes like *-ite* and *-ian* in other varieties. It compounds with (local) English words *rickshaw-wallah* 'rickshaw driver', elements from South Asian languages: *panwallah* 'seller of betel-chewing ingredients' and proper names: *Congresswallah* 'member of the Congress Party', *Delhiwala* (sic) 'person from Delhi'.

Where heteronymy and tautonymy interact within the same area of meaning confusion can arise, and replacement by a General English or American term seems common. Thus South Asian English *wafer* 'US chip, UK crisp' seems to be obsolescent.

Finally, we note that idioms are often restructured in IndE usage relative to their General English form. The article from *The Hindu* cited above includes the sentence *In Mumbai schools, Marathi and Hindi are compulsory and there is no way the children can wag their mother tongues,* where *wag one's mother tongue* seems to be a restructured idiom.

5.3.2.5 Style and pragmatics

The stylistic values attached to words and expressions are often different in Indian English from those in British or American usage, or perhaps stylistic distinctions are neutralized. The article from *The Hindu* quoted above also includes the sentences:

> A cousin of mine has married a Marathi lady and the lingo at home is Marathi. My aunt finds it amusing to keep up a conversation with the kid. . . .
>
> . . . The primary school teachers are not surprised, as the kids mix well the garbage Hindi of Mumbai with Marathi to effect communion . . .

Garbage Hindi and *kid* sound informal to British/American ears; *finds it amusing to* and *to effect communion* sound formal. Similarly *lingo* sounds old-fashioned British and *garbage* sounds American. It is possible that Indian English has stylistic differentiation, just using different markers from other varieties but it is also possible that stylistic effects are achieved by switching to another language in the multilingual repertoire, and the stylistic range of English is thus narrowed.

The pragmatics of English in the subcontinent derive, of course, from the sub-continental cultures, and so pragmatic behaviour may be very different from British or American. Possible examples are that *Sir* and other polite forms may be more used in speech, and, as Bhatia (1993) has shown, that positive politeness (praise of the addressee, self-denigration) is more common in letters of application than in their American or British equivalents.

According to Y. Kachru (1997), South Asian English texts may show 'non-linear' patterns of development unlike the 'linear' pattern of US English. Since Kachru argues that there is more variety in South Asian patterns of development than in US ones, this may be another instance of lower prescriptivism or codification in South Asian English.

Even where two cultures create the same niche for an utterance, they may use different verbalization in it. Thus when the person spoken of enters the room British English speakers use the jocular phrase *Speak of the devil,* but Indians in this context sometimes say the rather more positive *A hundred years to you.*

5.3.3 Further reading

Further information can be found in the relevant chapters of Cheshire (1991) and in Baumgardner (1996).

5.4 AFRICA

The basis of any independent government is a national language, and we can no longer continue aping our former colonizers ... Those who feel they cannot do without English can as well pack up and go. (President Jomo Kenyatta (1894–1978), Nairobi, Kenya, 1974)

I have been given this language, and I intend to use it. (Chinua Achebe, novelist, Nigeria)

One of the things we want to avoid is to give the impression that we are promot-ing English and downgrading Afrikaans ... we know this is a highly sensitive matter. (President Nelson Mandela, South Africa, original in Afrikaans)

> Person no fit tire for dis Nigeria
> Because why?
> look your rivers and de ocean
> Full of fish and oder good tings
> Look as every time de sun dey shine
> And for night de moon come fine
> And even de rain wey dey fall plenty'
> No be him dey make de food come plenty?
> Ah, Nigeria, you too fine for my eye.
> (Ken Saro-Wira, Nigeria, executed 1996 by the military government)

Fig. 5.3. African countries discussed in 5.4 and 4.9/10
Source: geography.about.com/library/blank/blxindex.htm

5.4.1 The countries and the history of the introduction of English

In Table 5.5 the West African countries are listed north–south round the coast of West Africa. The borderline between Eastern and Southern Africa as linguistic regions is fairly arbitrary (Bobda 2000b). The countries in that area are listed roughly north–south.

Four countries in East and Central Africa have some connections with English but are not discussed in detail here:

■ Rwanda, where English is only a joint official language 'on paper'. French and Rwanda, the language of most Rwandans, are in actual use.
■ Somalia, where the Somali language co-exists with English and Italian.
■ Ethiopia, where secondary and higher education are mainly in English, but most other state functions are in Amharic or a regional language.
■ Southern Sudan, where English was well-established, but has been replaced at least officially by Arabic.

Table 5.5. African countries and their proportion of English speakers

Country	Area (sq.km.)	Population (1995) (thousands)	Capital	Mother-tongue English	Functional command of English (thousands)
West Africa					
The Gambia	10,690	1115	Banjul	–	33
Sierra Leone	72,325	4509	Freetown	450	3830
Liberia	111,370	2380	Monrovia	60*	2000
Ghana	238,305	16,472	Accra	–	1153
Nigeria	923,850	95,434	(Lagos) Abuja	some creolizing	43,000
Cameroon	475,700	13,233	Yaoundé	–	6600
East Africa					
Kenya	582,645	28,626	Nairobi	some	2576
Uganda	236,580	18,659	Kampala	–	2000
Tanzania	939,760	28,072	Dodoma	–	3000
Southern Africa					
Malawi	94,080	9939	Lilongwe	–	517
Zambia	752,615	9456	Lusaka	50	1000
Zimbabwe	390,310	11,261	Harare	70*?	3300
Botswana	575,000	1549	Gabarone	–	620
Lesotho	30,345	2050	Maseru	–	488
Swaziland	17,365	913	Mbabane	–	40
Namibia	824,295	1651	Windhoek	13	300
South Africa	1,184,825	41,465	Pretoria	3600	10,000

*2002 figure

Reference figures

Barbados	430	265
Ireland	68,895	3.8m
UK	244,755	59.5m
USA	9,363,130	282.0m

Source: *The Times World Atlas*, Crystal (1995)

5.4.1.1 Languages

Most sub-Saharan African states are extremely multilingual. In each state there are typically two or three major languages, a dozen or so minor ones, and many spoken only by a few thousand people. Ghana, for example, is the size of the UK, with less than a third of its population, yet it has 42 different languages. On the other hand, in

Kenya and Tanzania (and to some extent Uganda) Swahili is a lingua franca and in at least Botswana, Swaziland, Lesotho, and Zimbabwe, one language is spoken by a majority of the population. Even in South Africa 70 per cent of people speak languages which are mutually comprehensible with Zulu.[8]

The indigenous languages in sub-Saharan Africa mostly belong to three groups: Afro-Asiatic, the group which includes Arabic, such as Hausa in Northern Nigeria and adjoining areas; Cushitic/Sudanic and Nilotic in Ethiopia, Somalia, and northern Kenya and Uganda; and Niger-Congo. The largest group is Niger-Congo – Wolof in the Gambia, Akan and Iwe in Ghana, Ibo and Yoruba in Nigeria for example. Rather surprisingly, most of the languages all over Southern and Eastern Africa, including the best-known, Swahili, are closely related and belong to the Bantu family within Niger-Congo, so that most of the varieties of English we shall be discussing, particularly in Eastern and Southern Africa, have a Bantu substratum.

The Niger-Congo languages in general are often tone languages in which tone is used to distinguish word forms such as tenses or lexical items in general. Katamba (1989) gives the examples *àwò* (two low tones) 'star' versus *áwó* (two high tones) 'guinea fowl' from Igala (Nigeria). Another characteristic feature of Niger-Congo languages is restrictions on consonant clusters and final consonants, so that English *street* appears as a loan into Yoruba as *títì*.

Within the Niger-Congo family, the Bantu languages of West, East, and Southern Africa are agglutinative, with numerous affixes, each with a well-defined meaning. Many morphemes are prefixes, so that the correct name for Swahili is KiSwahili 'Swahili language'. Similarly, in Luganda, the language of much of Uganda, *Luganda* speakers are *Baganda,* their kingdom (whose king still 'reigns, but does not rule') is *Buganda*, an individual member of the group is *Muganda*, etc. Crystal (1997b) is an excellent source for this type of background.

5.4.1.2 History

African tropical agriculture seems to have begun in the Nigeria-Cameroon area with the beginning of the Iron Age, perhaps with the Nok culture of around 500 BC in central Nigeria or maybe even earlier. Bantu languages seem to have started expanding south and east from roughly this area at this time, perhaps as a result of this technical progress. In the extreme south, which was difficult for Bantu-speaking arable farmers to occupy because their tropical crops were unsuited to the Mediterranean climate, there are still some people speaking pre-Bantu languages – the San ('Bushmen') – and there used to be another group called Khoi ('Hottentots').

By around 1000 AD there were (ignoring Christian Ethiopia) two kinds of African states south of the Sahara: Islamic ones in contact with the Arabic-speaking world along the southern border of the Sahara and the east coast, and pagan ones to the south and west of them.

---

8 These conditions, it should be remembered, are not radically different from the multilingualism of European states in, say, 1700. The modern European 'monolingual' states are the result of several centuries of aggressive language policy, border adjustment, ethnic cleansing, etc. and nearly all include substantial linguistic minorities even so.

In West Africa, successive cultures produced sophisticated bronzes from the ninth century AD. By the time the first Portuguese envoy entered Benin City in 1485 West Africa was a patchwork of empires and small kingdoms.

On the east coast, trade with Egypt and Arabia had started by 200 BC. By 1000 AD there were Muslim African trading cities and ports along the coast, importing cotton and luxury goods (including a great deal of porcelain from China) and exporting metals and ivory throughout the Indian Ocean and beyond. The products which the coastal cities traded came from states (presumably pagan and Bantu-speaking) in the interior. The city ruins at Great Zimbabwe and other sites in Zimbabwe and Zambia are relics of these inland commodity-trading states.

Swahili developed during this time on the coasts of what are now Kenya and Tanzania. It is a Bantu language with extensive borrowing of vocabulary from Arabic and Persian (rather as English is a Germanic language with extensive borrowings from French and Latin) and without tones.

On the west coast seaborne trade with Western countries increased quite steadily. In the course of the seventeenth and eighteenth centuries trade shifted from gold and ivory to slaves, and from the Portuguese and Dutch to the French and British. By the beginning of the nineteenth century English had become a useful foreign language. Traders at centres like Calabar in Eastern Nigeria sent young men to learn English and book-keeping in England and some locals in the main trading cities knew English well. Written Nigerian English dates from as early as 1786 (Banjo 1993), and it is likely that some form of pidgin existed.

The slave trade was abolished in the British Empire in 1807. In the West this led to its gradual end as other countries decided, or were forced, to follow. There was also some resettlement of freed slaves. From 1787 ex-slaves from Britain, North America, and the Caribbean settled or were settled at Freetown in Sierra Leone (and some at Banjul (Bathurst) in Gambia). They spoke various kinds of Creole English. English-language higher education was available at Fourah Bay College in Sierra Leone from 1827, and Sierra Leonean English and/or Creole speakers spread as officials, teachers, and missionaries all over West Africa, probably contributing decisively to what is now West African Pidgin. From the 1820s freed slaves from the US settled in Liberia and created a community speaking a variety of American English (see 4.10).

With continuing trade, missionary activity, and political intervention, English became more than a foreign language in the coastal region. Many of the intermediaries were West Indians and others from the African diaspora. Thus the first mission station in Cameroon was opened in 1843/44 by Joseph Merrick, a Jamaican, (Todd 1982a) and Echeruo (cited in Banjo 1993) speaks of 'the Lagos of ... the returning Brazilians, Americans, and West Indians, and later of Sierra Leoneans and West Indians, not the Lagos of Nigerians'.

On the east coast the first half of the nineteenth century saw a large and destructive increase in the slave trade (by Portuguese and Arab merchants), and the states in the interior were destabilized. During this period missionaries started to spread

Christianity, English, and Swahili inland from the coast. Given the existence of Swahili, as a lingua franca, no pidgin developed.

At the beginning of the nineteenth century a Bantu clan in Southern Africa called the Zulus united a large number of Bantu-speakers into one state (Davidson 1984). Meanwhile, as noted in 4.9.1, Britain took possession of the Cape at the end of the eighteenth century, and launched an assimilationist policy towards the Afrikaners, Dutch-speaking settlers who had been in the Cape since the seventeenth century. This encouraged the Afrikaners to move north and create independent states in Bantu territory. As noted in 4.9, before the discovery of gold and diamonds, British settlement was largely in the Cape and – after the Zulus had been defeated – in Natal (now KwaZulu-Natal).

Late in the nineteenth century rivalry among European powers led to a 'scramble for Africa' and the Congress of Berlin in 1884–5 ratified the division of the continent into zones belonging to seven European powers. One by one nearly all the states in Africa were conquered by military expeditions and incorporated into European colonial structures, among them the Afrikaner states in South Africa. After some adjustments the countries listed in 5.4.1 came under various forms of British control.

In West Africa the new rulers appointed local clerks and policemen who spoke English, creole (Krio from Sierra Leone, perhaps), or pidgin. In East Africa some use was made of Swahili, especially by the Germans in Tanganyika (now part of Tanzania), but most higher administration was through English. The pattern was the same in Southern Africa, even in South Africa proper, where Afrikaans was recognized but in practice not equal with English. British policy towards the Africans was not openly assimilationist[9] but in British-controlled territories, English was generally now the language of administration and the higher courts, and a key language for career success in business and the extractive industries of Southern Africa. In the early part of the century schooling was mainly carried out by missionaries from Britain, other European countries, and the West Indies, who were partly concerned to ensure that people could read the Bible in their own language. During the colonial period schooling was limited (out of 10 million people in Tanganyika in 1958, only 318 (Davidson 1984:304) finished secondary school), but what there was took place both in English and in local languages. In fact, although government policy aimed at primary education in African languages, English often played a part from the first years of education in response to mixtures of mother tongues among pupils, lack of material in a particular language, and parental demands (Todd 1982b).

5.4.2 English in Africa today

In all the ex-British colonies throughout Africa (apart from Cameroon and to some extent Tanzania, see below) English remains the main language of education, admin-

---

9 In the nineteenth century colonized white people like the Boers, the Scottish Highlanders, and the Irish suffered assimilationist policies but otherwise (despite Macaulay's *Minute* (5.3, motto)) the British tended to have a laissez-faire attitude to local languages and cultures.

istration, and business, although it is not always the link language for informal communication between ethnic groups.

5.4.2.1 English as a native language

There are at least three groups in Africa that have always had English (or creole) as their mother tongue: the black settlers in Liberia, with a variety descended from something like AAVE (discussed in 4.10), and those in Sierra Leone, with a creole which is fairly remote from English and ultimately more related to West Indian creoles, and the white settlers in South Africa (and the 700,000 or so in Zimbabwe), whose variety is a typical southern hemisphere one (discussed in 4.9). The Indian settlers in South Africa have now shifted to English (Mesthrie 1996) and have a distinctive variety (while those in Kenya seem to speak Standard English, sometimes with an Indian accent). There are also indigenous groups who are going over to English or pidgin (thus creolizing it). The Cape Flats coloured community in South Africa has traditionally spoken nonstandard Afrikaans, but parents are now speaking second-language English to their children, so that a variety of mother-tongue English with an Afrikaans substratum is developing (Malan 1996). In multilingual areas of West Africa with no local lingua franca communities seem to be shifting to pidgin (which they do not distinguish from English). Schaefer and Egbokhare (1999) describe speakers of Emai, a language with 20–30,000 speakers,[10] no written form, and no use at all in school, as gradually giving up the language. At the other end of scale, the urban elite in countries like Zambia may also speak English to their children, so that they become native speakers of African English.

5.4.2.2 Domains for English and other languages

As in other places, the languages used in the African countries under discussion can be placed in a hierarchy. At the top[11] comes English and at the bottom unwritten languages like Emai with no function in school or in wider communication. In between are languages which have all or some of literatures, official uses, roles in school or religion, and lingua franca functions. English is usually in practice the sole language used for official and public purposes. Attempts to expand the use of vernaculars in these domains have not been particularly successful (Oladejo 1993), although they are vital and widely used in others.

The Englishes of West Africa have formal similarities and the sociolinguistic situations in the various countries are somewhat similar. There was never any significant group of European settlers. In most West African countries pidgin is widely spoken between speakers of different African languages, although in Northern Nigeria, Hausa, rather than pidgin, functions as link language for those without formal education, and in The Gambia it is Wolof. Another factor producing common features

---

10 Contrast Faroese, spoken on islands in the North Atlantic south of Iceland, with some 40,000 speakers, and all education up to secondary level, all political activty, etc. carried out in the mother tongue.

11 None of this applies to Cameroon, which is officially 'bilingual'; it uses English and French as official languages and languages of education, but four-fifths of the population is in the 'French zone' and that language predominates.

is that the main site for learning English is the school and teachers typically move about a good deal, both from country to country (Ghana has traditionally exported teachers, and earlier Sierra Leoneans spread their versions of English and pidgin) and from one part of each country to another (so that Northern Nigerian Hausa speakers might have a Southern Ibo speaker as teacher). Electronic media spread the same US, British, and local models over whole countries. More subtly, it is said that the motivation for learning English is integration with the local elite, and there may be one usage or pronunciation that supports this.

So the language pyramid for Nigeria would look like this (Fig. 5.4):

Fig. 5.4. Language pyramid for Nigeria

The varieties of English in the other countries in eastern and southern Africa also have many features of form in common because of the common Bantu substratum (except in the extreme north), and a tradition of movement for work within the regions. Although we do not have space to discuss them in detail, the sociolinguistic situations vary widely. In Kenya, Uganda, and Tanzania, Swahili has a strong position, but history has meant that each country has a different policy towards it – the language is dominant in Tanzania and least used in Uganda (Abdulaziz 1991, Mekacha 1993).

In Zambia and Zimbabwe English is very dominant and local languages have little or no public role, though they are of course very widely used. The situation is similar in Malawi although the government there has also supported Nyanja (also called Chichewa), a language understood by 50 per cent of the population, as a medium for primary education and a national lingua franca – in broadcasting for example. This policy was resented by speakers of other languages (as the choice of Hindi was in India cf. 5.1) (Bernsten 1998) but there seem to have been educational benefits (5.4.2.3 below).

According to the 1996 census there were 40,58 million people in South Africa in 1996. 76.7 per cent described themselves as African, 10.9 per cent as white, 8.9 per cent as coloured, and 2.6 per cent as Indian/Asian. Although the government has launched an extremely ambitious language-rights policy (see below), English remains in wide use. Similarly, Namibia chose English as the official language, although a majority of the small population speak the Bantu language, Oshiwambo and Afrikaans had been the previous language of administration and education.

There are three fairly monolingual states in southern Africa which represent continuations of precolonial entities (Botswana, Lesotho, and Swaziland – the last two actually retaining royal families and sovereigns), but even they continue to use English in education and much public life despite having clear majorities speaking the national language.

Since the 1950s, Africa has produced a large literature in English, honoured in the 1986 Nobel Prize for Wole Soyinka and in the international success of novels by Chinua Achebe and others. Kenyan literature in both Swahili and English flourishes, but literature in English by Africans is not uncontroversial. Kenya's best-known writer, Ngũgĩ wa Thiong'o, who has written in English, Swahili, and Gikuyu but lives in exile, believes that African writing must be in African languages if it is to reach a valid audience, and has given up using English for his creative work. Chinua Achebe's response to such arguments is one of our mottos above.

To sum up, English seems to retain a public position in all these states, even when it is not particularly functional. This can be illustrated by surveys of 'who speaks what language to whom about what'.

Sure (1989) carried out a survey of teaching trainees in Kenya. He gives tables for use of English, Swahili, and the mother tongue in Kenya, with different individuals and in different places. These show that Kenyans use their mother tongue almost exclusively with their parents, use the mother tongue, English, and Swahili in that order of frequency with their brothers and sisters, and use the mother tongue (mainly), Swahili, and English in that order with their children. With a doctor in a clinic they would most often use English (though Swahili and the mother tongue were also possibilities). With a priest all three languages seem equally likely, but with a colleague at work English is most frequent. He also gives figures for languages in different places: Swahili or the mother tongue in the market, English in the library, the bank, or a government office, English or Swahili in the bookshop or post office. Everybody Sure investigated was trilingual and would suit the language spoken to the setting, interlocutor, and domain.

Adekunle (1995) surveyed language use in Jos, a linguistically mixed town in the Plateau region of Nigera, where Hausa is a lingua franca. He interviewed and observed people there about their language use in different situations, classifying his subjects by their ethnicity, domains as 'personal' or 'official' and interlocutors as 'intimates' (mainly of the same ethnicity as the speaker), 'acquaintances', and 'officials'. The results show that both domain and interlocutor affect language choice. With intimates personal affairs will be discussed almost exclusively in the mother tongue, but official matters may also be discussed in English. A Hausa-speaking official will use Hausa with those who can speak Hausa, English with others, and pidgin only with those who can speak neither Hausa nor English. Nevertheless, written records will be kept exclusively in English. Similarly a Yoruba in Jos – where Yoruba is not a local language – will use Yoruba with other Yorubas, and English, Hausa, or pidgin, whichever is effective, with acquaintances on personal matters. Three or four languages interpenetrate in all daily interaction and the English that may dominate on paper is not dominant in speech, because it signals social distance as well as impersonal subject matter.

South Africa is as multilingual as most African countries, but it has made unique efforts to validate local languages and have them all used in all domains, including administration and education. This is an attempt to overcome a history of linguistic oppression. After the establishment of the independent Union of South Africa in 1910 English speakers were dominant in the cities, in government, and in the economy, even though Afrikaans was equally official in theory, and the other languages of the country were used only for primary education. From 1948 to 1991 the Afrikaner-dominated National party was in power and pursued a consistent policy of making Afrikaans usable in all domains and, where possible, replacing English. It also aimed to limit opportunities for blacks to be educated, particularly in English, and so encouraged (primary) vernacular education. Consequently English (ironically) acquired an aura of 'freedom' and resistance, and education in English appeared better than vernacular education. South Africa was liberated in the early 1990s and reconstituted as a pluralistic society whose constitution establishes 11 official languages. The constitution asserts the right of citizens to be educated and deal with authorities in any of these languages. Serious efforts have been made to put the policy into practice, and government documents are translated into many of the languages. Nevertheless, market forces favour English as a high-status language likely to appear neutral in most situations and institutions like the army and government seem to be adopting English as link language. There is no language like pidgin or Swahili which rivals English. This is illustrated by the quotations from speakers of Tshivenda and Afrikaans given by Barkhuizen and de Klerk (2000):

> It would be difficult for me to go to the office or where to a certain place and try to talk Venda . . . there must be top language.
>
> What do you think that should be?
>
> That should be English. That is the only language that is the communication language.
>
> Okay, I'm growing up Afrikaans. I don't expect it from anybody else to speak to me in Afrikaans, but can't we now just communicate in English and we've got a middle medium. Everybody can be happy.

Even in South Africa, English has a specially favoured position. But the mother tongues have a place in the mosaic of a multilingual environment as well, and it is shown in this quotation from the interviews of de Klerk and Barkhuizen with a soldier whose mother tongue is neither TshiVenda (a Bantu language), nor English.

> For myself, there is some period when maybe I want cigarette and a Venda has got a cigarette then I get a problem how am I going to get a cigarette from the Venda guy. Then I introduce myself to other Venda guy and ask him, then they told me how to ask for a cigarette in Venda.
> But then why didn't you ask him in English?
> You see I want to soften him up.

English is useful, that is, but in many circumstances other languages are a possibility and appropriate choice is a vital skill of multilingual Africans (Bisong 1995).

5.4.2.3 English in education

The debate between westernizers and orientalists (5.3.2) about the correct medium for education in a colonial environment responds to an insoluble problem created by colonization. If education is offered in the language of the colonizers it alienates the local educated from their own community and creates an elite. But if education is offered in the vernacular, the colonized people suspect an attempt to keep knowledge from them and provide second class service.

Educationalists basically agree that it is better to acquire literacy in a language one is familiar with, rather than struggle to learn literacy and a new language at the same time (Cummins 1983, 1986), and there is a good deal of evidence that children learn content ineffectively in languages that they and their teachers have not fully mastered. A useful comparison can be made between Zambia and Malawi. In Zambia, English is the only potential link language and is the medium of education even at primary school, so that Zambian children normally do not learn to read their mother tongue. In Malawi Nyanja/Chichewa was made an official language and primary education was carried out in it, with English as a subject. But this language is also spoken in Zambia, so it is possible to compare the policies. Williams (1996) showed that while Zambian children could only read English, Malawian ones not only read as well in English as Zambian ones, but also were literate in Nyanja/Chichewa, which was their mother tongue.

Parents on the other hand remember colonialist policies aimed at excluding blacks and can generally see that knowledge of English is a key to success in their society. So they tend to be anxious for their children to get as much of the language as they can in the few years of schooling they can afford (Arthur 1997). Furthermore there are practical difficulties in the way of vernacular education. Zambia has many mother tongues, and large urban areas where people of different ethnic backgrounds mix. It would not be politically possible to choose just one or two vernaculars. But in a country with 30 mother tongues and limited resources, it would be very expensive to provide even primary textbooks in every mother tongue, or even five or six. Foreign aid money might be used in theory, but in practice it has normally been directed to English-language materials, cheaper to produce because of economies of scale, and frequently written by the aid-giver's own experts and published by their own publishers (Banda 1996).

Even in multilingual and supportive South Africa there are practical problems in providing education in all 11 languages, and very many parents prefer English-medium schools to those in their own language. The unfortunate thing is that in fact they may be making it more difficult for their children to get an education in competition with children who come to school with a good knowledge of the language of instruction.

The result is that middle-class children come to school knowing its medium and poorer ones do not, and that the books they read, even if not published in the West, say by their choice of medium that the West is best. These circumstances give a good deal of support to the argument of the radicals (3.4.1) that the language policies – and still more so practices – which have been adopted in Africa benefit Britain, the USA and the local elite much more than local people, but they also show how difficult it would be to supply Africans with the primary education in the mother tongue (or at least majority local language) that Europeans and most Asians take for granted.

5.4.3 African Englishes – a descriptive account

5.4.3.1 A preliminary sketch

- Some common features, partly because they often have a substratum in Bantu languages.
- A smaller vowel set than inner-circle varieties, compensated for by spelling pronunciations and nonreduction of vowels. Spelling pronunciations are normal and predominant. As an example of how different the vowel patterns of African English can be, and yet how distinctiveness and redundancy are retained, Ebot (1999) cites Cameroon English *purpose* /pɔpɔs/, *perpetrate* /pɛpɛtret/ compared with GA /pɜrpəs/, /pɜrpətreɪt/ or RP /pɜ:pəs/, /pɜ:pətreɪt/ where every vowel is different both in realization and systemically and yet both varieties have three different vowel phonemes in these two words.
- Some vowel pronunciations used as identity markers. In discussing NURSE, *first* realized as [nas] [fast], Schmied (1991) quotes Kenyans saying ' I don't want to strain myself so much to say [fɜ:st] only to sound British . . . This would seem snobbish to my colleagues'.
- Word stress sometimes assigned according to local rules (Peng and Ann 2000, Bobda 1994), as in West African *indi'cate* vs RP/GA *'indicate* perhaps because stress is attracted to certain types of strong syllable.
- Figurative expressions based on the substrate languages. Chisanga and Kamwangamallu (1997) cite *I have killed many moons in that hut* from Zimbabwe.
- In casual speech, long words which sound formal to inner-circle ears but do not necessarily have that value, since casual styles have had to be 'reconstituted' from language learnt at school.

5.4.3.2 Phonology

The accents of individual African speakers depend on their mother tongue, the area they grew up in, and how acrolectally they are speaking. However, there are similarities among the varieties of English that have a Bantu, or at least Niger-Congo substratum, and those with Afro-Asiatic or Nilotic (or Krio) substrate seem to have similar phonological characteristics. The exceptions to this overall very rough similarity are varieties in South Africa with Afrikaans (Germanic) and Indian substrata.

Schmied (1991) and Bobda (2000a,b) have attempted overall summaries of the vowel systems of speakers with African-language substrata, and the result, describing a mesolectal accent, is something like this (Table 5.6), with interesting mergers and splits:

Table 5.6. African lexical sets

KIT = FLEECE = happY	[i]
DRESS = FACE	[e] see below
TRAP = BATH = PALM = START	[a] or [ɛ, e] in East Africa
LOT = STRUT = CLOTH = THOUGHT = NORTH = FORCE	[ɔ] , [o] see below
FOOT = GOOSE	[u]
NURSE	split, see below
GOAT	[o] see below
PRICE	ai
CHOICE	oi
MOUTH	au
NEAR	[ia]
SQUARE	[ea]
CURE	[ua]
lettER = commA	split, see below

DRESS is [ɛ] in West Africa and FACE is [e] (Wells 1982, Schmied 1991, Ebot 1999), but this distinction is lost in eastern and southern Africa. Similarly LOT/THOUGHT/CLOTH/NORTH are distinct from GOAT in the West (as [ɔ] and [o]) but merged in the East and South.

Bobda (2000a,b, 2001) has an elegant analysis of the regional differences in NURSE. He says that the vowel is normally [ɛ] in the South of eastern-southern Africa (Zimbabwe and south) and [a] in the north (Kenya, Uganda), with zones where both forms occur, sometimes with lexical differentiation, in between. In West Africa, he says, pronunciation depends on an interaction of spelling and region/mother tongue. People who pronounce *first, bird, third* as /fɔst, bɔd, tɔd/ are from southern Nigeria, Sierra Leone, or Gambia, people who pronounce *work, journey, church* as /wɛk, dʒɛne, tʃɛtʃ/ are from Ghana, and people who pronounce *bird, murder, world* as /bad, mada, wald/ are Hausa speakers from northern Nigeria.

Finally, because African English is less stress-timed than inner-circle varieties, *commA* and *lettER* have split (Bobda 1994).

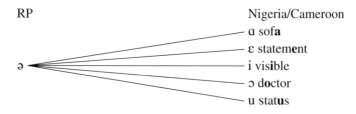

Fig. 5.5 West African realizations of syllabus which have shwa in RP

This reflects the general tendency in school-learnt English to spelling pronunciation mentioned above.

As for consonants, many varieties of African English realize /θð/ as [td] as one would expect (Ebot, Wells), though this is regarded as nonstandard by Wells. Given their origins in school British English and pidgin, it is not surprising that the varieties are nonrhotic, although rhoticity has been noted in Kenya, ascribed to the influence of American tourists, and in Malawi, ascribed to Scottish missionaries.

Final voiced fricatives (which are somewhat unusual in the world's languages) may be unvoiced: [laf] 'love'. Consonant clusters may be broken up with epenthetic vowels, especially in East Africa: [kɔnɪfɪdɛns] 'confidence', or simplified, especially in the West: *pos' office*. Final /l/ is often vocalized. Otherwise, consonant variation seems to depend on the substrate language. For example, many individual languages have a single phoneme covering [l] and [r] and so confusion of English /l/ and /r/ occurs sporadically, for example among Asante speakers in Ghana and speakers of the central Bantu languages in Kenya (Kanyoro 1991). This can be illustrated by the spelling *Ordinally Level* 'Ordinary Level' from a web page written by pupils of an elite school in Uganda. Some languages, like Hausa in Nigeria, have no /p/, or like Luyia in Kenya, no /b/. Some have no distinction between /b/ and /v/. According to Ebot the 'ethnically characterized features' of English pronunciation that may arise 'are hardly accepted by educated Cameroonians as good usage'.

Most African English is syllable-timed with stress marked mainly by high pitch (Wells). When one of the authors suggested that Nigerians should teach stress-timed speech with marked sentence stress he had the response 'The students would just laugh at me if I tried to speak like you people.' This means that syntactic devices rather than contrastive stress have to be used to indicate focus: *For Peter, he won't come* may be used to emphasize *Peter* rather than stress on *Peter*.

Words are very often stressed differently in African English (partly because stress is a less prominent feature and rarely distinctive). Bobda (1994) says that stress is generally further forward in the word than in British English. He is able to give some rules predicting Nigerian/Cameroonian stress placement from the form and word-class of the item, analogous to, but different from those which operate in RP/GA. Here we just give some examples:

W.Af	RP/GA	W.Af	RP/GA	W.Af	RP/GA
indi′cate	′indicate	Ire′land	′Ireland	holi′day	′holiday
an′cestor	′ancestor	or′chestra	′orchestra	indo′mitable	in′domitable
plan′tain	′plantain	cate′chist	′catechist	photo′grapher	pho′tographer

5.4.3.3 Syntax

The syntax of written standard African English is close to that of other Standard varieties. In a text from the *Accra Mail*, 8 August 2001 we noted three local features of syntax:

> …This places enormous responsibilities on the party, because it will be partisan affair but also a non-partisan flavour would be expected. It is not too early for us to sound our concern. The congress should be so organized that it would give the whole country a sense of purpose and direction.
>
> It will not do for the congress to for example downplay the importance of the NPP's allies in Election 2000, nor would it serve any purpose for the congress to degenerate into squabbles that would be seized upon by detractors to distract....

- *because it will be partisan affair*, where one might expect *a partisan affair*, reflects a local, or unsystematic, use of articles
- *a non-partisan flavour would be expected* and *so organized that it would give* contain a characteristic outer-circle use of *would* as a formal or polite version of *will* rather than something required by the sequence of tenses
- In *seized upon by detractors to distract* the verb *distract* is intransitive, where inner-circle varieties might use an object such as *attention*.

In more mesolectal varieties more local characteristics might appear, most of them typical of New (or simply unedited?) English: non-standard patterns of verb agreement, avoidance of complex tenses, extension of progressive forms to stative verbs, different patterns of preposition use and complementation with verbs, non-marking of noun number, conflation of count and non-count, and of definiteness categories, invariant tags, pronoun copying *(Mr Chongwe said his client he did not want)* and simplified word order conventions (Schmied 1991: 64–76).

Mesthrie (1996) gives three syntactic characteristics of South African Indian English: consistent plural marking in the second-person pronouns *you* singular and *y'all* plural; inversion in indirect questions (*I don't know when's the plane going to land*); and extended use of *of* in constructions like *She put too much of nuts in the cake*. All three seem logical regularizations, but only the second is widely reported from other African Englishes.

Afrikaans English differs in syntax from 'Anglo' South African English mainly in features like concord and article use that affect all second-language speakers, though Watermeyer (1996) mentions a tendency to use *a* as an invariant indefinite article even where other varieties use *an* (also reported from New Zealand and Tristan da Cunha).

5.4.3.4 Lexis

We saw that South Asian English was characterized by frequent code mixing, in the sense that words from Hindi and Urdu can be quite freely used in English, because one can rely on one's reader being bilingual. The situation for African speakers varies from country to country. In Kenya and Tanzania one can assume that one's reader or interlocutor knows Swahili, and according to Hancock and Agongo (1982) 'Practically any local word can turn up in East African English'. Similarly in the monolingual states of Southern Africa (Swaziland, Lesotho, Botswana) one can assume some knowledge of the national language. But in Ghana, Nigeria, or Zambia,

English is genuinely a link language, and any borrowed word must be genuinely 'local English' rather than code mixing.

Borrowed foreignisms are common,[12] like *people who khonta-ed* ('apply for land from royal family') from Siswati in Swaziland. From South African English one could cite *bredie* 'type of stew' (from Afrikaans), and *maas* 'dairy product' (from a Nguni language). In Nigeria there are foreignisms which are also borrowings from local languages – often the names of foods such as *dodo* 'fried plantains/bananas', *foofoo* 'yam porridge', or garments like *agbada* 'male gown'. Others are loan-translations like *waist beads* for a form of decoration. Many are extensions within English: *social wake-keeping* 'part of the funeral ritual', *chewing stick* used for cleaning the teeth, *introduction* 'type of ceremony to formalize engagement to marry', *senior wife* in a polygamous marriage (cf. Southern African *right-hand wife, principal wife), black soap* 'locally made cheap soap', *pounded yam* food.

Among local lexicalizations, one could cite borrowings like *will be bulewa-ed* ('promoted, impliedly to an unrefusable but difficult post') from Swaziland and local developments like *bisley* 'shooting competition' from South Africa. Here too belong the loan-translations from Siswati *young father, young mother* 'father's younger brother, mother's younger sister'.

Among tautonyms – words which have a different or extended meaning in one variety compared to another – Nigerian English has *escort* 'show/accompany someone out of the house', *travel* 'be away' and *go-slow* 'traffic jam', *fatal accident* 'serious accident, not necessarily leading to death' and *teller* 'bank paying-in slip'. Kinship terms have extended reference in many African cultures and languages: *brother* 'member of same tribe/friend' in Nigeria which could be compared with a quotation from Zambia '*I went to see my sister, same father same mother*' where specification is necessary since it could otherwise be a cousin, half-sister, or more distant relation. In Uganda there are usages like *balance* 'change in a shop' (also reported by Nihalani *et al.* 1979 from India), which is perhaps just an example of the use of what in other varieties is a rather formal term, *eat money* 'embezzle', a local figurative expression, *avail* 'provide' (us with documents, for example) and changes of complementation such as *rob* 'steal'. Many varieties, including Afrikaans English, conflate *lend* and *borrow,* and Afrikaners also conflate *loaf* and *bread, ride* and *drive, when* and *if* under mother-tongue influence.

Among heteronyms (items or activities which have different names in different varieties), a distinction can again be made between borrowings, loan-translations, and new coinages. There are borrowings from local languages and pidgin like *chop* 'food' from pidgin, *lobola* 'bride-price' from Siswati in Swaziland. Others are loan-translations like Nigerian *long legs* 'undue influence/string-pulling', *hear a smell,* 'smell something', *not on seat* 'out of the office'. Many of these are idioms like *the girl is ripe* (for marriage), *the woman has jumped him* (betrayed with another man)

---

12 Examples are quoted here from our own observations and from Chisanga and Kamwangamallu (1997), Branford and Branford 1991, Adegbija (1989), Schmied (1991), and Fisher (2000).

from Southern Africa. Most common seem to be extensions or new collocations: Nigerian *off the light* 'turn off the light', (compare *forwarded* 'put forward' in a newspaper from Sierra Leone), *kola* 'bribe', *tight friend* 'close friend'. Some well-known East African borrowings are: *jambo* 'hello' and *safari*, 'journey of any kind' (confusingly tautonymous with General English *safari* 'tropical wilderness journey'.

Tautonyms combine with heteronyms in the many French-influenced usages in Cameroon lexis: *formation* for 'training', *licence* 'university degree', etc. Other local developments have the same effect: South African *stroller* 'street child' is tautonymous with a US English term for a child's pushchair.

Skandera (1999) warns us to be sceptical of lists of the kind above. They usually derive from anecdotal observation or intuition and may include very ephemeral items. It is therefore interesting to note that Adegbija asked his students what *trouble shooter* (5.2.4 above) meant and virtually all gave only the Nigerian (and Indian) meaning: this tautonym at least has been tested.

5.4.3.5 Pragmatics and style

Behaviour and discourse patterns are transferred direct from one's own culture and therefore will be very different across Africa.

One common stylistic feature of African English is the use of idiomatic expressions in different forms from their inner-circle originals, often merging two expressions. Thus in the *Accra Mail* text quoted above we have *pool our resources together* (= UK, US *put our resources together* mixed with *pool our resources), sound our concern* in the above (= UK/US *voice our concern* mixed with *sound a warning*). Another shows the effect of independent development of formality and tone: formal (even biblical) phrases that have become old-fashioned or clichéd in the inner circle occur alongside others that seem slangy and colloquial. Thus in the *Accra Mail* article we see *chipped in their widow's mite*. Corresponding to this is the use of unexpected and fresh figurative phrases from the substratum languages or cultures: Adegbija quotes the novelist Achebe 'Proverbs are the palm oil with which words are eaten'.

Apart from the characteristic use in Nigeria (5.2.5) of *Sorry!* (at all levels) and *Well done* (only mesolectal and below, according to Banjo) there are many other pragmatic features. Some are culturally determined, like the reluctance to refer seniors by name mentioned by Adegbija (*My senior brother* rather than his name), or loan translations like the greeting sequence *How? Not bad?* Others are different verbalizations of recognizable situations. Thus when someone happens to come into the room while being spoken of, Nigerians say *true son* (UK/US *talk/speak of the devil*, Indian *a thousand years to you*).

Similar developments sometimes happen in widely separated areas. Adegbija (2001) gives examples of characteristic Nigerian uses of *OK* to mean things like 'I have made up my mind' and 'what did you expect?' Writing about a country in Southern Africa in about 1990 the Zimbabwe-born British novelist Doris Lessing highlights similar extensions:

'What's wrong, Rebecca?'

'Okay' said Rebecca, meaning, I shall tell you.

. . .

'Okay' said Sylvia, in her turn using this new or newish idiom which now seemed to begin every sentence. She meant that she had absorbed the information and shared Rebecca's fears. (Doris Lessing, *The Sweetest Dream* 2001:348–9)

5.4.4 Further reading

African history is described in Davidson (1984). Schmied (1991) gives a fuller account of what we have said here. Ngũgĩ gives the classic arguments against English in Africa. De Klerk (1996) gives a view of what is happening in South Africa.

5.5 SOUTH EAST ASIA

When one is abroad, in a bus or train or airplane and when one overhears someone speaking, one can immediately say this is someone from Malaysia or Singapore. And I should hope that when I'm speaking abroad, my countrymen will have no problem recognising that I am a Singaporean. (Professor Tommy Koh, quoted by Tongue 1974)

5.5.2 The countries

Table 5.7. South East Asian countries and their population of English speakers

Country	Area (sq.km.)	Population (1995) (thousands)	Capital	Mother-tongue English (thousands)	Functional command of English (thousands) as non-mother-tongue
Hong Kong, China	1062	6205		125	1860
Malaysia	332,965	19,948	Kuala Lumpur	375	5984
Philippines	300,000	70,011	Manila	15	36,400
Singapore	616	2989		300	1046

Reference figures

Barbados	430	265			
Ireland	68,895	3.8m			
UK	244,755	59.5m			
USA	9,363,130	282.0m			

Source: *The Times World Atlas*, Crystal (1995)

5.5.2 Background

In moving from Africa and India to South East Asia we move to a different economic environment. Singapore is a developed country with levels of education which are among the highest in the world (and with infrastructure, computer use, health, welfare, etc., at or above European and North American levels). The Hong Kong region of China is a fully developed world financial and business centre with a high standard of living. Malaysia is a rapidly developing 'Asian tiger' economy. The Philippines are poorer, but better off in terms of average income than the African or South Asian countries. Consequently the resources available for education and implementing language policy in these countries are incomparably greater than in sub-Saharan Africa or even (per head) in South Asia.

The precolonial languages of the Philippines, Malaysia, and Singapore were Austronesian languages. These are usually not tonal (unlike Bantu languages and Chinese), have polysyllabic words which may have inflections, and a phonology with few consonant clusters and relatively fewer consonants than English. In Malaysia (and Singapore) the precolonial language was Malay, which in its modern standard-ized form has many loanwords from Sanskrit, Arabic, and English, and often coins words from Sanskrit roots as English does from Latin or Greek. It can be written in characters derived from the Arabic script, but is now more commonly written in Roman letters. The various precolonial languages of the Philippines had less influence from other languages.

The local language of Hong Kong is Cantonese, a 'dialect'[13] of Chinese. Cantonese and the other 'dialects' are tonal, typically have words of one or two syllables with few or no inflections, and have few consonant clusters and few possible final conso-nants. Most people in modern Singapore, and many in Malaysia, are of Chinese descent and speak Cantonese or Hokkien or another 'dialect' of Chinese as their ancestral language. In both countries there are substantial numbers of people of Indian descent, mostly with Dravidian language backgrounds.

5.5.2.1 History

The earliest civilizations in Malaysia and Indonesia arose as a result of Indian expansion starting 2000 years ago. From the eleventh century onwards Islamic missionaries and traders appeared in the area and gradually Malaysia and most of Indonesia became Muslim, often with a striking mixture of Indian and Islamic traditions and styles. However, neither Hindu nor Islamic culture affected most people in the Philippines. In 1565 they became a Spanish possession (under the viceroy of Mexico) and consequently it was Spanish Catholic missionaries rather than Hindu/Buddhists or Muslims who brought 'higher religion' to the islands. Most of the population became Catholics (though some were reached first by Islamic missionaries and became Muslims) and Spanish was used for education for the small upper class.

The fishing settlement on Singapore was converted to a strategic British trading and military centre at the beginning of the nineteenth century. The spices, the main goal of Europeans in South East Asia, grew further east, and it was not until the later

---

13 'Dialect' has its quotation marks because 'dialects' like Cantonese or Hokkien are as different from one another as Spanish and French, but are regarded as dialects of Chinese because (simplifying) all dialects are written in the same way, as Standard Chinese – as if Spanish and French were written down as Latin.

nineteenth century that the peninsula itself became valuable to Europeans. British interests then started to exploit the tin deposits and tropical products including palm oil and rubber. The ten or so small Malay sultanates were gradually taken over by Britain, and Chinese and Indian labourers and business people came to operate the mines and plantations.

During the twentieth century the Malay peninsula was a multilingual society. The Malays spoke different local varieties of Malay, and used a standard written form; the Chinese used their 'dialects', the Indians Tamil and other Indian languages, and the colonial authorities used English. Arabic and Sanskrit were known as languages of religion. A lingua franca variety of Malay, 'Bazaar Malay', and types of English functioned as link languages. English was spread by the education system and educated people became very fluent because they used the language for everyday communication across communal boundaries. Less educated people in towns also used English for this purpose. The result was that lingua franca English existed in a range of varieties from an 'acrolect' (3.4.2.4) which was a Standard English with local phonology to a 'basilect' which had many of the characteristics of an extended pidgin or creole (even if it was no one's mother tongue and hence has been called a 'creoloid'). Because more basilectal varieties were used in the school playground, they began to connote intimacy for many people who also mastered the acrolect, and the lectal range from standard to markedly local began to imply a stylistic range from formal to informal.

Hong Kong came under British control as a result of the Opium Wars with China and developed as a trading centre. Throughout the colonial period a minority of British administrators and traders co-existed with a large majority of Chinese traders and labourers. Since most Chinese could speak Cantonese, there was no need for a lingua franca, only for a language to use with powerful foreigners. Knowledge of English was spread almost entirely through the education system, which increasingly used English as a medium.

In 1898 ownership of the Philippines passed to the USA. The Americans launched a vigorous campaign of education though the medium of English, so that by independence in 1946 a rhotic variety of English with US vocabulary was widely known for administration and education, and used among Filipinos with different mother tongues. Virtually all Filipinos spoke one or more local languages alongside it, of course.

5.5.2.2 The current situation: Malaysia and Singapore

The former British possessions in the area are mostly now part of Malaysia, which finally emerged in 1964 as a federation combining the old sultanates on the peninsula with the parts of Borneo which had been British. Singapore became an independent city state.

As noted above (5.1), at independence Malaysia adopted a policy favouring Bahasa Malaysia, a synthetic language close to written literary Malay, and not very distant from the Malay vernaculars. Singapore, with a population speaking a variety of

Chinese 'dialects', Indian languages, and local Malay, emphasized English as the main official language. It has subsequently moved towards a policy which aims at the Chinese community dropping the 'dialects' and becoming bilingual in Mandarin Chinese (the official language of mainland China and Taiwan) and English, Indians in an Indian language and English, and Malays in Bahasa Malaysia and English.

In Malaysia, English is used for some tertiary education, and quite widely as the language of business, where many firms are still dominated by Chinese or Indian personnel. Nair-Venugopal (2000), Gill (1999), and Morais (1998) examined workplaces in Malaysia and showed that English is frequently used, often with codeswitching into Malay and variation between standard and more localized forms according to situation and conversational partner. In 2002 the government, eager to benefit from globalization, signalled a swing back to English-medium primary and secondary education, at least for science and mathematics.

In Singapore in 1990 a quarter of parents of children entering school claimed that English was the most frequently used language in their home, and this reflects the very different status which English has in Singapore from Malaysia and Hong Kong. An increasing proportion of speakers have English as a mother tongue – but the local variety rather than Standard English. As in preindependence Malaya, Singaporeans can move up and down a continuum from acrolect to basilect according to the formality and intimacy of the situation, though of course only the most educated have full access to the acrolect and only the least educated use the deepest basilect.

5.5.2.3 The current situation: Hong Kong

Hong Kong was returned to Chinese sovereignty in 1997. Today, English is very widely used in the education and legal systems and to deal with international business, and is becoming 'localized', and used to some extent for everyday interaction among locals who all speak Cantonese (Bolton 2002). Mandarin Chinese (putonghua) is becoming more and more important in administration and for interaction with people from the rest of China.

5.5.2.4 The current situation: the Philippines

The Philippines became independent of the USA in 1948. There were indigenous lingua francas, and one of these, Tagalog, the language of the Manila area, was chosen as the national language (and, after some negotiation, renamed Filipino). The local languages are all related to Tagalog, so Filipino is easier than English for local people to learn. Since 1984 the principle has been that the first years of education may be in the vernacular – the local language – but after that the humanities and social sciences must be taught in Filipino and the natural sciences in English. Tertiary education is largely in English. Thus successful school leavers are proficient in English and Filipino.

In fact nearly all adults understand Filipino and a high proportion can speak it. Knowledge of English is also widespread (56 per cent of adults can use it, according to Gonzales (1998)), but the upper classes have the highest proficiency in English and the advantages that go with it. Filipino is the language of many publications and much entertainment, the thriving film industry for example. Television is said to be 60 per cent Filipino (including Mexican soap operas dubbed into Filipino) and 40 per cent (imported) English, and it is said that Filipinos prefer the programming in the national language (Clampitt-Dunlop 1995).

Nevertheless the choice of a local lingua franca as national language sets up a language pyramid of a type we recognize from parts of Africa and India (and Malaysia), with the national language intended to take over functions from English, but not automatically accepted by those who do not have it as their mother tongue. In fact full implementation of the bilingual education policy is hindered both by English-medium universities unwilling to use Filipino as a medium, and by speakers of Cebuano, another lingua franca, who have used the courts to prevent school exams being held in Filipino rather than English, on the grounds that this would give native Tagalog speakers the advantage of exams in their own language (cf. Chichewa/Nyanja in Malawi in 5.4.2).

5.5.3 Malaysian/Singaporean English – a descriptive account

5.5.3.1 A shortlist of particularly salient features
This is a variety which varies much within itself in terms of styles and speaker proficiency. While Singapore English seems to vary on a one-dimensional scale from a formal, educated acrolect to an informal, uneducated basilect, with education a key variable determining a speaker's lectal range, modern Malaysian English seems to vary according to ethnicity as well as education. For some, many of them Malays, English is almost a foreign language used with varying proficiency in work-related situations. For others, many of them educated non-Malays, it is a local lingua franca or even mother tongue, used in a variety of situations with appropriate lectal variation. For others even, less educated non-Malays perhaps, it is a lingua franca to be used in basic communication, generally at mesolectal or lower level. In what follows we can only give examples of features which, while local, occur across a range of varieties and lects. 'Singlish' – basilectal/mesolectal Singapore English – is well described (for example on Anthea Gupta's web page (http://www.leeds.ac.uk/english/staff/afg/singeh2.html)) and, in terms of salient features, at least, close to basilectal/mesolectal Malaysian English.

- a reduced set of final consonants and consonant sequences as compared with most other varieties and consequently words which end with glottal stops, voiceless fricatives, or nasals ([iːʔ] 'eat', [bæŋ] 'bank')
- stereotyped Singapore vocabulary items: borrowings from Malay like *ulu* 'old-fashioned, provincial', and from Chinese like *kiasu* 'selfish' (see below), and local coinages like *blur* 'confused'
- the particle *lah* (borrowed from Chinese) which is used to emphasize confidently made statements or shared knowledge
- omission of sentence subjects (and objects) that can be inferred from the context.

5.5.3.2 Phonology

The vowel inventory is typical of a 'new English' (Table 5.8).

Table 5.8. The vowels of South East Asian Englishes

Philippines (Wells)	Hong Kong (Yung)	Singapore/Malaysia (Gupta)	Key word	Ga GA (Wells)	RP (Wells)
ɪ	i	i	KIT	ɪ	ɪ
e	ɛ	ɛ	DRESS	ɛ	e
æ	ɛ	ɛ	TRAP	æ	æ
a	ɔ	ɔ	LOT	ɑ	ɒ
ə	ʌ	ɐ	STRUT	ʌ	ʌ
ʊ	u	u	FOOT	ʊ	ʊ
æ	ɑ	ɐ	BATH	æ	ɑː
ɔ	ɔ	ɔ	CLOTH	ɔ	ɒ
ər	ɜ	ə	NURSE	ɜr	ɜː
i	i	i	FLEECE	iː	iː
eɪ	eɪ	e	FACE	eɪ	eɪ
a	ɑ	ɐ	PALM	ɑ	ɑː
ɔ	ɔ	ɔ	THOUGHT	ɔ	ɔː
ou	ou	o	GOAT	o	əʊ
u	u	u	GOOSE	u	uː
aɪ	ai	aɪ	PRICE	aɪ	aɪ
ɔɪ	ɔi	ɔɪ	CHOICE	ɔɪ	ɔɪ
aʊ	ɑʊ	au	MOUTH	aʊ	aʊ
ɪr	iə	ɪə	NEAR	ɪr	ɪə
er	ɛə	ɛ	SQUARE	ɛr	ɛə
ar	ɑː	ɐ	START	ɑr	ɑː
ɔr	ɔ	ɔ	NORTH	ɔr	ɔː
ɔr	ɔ	ɔ	FORCE	or	ɔː
ʊr	ʊə	uə	CURE	ʊr	ʊə
ɪ	ɪ	ɪ	happY	ɪ	ɪ
ər	ə	ə	*lettER	ər	ə
ə	ə	ə	*commA	ə	ə

*Vowels reduced in GA/RP are often not reduced in these varieties.

The consonants are rather more distinctive. Final consonant clusters are simplified, so that *think* is [θɪŋ] or [tɪŋ] and *effect* is [ɪfek] or [ifɛʔ]. Word-finally, most plosives/stops are omitted or reduced to glottal stops, especially if voiceless – *that* may be [ðæʔ] and *word* may be [wɜ] or[wɜʔ]. Final fricatives – especially /s/ and /z/ –

may be all voiceless, so that *cease* and *seas* are homophones, and *expensive* is [ekspen↓ sif]. Relatively few vowels are reduced to [ə], as in other syllable-timed varieties, so that vowel pronunciation may be close to the spelling. A number of words have local stress patterns, some of which, like *pur'chase*, look like regularizations based on the spelling (cf. *pursuit, chase*).

Having an accent that is too Chinese is a mark of not being cool in youth culture. The *Guide to Singlish* (http://www.geocities.com/Colosseum/Park/1999/singlish.htm) gives these utterances of uncool youths, which actually seem mainly to illustrate normal mesolectal pronunciation with the addition of loss of /θ/ and/r/ in *withdraw*, and the South Chinese conflation of /lrn/ in *nine, number,* and *road.*

I one too wee door some money. 'I want to withdraw some money'
Blok lie-tee-fi, lumber tree-too-egg, Ang Suah load; 'Block 95, No. 328, Ang Suah Road'

By contrast, an American accent may be becoming more fashionable: originally US pronunciation of individual words like *schedule* are said to be becoming more common.

5.5.3.3 Syntax

Basilectal and mesolectal Singapore-Malaysian English differs rather dramatically from the standard in terms of syntax and we just give some examples of common features which can be encountered.

Subjects and objects can be omitted where they are clear from the context, as in Chinese and Malay. For example as an answer to the question *Do you get overtime pay, or can you take time off in lieu?* Richards (1977:79) recorded *You want to overtime also can, take off, also can* 'If you want (to take) overtime, you can, but if you want to take time off, you can do that too'.

Correspondingly, as in Chinese, Malay, and many creoles, *be* as copula (and auxiliary) can be omitted. Richards recorded, as an answer to *It's pretty quiet running this car park at night, isn't it? This one Ø near the shopping centre, night club, there the good business Ø, that Ø why the government operate the parking here.* 'No, it is near the shopping centre and night clubs, there's good business there, that's why the government has a parking lot here.'

Gupta (1994) says that the syntax of questions in Singapore Colloquial English – what we are calling the basilect and mesolect – is simpler than that in Standard English and also than that in Malay and Chinese. Question words other than *why* and *how* are not usually fronted, and inversion is only usual when the verb has the BE or CAN auxiliaries, so that the following question forms are normal:

Why you take so many?
Go where?
She eat what?

Given the possibility of omitting the subject and not inverting, questions of the form *What to do? Where to go?* ('What can/should I/we/she do?', 'Where can/should

I/we/he go?') are common and characteristic of Singapore/Malaysian usage. In Chinese and South East Asian languages questions often include the equivalent of *or (not)*? as a question word, and correspondingly local English often has questions like *Want or not? You want tea or what? Can or not? Pain or not?* (Gupta 1994).

Singapore English is well described and its syntax is of great interest. Anthea Gupta's *The Step-tongue: Children's English in Singapore* is a good introduction.

5.5.3.4 Lexis

The various lects of Singapore/Malaysia English include a great deal of local vocabulary. Singlish has a rich supply of local lexicalizations derived from Chinese dialects, of which we only discuss three:

- *chim/cheem* 'excessively complex/difficult/serious'. The *Guide to Singlish* gives this example: '*Usually when confronted with something that appears to be more complex than 1 + 1, the S'porean would exclaim, "Why so CHIM one?" even before s/he begins to read or think about the "something" . . .*'
- *chope* 'reserve a chair, etc. by putting a bag or garment on it'.
- *kiasu* 'person with a fear of losing out to others'. The *Guide to Singlish* gives these typical traits of a *kiasu*, expressed in charming basilect:

1. *Everything also must grab* 'He/she has to grab everything'.
2. *Must chope seat when you go everywhere* 'He/she has to *chope* a seat on all occasions'.
3. *Anything that is free must get* 'He/she must get some of anything that is going free'.
4. *Must be number 1 in everything* (self-explanatory).

Foreignisms formed from English lexical material include:

heaty, cooling, 'foods regarded in Chinese tradition as yang (male light positive) and yin (female dark negative) respectively.
red packet 'envelope containing money given at a festival'.

Among tautonyms one could mention *send* with the meaning of 'take' as in *send him to the airport, peon* 'office boy, office porter', *blur* (adjective) 'out of touch', *that time, last time* 'in the past, formerly'. Among heteronyms one could mention borrowed words, which give local colour to universal concepts: *makan* 'food', *jaga* 'watchman'. Of course the General English terms are known and used alongside the local ones, with a different stylistic effect.

Probably more specifically Malaysian are the foreignisms *outstation* 'provincial office' and the official term, *bumi putra* a foreignism borrowed from Malay meaning 'a person with the Malaysian legal ethnic status of a "native" (as opposed to a Chinese or Indian, for example)'. *Bungalow* is used in its General English sense of 'tropical villa' rather than its British one of 'one-storey house', and *stay* is in used in the Scottish, African, etc. sense 'reside permanently' as well as its English/US one 'be based temporarily'.

5.5.3.5 Pragmatics

One of the most striking features of much Singapore/Malaysia English is its use of pragmatic particles, mainly borrowed from dialects of Chinese. Gupta (1992) identifies 11 particles used to mark tentativeness, definiteness, or contradiction to identify directives, and to establish solidarity, etc.; *la(h)* 'definiteness' is part of the stereotype, illustrated in the following dialogue from Platt *et al.* (1984). (A is an ethnically-Indian, English-educated Malaysian, so the text also illustrates that this variety is an independent form, not English in the mouths of Chinese or Malay speakers. This could be called upper-mesolectal):

> Do you use Tamil at all?
> A. I'm afraid [əfrɛ] we know little. Don't [dɔn] speak [spiʔ] at home. To my maid, I have to speak to her. We have learned, lah, since she came.

Gupta's example of *ma* 'rejoinder' is quite striking as it shows a child who is a native speaker of Singaporean English interacting with her mother, reminding us that here at least the term 'non-native variety' is meaningless:

EG: *Why Meimei head like that one?*	'Why is M's head like that?'
MG: *Mei-mei's head is on the bed.*	(utterance is StE)
EG: *He why o-oi like that one?*	'Why is she sleeping like that'
MG: *Why? Sideways **ma***	'Why? sideways, obviously'
EG: *Why?*	'Why?'
MG: *Because her way of sleeping*	'Because that's her way of sleeping'

The example also shows that the mother moves from acrolect to mesolect (retaining pronoun gender for example even in the Singlish utterances), while the child speaks the basilect she has learnt from her peers, referring to her sister as *he* for example.

5.5.4 English in Hong Kong

Thirty-eight per cent of people in Hong Kong apparently know and use English (Bolton 2000). However, it is mainly used in education and interactions with 'outsiders' and so Hong Kong English is somewhat closer to a foreign-language variety than the Malaysian/Singapore variety. Hong Kong English does not seem to have a capacity to use lectal variation for stylistic effect or the same wealth of local vocabulary and slang that seems to characterize Singapore English. Hong Kong Cantonese seems to have many loanwords from English, and many unassimilated English words occur in Cantonese discourse, but this is quite common in languages like Japanese or German and so can be regarded as a 'foreign-language' phenomenon. On the other hand, as more and more young people in Hong Kong are English-educated and have friends and relations in Canada, the USA, and Britain, English is more and more a natural means of expression (Bolton 2000). Literature has started to be written in English, and on the Internet Cantonese and English have started to interpenetrate one another, as in these comments on a home page:

Comment: lo por jai: sorry ah . . . i know fault la . . . forgive me la . . . hmmm . . . your hp write duk ho ho ah . . . but y mo ngor gah??? hope lo por jai ng ho angry la . . . lo por dai yan :P lo kung jai

Comment: Good homepage wor . . . . . will be (haha. . . since u haven't finished it ma). CutieGal really has a cutie homepage with cutie music wor. But. . . . why don't you put your cutie photos here ah?

The first comment simply mixes transcribed Cantonese with English; the second uses English clarified with the Chinese attitudinal particles *wor, ma,* and *ah* as in 5.5.3.5.

The phonology of this variety of English (or more precisely of one type of mesolect) is shown by Hung (2000) to be distinctive and consistent. The vowel system is given in Table 5.8 above. It is striking that although length/tenseness distinctions like RP/GA /ɪ/ /iː/ are not present, the set of diphthongs is quite large, and /eɪ/ and /oʊ/ do not appear as monophthongs as they do in Singapore and in many other varieties. The consonants are quite different from those of our reference varieties, and the set is given as:

- ▪ p t k b d (in words which have /d/ and /ð/ in RP/GA) g tʃ dʒ
- ▪ f (in words which have /f/, and for some speakers /θ/, in RP/GA and some words with /v/) θ for some speakers, s (= RP/GA /s/ and /z/), ʃ (= RP/GA ʃ and ʒ)
- ▪ ɹ j w (= RP/GA w, and /r/ after consonants and some words with /v/) l (realized word-finally as [w] after non-back vowels and as zero after other vowels)
- ▪ m n (in free variation with l word initially) ŋ.

The v-split seems particularly interesting. Morphemes with orthographic <v> at the beginning of a usually stressed syllable are pronounced with /w/, other orthographic <v> pronounced with /f/ (/ɛˈdwɜtismən/ 'advertisement', /lif/ 'leave'). But if the stress shifts the pronunciation of <v> does not change: /ˈɛdwɜtais/. So /w/ and /f/ here are different phonemes, not realizations of /v/.

The syntax of Hong Kong English includes many typical 'new English' simplifications, particularly in the noun phrase: systems of countability and singular, definiteness, etc.

There does not seem to be much distinctive lexis, rather distinctive uses of general lexis like *triad* 'Chinese gang', *localization* 'replacing expatriate workers' or *karaoke bar* 'near-brothel' (Benson 2000). Local Westerners may use borrowings from Chinese like *dim sum* (snacks served in local restaurants) and *gwailo* ('Westerner'), but also, reflecting imperial connections, from South Asian languages including *chit* (for 'bill' or ' receipt'), *nullah* (an open drain or 'water course') (http://www.hku.hk/ english/research/icehk/overview.htm). The word *chop* has two homonymous local meanings 'stabbed/slashed' and (borrowed from Chinese and frequent throughout South East Asia) 'stamped/certified'. These are tautonomous not only with the General English lexeme, but with Indian *chop* 'cut hair'.

5.5.5 Philippine English – a descriptive account

5.5.5.1 A shortlist of particularly salient features of Philippine English
Unlike all the varieties discussed in this chapter so far, Philippine English derives

from US varieties, normally uses US spelling conventions and vocabulary variants, and is rhotic. However the /r/ is an alveolar flap, not a semivowel. The vowel inventory is reduced in ways typical of 'New Englishes'. Philippine speakers are said to have a 'sing-song intonation' and definite syllable timing.

There is a range of typical Philippine vocabulary: borrowings from Spanish (*merienda* 'afternoon tea'), Tagalog/Filipino (*kundiman* 'love song'), loan trans- lations from local languages (*since before yet* 'for a long time') and local coinages (*batchmate* 'person who studied, did military service, etc. with the speaker'). Since nearly all speakers of Philippine English also speak Filipino, codeswitching is common in informal and intimate situations. Use of this 'mix-mix' language corre- sponds partly to movement down the lectal scale in Singapore.

5.5.5.2 Phonology

As Table 5.8 shows, the vowels of Philippines English are based on General American: educated speakers distinguish most of the vowels Americans do, though not necessarily with the same qualities: /i/ and /u/ are pure vowels without the diphthongal quality typical of British and American 'long' vowels, for example. Because Philippine English is largely syllable timed, unstressed vowels are often given their full spelling pronunciation and indeed vowel reduction is a mark of formal speech and careful style rather than the other way round.

Reduction and simplification of final consonants seems less extreme than in the varieties discussed above, but voicing distinctions are often lost between /s/ and /z/, /ʃ/ and /ʒ/. Under influence from the indigenous languages, Philippine English often has unaspirated voiceless stops at the beginnings of words and unreleased stops at the end of words. It also has dental /t d n l/.

5.5.5.3 Syntax

Written Standard Philippine English does not vary syntactically from other standard versions, and because its domains of use are more limited than those of Singapore English it has not developed the lectal range and exotic syntax of colloquial Singapore English.

Typical features of informal writing and speech include omission of 'redundant' subjects, and optional marking of verb agreement and plurality. It is characteristic that these features co-exist with sophisticated journalistic constructions – although not standard, they are not necessarily marks of unsophisticated writing. We can cite from the website http://www.ala-eh.net/lipa/language.html:

> Trailing behind with a big difference in the frequency are residents who speak Bicol totaling some 684 followed by some 517 residents who speak Ilokano. Other dialects spoken are Hiligaynon, Ilongo, Cebuano and other dialects that are minimal spoken.

There are also individual constructions typical of South-East Asian English in general: *Almost of the Tagalog speaking population* (= 'almost all of . . .').

5.5.5.4 Lexis

Philippine English tends to be so full of codeswitching and mixing that it is hard to tell what is simply Tagalog and what is borrowed into English. Nevertheless one can identify local lexicalizations, either coined in English like *bedspacer* 'person who is sharing a flat' or borrowed, like *barkada* 'circle of friends'. Among foreignisms borrowed from Tagalog are *barong (shirt)* 'traditional smart shirt made from embroidered cloth', *dalagang Filipina* 'traditional "good girl"' and *lechon* 'roast pig dish' – as usual foreignisms cluster round food, costume, and traditional values. From Spanish (apparently) comes *maja blanca* 'coconut pudding'. The best known foreignism formed from English lexical material is *jeepney* 'taxi on a jeep chassis'. An interesting tautonym is *standby* 'idler, bystander' (Platt *et al.* 1984). Among heteronyms one could mention the following borrowed words: *carabao* 'water buffalo', *calamansi* 'lime', *yaya* 'nanny, nursemaid' *lumpia* (ultimately from Chinese) 'spring roll', and *sari-sari* 'corner shop/neighbourhood store'.

5.5.5.5 Pragmatics

Functional phrases differ between varieties, and in the Philippines one can say *for a while* when answering the telephone, where other varieties might use *just a moment* – a sort of pragmatic tautonym.

Like other varieties that do not occupy all the domains of their local culture (5.3.2.5), Philippine English can be stylistically underdifferentiated in the sense that language which other varieties would regard as rather formal can be mixed with apparently informal phrases. Thus the informative text on Adel Rey's website (http://reyadel.tripod.com), about the lives of a *bedspacer* who shares a flat and room with other students and a *homebody* who studies from home, mixes phrases which would sound formal in American English with others which would sound informal.

> **Let us then trace** their movements in one typical school day.
>
> The HOMEBODY wakes up early if he is a commuter, then helps in household chores, eats breakfast, and he's off to school. After the morning classes, he's back home helping do the chores, then **partakes of lunch**. After his meals, he might wash the dishes or he is immediately back to school.

Code-mixing English and Tagalog is, as noted above, a characteristic way for educated people to vary style. The following extract gives No. 10 of 'ten things I like about the US' from an Internet chat site:

> Number 10 ko, camping. camping dito. . .akala ko, OK.
>
> Roughing it out daw. Tapos, when my gf and I got to the camp, naka-RV ang mga hinayupak na Kano; may barbecue grill pa sa pick-up trucks nila!
>
> Walang hiking involved to get to the campsite. . .pupunta pa ako sa upstate New York para lang makapunta sa mga lugar na ganon, bear country pa!

Finally, nonverbal communication (paralanguage) is of course different in different cultures. Filipinos asked directions may simply point with their eyes and lips rather than either pointing with a hand or giving verbal directions.

5.5.6 Further reading

For Singapore English Anthea Gupta's *The Steptongue* and Shirley Lim's short stories (particularly 'The Taximan' and 'The Teacher') are good further reading. Bolton (2002) describes many aspects of Hong Kong English, and Gill (2002) describes current language issues in Malaysia. Gonzalez (1991) (in Cheshire's *English Around the World)* deals with style in the Philippine media.

5.6 OTHERS

British and American influence affected many parts of the world and led to the use of English for education and administration in many states other than those we have discussed above. Here we give brief descriptions of a few examples, which illustrate the interaction of several factors in determining the impact of English as a colonial language. First is the degree of development of the local language – the number of domains in which it has been used. Where the local language is already used for religion, in a school system, for a written literature, for university study, for news-papers, for modern entertainment, etc., there will be less tendency to use English in these domains, and the local language will have greater vitality, and also normally higher status. Second is the degree of multilingualism of the community, which leads to the use of English at the popular level as a link language. The inverse of this is the extent to which English is used in contact with native speakers (normally from the colonial power). Finally there may be some effect from attitudes to the colonial power.

5.6.1 The Mediterranean

Three territories in the Mediterranean were occupied by Britain long enough for the English language to have retained some official or at least public functions there: Gibraltar at the southern tip of the Iberian peninsula, the island of Malta between Italy and Libya, and the island of Cyprus. All three territories are at least bilingual. Gibraltarians speak Spanish at home and English on official occasions, and use both languages at school. The Maltese use Maltese for most purposes but have English as an official language and operate a bilingual education system. The broadcast media, on the other hand are largely in Maltese or Italian, and films are often dubbed into Italian. Similarly, the media in Cyprus are mainly in Greek (foreign films subtitled into Greek), but Cyprus combines bidialectalism with bilingualism. It is said that although (standard) Greek is the sole official language in the Greek sector, Cypriots may write a letter applying for a job in English, but would expect to be interviewed in Standard (Athens) Greek, and then chat with their colleagues in Cypriot Greek, which is characterized among other things by a large number of loanwords from English.

A contrast between Cyprus and Gibraltar shows that the survival of English is not particularly closely related to attitudes to the British. Gibraltarians are generally in favour of links with Britain, and so it is not surprising that English is official, well known, and widely used. By contrast, there is much resentment in Cyprus against the British presence and the treatment Cyprus has received from Britain. English is not an official language, but it is still widely used in business and education; the utilitarian value of the languages outweighs attitudes.

5.6.2 The Caribbean

The island of Puerto Rico was captured by the USA during the Spanish-American war of 1898 and has remained a US possession (a self-governing 'commonwealth') until now, with its inhabitants fairly evenly divided among advocates of statehood, independence, and the status quo. Puerto Rico had a rich literature and an intellectual elite educated in Spanish when the Americans arrived, and, despite early attempts to impose English as the medium of education, the position of Spanish has never been seriously threatened on the island.

Spanish is used for virtually all internal purposes, and although (US) English is widely known, it is only spoken fluently by educated people. Thus in 1992 only 11 per cent of respondents to a survey claimed to use English frequently at work, and only 24 per cent of the population said in the 1990 census that they could speak English easily (Clampitt-Dunlap 1995). The media are mainly in Spanish, although US television, etc., is also widely available.

5.6.3 The Indian Ocean

On the Indian Ocean islands of the Seychelles and Mauritius, English is again in contact with a pre-existing well-developed European language. They were first colonized by France in the eighteenth century and developed for the production of cotton and sugar using slave labour. At the beginning of the nineteenth century they became British with no significant change of population. When slavery was abolished the Seychelles went over to less intensive agriculture, while on Mauritius slaves were replaced by indentured Indian workers. In both territories the majority language remained creole French with the upper classes speaking French, and the Indians their own languages.

However, just as Indians in South Africa are going over to English, and those in Guyana and Trinidad have largely adopted creole or English, the Indians on Mauritius are going over to French creole or French. *The Times of India* for 7 February 2000 gave these interesting quotations:

Yashdev Sharma Rutha, an engineering student said: 'Some youngsters consider it degrading to use either Bhojpuri or Hindi at home and would rather speak French, which is more fashionable than English.'

A government official said: 'I may use Bhojpuri to communicate with the elders in the family but with my children – it's French or Creole.' The youngsters don't like Bhojpuri at all.

The situation in the current independent states is that French creole remains the dominant everyday language. French is widely known and spoken (and a compulsory subject from the beginning of primary school), and English is an official language, and a main medium of education, but less 'popular' than French, (or the French–creole continuum). The result seems comparable with that in Puerto Rico.

5.6.4 Papua New Guinea and the Pacific

New Guinea was one of the eight or 10 areas in the world in which agriculture developed independently and the farmers of inland New Guinea continued to pursue their intensive agriculture unaffected by outside influence until the twentieth century. The island is extremely rich in relatively unrelated languages, although many are now dying as a result of increased communication. Other islands of Melanesia like the Solomons and Vanuatu have similarly been settled for a long time and have a rich variety of (Austronesian or New Guinean) local languages. Western traders, administrators, and missionaries introduced pidgin Englishes in the nineteenth century and these have developed as lingua francas. Several have become official languages and are used for some education and administration, like Tok Pisin in New Guinea and Bislama in Vanuatu.

In New Guinea, English and Tok Pisin (the local pidgin) are official languages and Tok Pisin is the medium of primary education, with transfer to English later. Tok Pisin is the best developed pidgin in the world, with standardized grammar and vocabulary and a very un-English appearance.

Unlike Puerto Rico and the Indian Ocean islands, New Guinea had very many local languages and none of them was used in 'modern' domains before colonization, so that the local languages are much 'weaker' than French or Spanish. Unlike in the Mediterranean islands, where English is used only with outsiders, in New Guinea English is used mainly with other local speakers for internal purposes, and consequently can become very nonstandard. Because of these factors the island is rather rapidly undergoing language shift. Smaller languages are dying. Tok Pisin is becoming creolized – acquiring native speakers – and as Tok Pisin borrows more and more 'modern' vocabulary and spellings from English, something like an English–Tok Pisin continuum is developing.

Mühlhäusler (1991:637) gives these examples of city boys calling out to girls (with unashamed sexism) in a mixture of English (roman), Tok Pisin (*italics*), and fixed phrases from Hiri Motu, an earlier lingua franca (<u>*underlined italics*</u>):

Yu, mipela givim long yu.	'You, we give it to you.'
laik ok one *eh* <u>*edeseni oi lao?*</u>	'I like the OK one. Hey, friend, where are you going?'
laik fresh one <u>*Tura, edeseni oi lao?*</u>	'I like the unattached one. Friend, where are you going?'
O laik gut wan. Olsem, olsem.	'I like a good one just like her, like her.'
Tambu, can I have the back one?	'Cousin, can I have the one at the back?'
. . . Ai, nogat mani ya, yu stupit.	'You have no money, you stupid.'

The situation in the much smaller islands of Vanuatu is in a way more complicated, since the islands were colonized jointly by the British and French, and both English and French are official alongside Bislama, which has developed as a link language among the 105 small languages of the island. Bislama is an English-lexified pidgin, but the Vanuatu government's website *Welkam long Tokbaot Vanuatu* (http://www.chez.com/webyumi/) provides examples of how different the two languages are: *Sapos yu wantem talem tingting, kross o glat blong yu* is glossed 'For any feedback, complaints, comments, corrections. . .' and *Plis jusum one samting blong luk luk long em* is 'Make your choice'.

Early (1999) reports that 80 per cent of spoken interaction among the 'educated' staff of the national broadcasting organization is in Bislama. Unlike New Guinea, however, Vanuatu does not use the pidgin as a medium of education, but has two streams, one English-medium, one French-medium. We saw that in the Seychelles and Mauritius the existence of French creole and French as a local international language (Madagascar, the Comorenes, Réunion) meant that English was less 'fashionable' than French. In Vanuatu analogous factors – an English-based pidgin, English-using neighbours – mean that English is gaining ground over French. The survey of language use by broadcasting staff showed that only 20 per cent of writing (and much less speech) was in French, with most being in English or Bislama. Early (1999) argues that focus on the maintenance of the two colonial languages distracts attention and resources from the development of the language nearly everyone understands – Bislama – and the maintenance of the rich heritage of Melanesian languages.

In Fiji a situation reminiscent of Malaysia has arisen. Colonization at the end of the nineteenth century left the traditional power structure of Fijian society in place. However, workers for plantations were imported from India, and to a smaller extent China, so that in modern Fiji a majority of the population is ethnically non-Fijian. The independence constitution gave privileges to native Fijians and one dialect of their Austronesian language is the official language. Nevertheless English is widely used and is the medium of education at most levels. The Chinese community is said to have gone over entirely to English as its daily language, and some Indians are moving in the same direction. Fijian English is definitely used for interactions among locals, at least in urban areas, and its lexis has therefore been localized. It includes local lexicalizations of relationships, either loan-translated from Fijian or Hindi like *big father* 'father's elder brother' or borrowed like *tavale* 'cross-cousin' (cf. 3.2), and foreignisms like *tyre* 'game played with a tyre and two sticks', *tanoa* 'traditional drinking bowl' (Tent 2000). In Fiji, unlike in Malaysia, political support for an official 'indigenous' language seems to have been unable to overcome a degree of societal multilingualism. Perhaps the reason is the limited scope of Fijian compared to Malay – the lingua franca of its area for centuries – and the absence of previous or current use of Fijian in modern domains.

French, Spanish, and, with political support, Fijian, seem to be holding their own against English, while the languages of New Guinea, the Solomons, and Vanuatu seem to be severely threatened by pidgin and/or English.

The extreme case of language shift seems to be illustrated by the small island of Guam, which was acquired by the USA from Spain in 1898 along with the Philippines and Puerto Rico. It was a strategic military base and English was at once imposed as the language of education and government. Teachers were mostly native speakers of English from the USA, and Guamanians came to identify strongly with the USA after the Second World War. Influxes of immigrants and US military personnel increased the use of English. Consequently Guamanians today mainly use English. As described by Clampitt-Dunlap (1995), the situation seems like New Zealand or Ireland, with revived interest in the local language, Chamorro, coming almost too late to rescue it. Children are said now hardly to understand the mother tongue of their parents and grandparents, even though it is a school subject nowadays. On Guam, with a language spoken by few people and used in no modern domains, education entirely in English, immigration from other islands requiring English as a link language, and a high proportion of prestigious inner-circle speakers in the community, there seem to have been all the conditions for rapid language shift without even a creole phase.

The factors that favour or limit the spread of English are to some extent 'market forces' and our three stereotyped ideological viewpoints might be interpreted as differing as to how far language planning should interfere with them – with the radicals arguing for aggressive government actions to ensure human rights, and the liberals essentially wanting to accept the inevitable and alleviate its consequences.

6 The expanding circle

6.1 THE RISE OF ENGLISH IN THE EXPANDING CIRCLE

One consequence of the rise of British power outside Europe was increasing use of English (and English-based pidgin) as a lingua franca even outside territories under British or US control. Even in the mid-eighteenth century there is evidence of a shift from Dutch and Portuguese towards English (and French). Until 1748 the official language of the Danish West Indies[1] (which was never Danish) was Dutch, thereafter it was English (Liebst 1996). On the other hand, English did not have the self-evident status it occupies now. When Stamford Raffles, the British commander in South East Asia around 1800, wrote to local kings and princes he naturally did so in their languages: Javanese, Malay, etc. However, as world shipping came to be dominated by Britain in the nineteenth century, English became the lingua franca of traders and sailors all over the world outside Europe, and pidgin Englishes sprang from their interaction with local people.

Within Europe, French had replaced Latin as the natural international language by the eighteenth century. The Treaty of Westphalia in 1648 ending the Thirty Years' War was the last major European peace treaty written in Latin. The next, the Treaty of Utrecht between Britain, France, and Spain (1713), was written in French only, and so was the Treaty of Vienna a hundred years later (1815). Robert Walpole, who became effective Prime Minister of Britain in 1718, still spoke Latin to the German-born King George I because George did not speak English and Walpole did not speak French or German. However, when an English princess married the King of Denmark in 1765, they spoke French to one another. The prestige of French was so high that the upper classes in countries like the Netherlands and Prussia started to adopt it as their home language.

However, towards the end of the eighteenth century several factors combined to lead to more use of mother tongues, and particularly to a kind of 'three-language system' where educated people read English, French, and German, as well as their mother tongue if it was another European language. Among these factors were increased nationalism, a Romantic turn towards the mother tongue, industrial and technical leadership in Britain, the superior German education system which made Germany the centre of science and scholarship, and the continuing status of French as the language of diplomacy and culture.

---

1 Now the US Virgin Islands.

In the second half of the nineteenth century the importance of English tended to increase as US industry, technology, and above all research and scholarship, were added to British power.

The wars of the first half of the twentieth century destroyed the intellectual basis for German as an international language and weakened French. It is significant that the Treaty of Versailles (1919) was written in English as well as French: American power had been decisive in winning the war and the language of the USA achieved a new status as a result. Even before the Second World War, the German and Italian foreign ministers (Ribbentrop and Ciano) found themselves communicating in English, the only language they both knew.

Throughout the twentieth century English became more and more widely known as a consequence of US military power, the attractiveness of US popular culture, the superiority of US technology, science, and scholarship, and the spread of knowledge of English within territories once colonized by Britain and the USA, which continued as we have seen, even after independence.

6.1.1 A note on terminology

Since we have used 'General English' for features common to all or most standard varieties we will call English that is not localized to any particular inner or outer circle country 'expanding-circle English', and we will reserve the term 'International English' for a complex of linguistic features and communicative practices which make the variety widely comprehensible. Thus expanding-circle English is defined by where it comes from, but International English is defined by its scope, as discussed in 6.5.

6.2 DOMAINS FOR ENGLISH

6.2.1 Introduction

Even where other languages are used for official purposes and as the normal medium among the citizens of a country, English often functions as an international language for communication with speakers of other languages from other countries. It may even be used in some fields within the country. For example, in the expanding circle English will not be used in primary education, religion, courts and the law, national politics, literature, national administration, or home and family life. However, it may be used (along with local languages) in international relations, communication with or within international organizations, research, education (especially university level), publicity, business, popular culture, the mass media, and in everyday interaction with foreigners of all sorts.

English comes to be used in these domains for a number of reasons. Some are functional: international diplomacy, international organizations, research publication, business negotiations, and chats with foreigners often make use of English because it is widely known and the interaction is likely to succeed in this medium. In other cases English seems to be chosen largely for its associations: advertisements intended entirely for a public with some other mother tongue often make use of English, despite its clear inefficiency as a medium (at least 20 per cent of the audience (Preisler 1999a, INRA 2001) in any country, and far more in most, will not understand at all), and song lyrics in English are often said merely to sound better. Neither factor is new. In the eighteenth century French was functional for international diplomacy because it was the language most diplomats knew. At the same time, Italian was the fashionable language of music, and operas in London and Paris were written in Italian, presumably because 'it sounded better', not for any functional reason (unless it is true that the high proportion of vowels makes singing easier).

Both function and fashion represent 'market forces' which tend to lead to spread of a dominant language. The main force that can act effectively to manage language use (and perhaps limit the spread) is action by governments and other public bodies. In the expanding circle governments often have policies to secure the position of national languages by, for example, subsidizing the local film industry or publishers, ensuring that democratic processes and legal actions are carried on in local languages, regulating the use of English in education, or even imposing codes for what languages can be used in particular media. Our three ideologies (3.4.1) will support different policies in this area, with liberals more inclined to bow to market forces and both conservatives and radicals looking for firmer action to protect particular languages or their users.

The school system – which is usually an instrument of national policy – is also affected by market forces. Once a language becomes widely known, schools tend to make its dominance self-perpetuating. If it is observed that English is a useful language on the world stage, then schools start to teach it. Once more people in more countries have learnt it at school, it becomes more useful, because there are more foreigners with whom it can be used. So, following the wishes of parents and pupils, schools teach the language even more, so even more people learn it, and it becomes even more useful. The evidence is that government policy cannot easily resist market forces at this level. The former Soviet satellite states in Europe taught Russian in the schools energetically without establishing the language as a self-perpetuating international medium.

At present the world's schools are forces to strengthen the position of English. English is the main foreign language taught in Japan, China, and other Asian countries. The EU issues education figures for 26 expanding circle European countries which are members of the EU or EEA or candidates for that status (Pilos 2001), and in all but two English is the most studied foreign language. The two are Hungary, where slightly more pupils take German than English, and Romania, where French predominates (but only, it is said by Iatcu (1999), because there are not enough English teachers yet). The age of beginning English study is gradually being lowered and it is not unusual to start before the age of 10 (Pilos 2001).

6.2.2 Mechanisms and results in the use of English in the EU

Before briefly examining the use of English in various domains worldwide we can illustrate the mechanisms that lead to wider use of English by considering an international organization and a subculture within popular culture.

Most international organizations define English, or English and French, or English and a regional language, as working languages. However, the European Union is in theory quite different, with a strong institutional policy commitment to multi-lingualism, and this makes it an interesting case study for the spread of English. The Treaty of Rome (1956) and later treaties are formulated in all the languages of the community of the times. The EU has no official working language and its official languages are the 11 national languages (German spoken as first language by some 24 per cent of the population, French, English, and Italian, each spoken by some 16 per cent, Spanish by 11 per cent, Dutch by 6 per cent, Greek and Portuguese by 3 per cent, Swedish by 2 per cent, and Finnish and Danish by 1 per cent). Anyone has the right to use any language and interpreting or translation will be provided, at least in theory. However, as an international institution the EU is faced with strong market forces leading to increased use of English. Generally speaking the more public fora, mainly the European Parliament and the Council of Ministers, are multilingual with simulta-neous interpretation into all 11 languages. However, at more informal meetings of ministers or representatives, and in most of the work of the Commission, (the EU civil service), market forces take over and only 'major languages', actually usually English or French, are used. The parliament is the most multilingual institution but even here Swedish members of the EU parliament use Swedish in plenary sessions and official committee meetings, but English in study groups and in informal interaction (Melander 2001). Although all documents with legal force are produced in all languages, in practice many MEPs consult documents in English rather than wait for versions in their own language.

Most of the day-to-day work of the Union goes on in English or French and Schlossmacher (1994) gives a vivid illustration of why this is so. More Europeans learn English than other languages, and in the EU French comes second. Hence, if a German representative or official addresses an unknown person in German, the interaction normally fails and the two have to resort to French or English. Next time the German will probably not bother to try in his own language but start off in French or English. Increasingly no one will hear German spoken, and the posi-tion of French and English will be strengthened, irritatingly for the German, who speaks the language which is the mother tongue of the highest proportion of Europeans.

When Sweden, Finland, and Austria joined the Union in 1995 the proportion of people likely to reply in French when addressed in French went down somewhat, as Swedes and Finns at least were more likely to know English than French, and when new countries join in 2004 or 2005 it will go down again. Young people in Europe as a whole are now more than twice as likely to have English as French from their education (Pilos 2001), and this has the same effect. So the process that has limited the use of German is already eroding the position of French, and market forces are pushing the Union (slowly) towards a single de facto working language.

The Union's policy to manage multilingualism is basically to provide translation and interpretation as often as possible. Its interpreting services have usually followed the principle that all interpreting should be into the interpreter's mother tongue. In the late 1990s the system broke down because of the difficulty of finding native speakers of other European languages who could interpret from Finnish. Increasing use started to be made of relay interpreting, in which a speaker's words are translated into a pivot language, usually French or English, and then from the pivot into other languages and of biactive or 'retour' interpreting in which the interpreter works out of his or her own language into the pivot (Gebhard 2001). Thus Finnish was often handled by native speakers of Finnish interpreting out of Finnish into English, with the other languages being served by their own native speakers interpreting out of English. Interpreters are vehemently opposed to these practices, but considerations of cost are likely to result in their becoming increasingly common.

Three interesting and symptomatic points arise from these changes in interpreting practice. One is that since the pivot will often be English, the position of English will be strengthened – all information will have 'passed through' the language. The second is that combining relay and biactive interpreting means that no native speakers of English will be involved: an expansion of English appears to result in a reduction of the significance of native speakers. Consequently, the third observation is that the English that occupies such an important position will be an 'offshore' variety not controlled by native speakers. This combination of increased use with a decreased role for native speakers and a variety defined by non-natives is a common one in considering English in the expanding circle, as it was in the outer circle.

6.2.3 Subcultures: English from the bottom up

A rather different set of functional factors lead to English being necessary and acquiring a high status in many subcultures, some of which would see themselves in violent opposition to the bureaucrats of the EU. Preisler (1999a,b) studied members of four youth subcultures in Denmark: hip-hop, computer nerds, rock music, and death metal music.

The subcultures turned out to be rather hierarchically organized, with highly skilled and knowledgeable individuals enjoying high status. Because the subcultures are international, one aspect of being skilled and knowledgeable is that one is part of an international network with links to other countries in Europe and back to the USA where the subcultures originate. This network operates in English, and the technical terms for different types of dance, etc., are English. Preisler gives these examples of the international vocabulary of hip-hop:

Breakdance: *boogie, electric boogie, windmills, back spin, head spin, turtle, foot work, shop, crocke* (Danish verbal suffix), *poppin', bobbin', back slide*, etc.
Rap/DJ: *ragamuffin, scratch, scratcher, mixer, cut-backs*
Graffiti: *tagge* (Danish verbal suffix) *tagging, bomb, bombing, jams, cypher, burn-off, wild-style, straight-letters, window-down-whole-car*, etc.

Consequently the high-status members of the subcultures are characterized by a reasonable knowledge of English, among other things of course, and knowledge of English acquires status within the subculture. Consequently English expressions and respect for English filter 'down' to lower-status subculture members and out into the general population because of the covert prestige of the subcultures. Knowing English is necessary for being a good hip-hopper, and is not just a mark of success within bourgeois society.

Four interesting points emerge here. First, English enters European society not only institutionally or top-down via European institutions, education, etc., but also individually or bottom-up via the subcultures. Second, the latter is a very different English from that of the European Parliament or world business – it is a version of US street slang, strongly influenced by AAVE (4.5.4.1). Third, although the technical terms in its vocabulary are strongly oriented to native-speaker models (the originators of the subcultures), grammar is probably less important and very varied, given the role of the language as an international lingua franca of the subculture. Fourth, this is also a variety that is often used between non-natives: Preisler describes how hip-hoppers from Poland visit Danish groups and communicate in English.

However, we should notice that these informal, even oppositional, subcultures actually have the same structure as groupings like business, academia, sport, and even the military (NATO). Because of globalization the same mechanism works in these fields, with the highest-status members operating on an international stage in English and thus lending the language their status.

6.2.4 Domains of English in the expanding circle

Having mentioned schools, song lyrics, and international organizations, we can briefly describe other domains occupied by English in the expanding-circle as follows:

advertisements, posters, trademarks, shop names, etc. Many television and print advertisements use (usually American, if spoken) English for its fashion value. SAS, the Scandinavian airline company, for example, produces television commercials which show long sequences of Scandinavian scenery and customs ending with the slogan 'It's Scandinavian'. Commercial services are given English names, like the notorious charge-classes of the German telephone company – *GermanCall, FreeCall, CityRate*, etc.

In this context it is difficult to resist quoting (from http://www.tokyotales.com/japlish/) an example of 'T-shirt English', the variety used in slogans on East Asian T-shirts, pencil-cases, etc., which is evocative rather than communicative:

STANDARD
ONESELF WHOM BE ACTUAL
IS CERTAINLY
FOUND

business: multinational companies, even those with few or no inner-circle subsidiaries often adopt English as the 'company language' for newsletters, correspondence, internal documentation, etc. Negotiations between companies, joint ventures, etc., also typically make use of English, often without interpreters. Market forces tend to move companies towards this solution. For example attempts to use Swedish in Finnish-Swedish multinationals have broken down and English has been adopted. On the other hand, nobody knows how efficient the 'English as company language' principle is, and there is evidence that executives have been promoted above the level of their competence, and over the heads of more able colleagues, simply because of their English proficiency.

films, television: in some countries (Scandinavia, the Netherlands, Syria, and Portugal for example) American and other imported films are subtitled, so that the original soundtrack is audible, and television becomes a channel bringing English into the home. In others films are 'dubbed' by a variety of techniques (some, in Latvia and Poland for example, quite cheap because they involve a single narrator) and films and television bring in US culture without the language. The extent to which subtitled films and television create a presence of English in the country depends of course on the volume of imports.

Tastes vary as to whether dubbing or subtitling is preferable. Preisler found that 80 per cent of people in Denmark, a subtitling country, preferred subtitling to dubbing, but surveys of the whole population of the EU (INRA 2001) – most of whom are used to dubbing – show that 75 per cent prefer dubbing.

interaction with outsiders: increasingly English is the default language to address foreigners or tourists in. Tourists who speak Asian languages assume that everyone in Europe knows English, and Europeans assume that people of Asian appearance will understand English if they do not appear to understand the local language.

medium of education: it is characteristic of expanding-circle countries that the national language is used as the medium of education throughout primary, secondary, and tertiary education. Market forces of various kinds are starting to erode this. At the highest level, PhD theses in many subjects are routinely written in English in many countries so that they become part of the international 'conversation of the discipline'. Even at undergraduate level, university textbooks in many subjects are too expensive to produce in languages with few speakers. Even in languages with many speakers, translations may be out of date by the time they are available. So increasingly university departments, particularly in the natural sciences and technology, prescribe set texts in English. At the same time universities are under pressure to attract students from overseas, either to earn money or as part of exchange programmes. University staff are also mobile, and universities employ the best researchers they can get wherever they come from. Students or their parents may like to see courses in, for example, business studies, taught in English so that they learn the language along with the subject. All these factors encourage universities to offer courses taught in English, and in the last few years these have become quite common in northern Europe, Turkey, and Japan, for example. Similar pressures have led to 'immersion' secondary education through English in some secondary schools.

printed press: newspapers and magazines in most countries are in the local language but there is often an English-language local newspaper like Thailand's *Bangkok Post* and Saudi Arabia's *Saudi Express* which is read by locals and is quite influential. American 'international' publications like *Time* and *Newsweek* (and many others, British or American) are read throughout the world.

Of course the key feature of the expanding circle is that most domains are unaffected by English other than in the form of occasional loanwords: religion, courts and the law, national politics, literature, national administration, home and family life, to name a few.

6.3 A SKETCH OF EXPANDING CIRCLE ENGLISH

6.3.1 Lectal variation

Much spoken expanding-circle English is unstandardized, a lingua franca made up in interaction between people with different proficiencies and substrates. Allan James (1999) gives this example of 'Austrian/Italian/Slovenian conversation':

A: I don wanna drink alcohol
B: Me too
C: I also not

and at a higher level of proficiency there is Alan Firth's (1990) example of Syrian (A)–Danish (B) interaction in which the meaning of a key vocabulary item has to be negotiated:

A: So I told him not to send the cheese after the blowing in the customs. We don't want the order after the cheese is blowing
B: I see, yes.
A: So I don't know what we can do with this order now. What do you think we should do with this all blowing, Mr Hansen?
B: I'm not uh (pause). Blowing? What is this, too big or what?
A: No the cheese is bad Mr Hansen. It is like fermenting in the customs' cool rooms.
B: Ah, it's gone off.
A: Yes, it's gone off.

Many of the lects at this level are strongly influenced by the local language, and this has given rise to a series of jokey labels for expanding-circle Englishes: *Chinglish, Italglish, Japlish/Janglish, etc.* Parallel names exist for outer-circle varieties – *Hindlish/Hinglish, Punglish* (Punjabi), *Singlish,* and even inner-circle ones: *Wenglish* (Wales), and, significantly, *Britlish*!

The point of these terms is that the variety is (to some extent) only comprehensible to those who know it or its substrate, and hence that the purpose of learning – international communication – is not achieved. The following example from the Internet is in Italglish, but perhaps not difficult to understand:

Since more time I collect the translation of the word 'Chess' in the different tongues (or dialects) in the World. This is not a scientific linguistic work, because I am a mathematician (Math Chess lovers) and not a linguist. Awaiting your welcome notes, I am very sorry in advance, for every my trivial error!

Send every your comment, correction, request, increment to my snail-mail address:

Crystal (1999) contrasts these local varieties with an international colloquial English which may emerge as an international spoken norm. One can imagine what an 'independent' international colloquial English would be like, but its features are generally still regarded as nonstandard 'mistakes' by its users. How such a variety, or at least a regional version of it, could develop is suggested by this quotation from a Spanish student in Sweden describing a colleague:

'... though here in Sweden he practices English every day, he practices it mainly with Erasmus students. People who are in his same linguistic situation. These students could speak better or worse, but they are not the better sample to follow. *But since they speak different languages from him, they are not making gross Spanish mistakes. He will develop a kind of Euro-English*'

But of course much international interaction, especially written, seeks to use a standardized variety. At present standard expanding-circle English is exonormative, that is, it draws its norms for correctness from Standard English as spoken in other areas, often Britain or the USA. However it may be becoming 'independent' and one can imagine two stages, one in which features of different varieties are mixed to create a norm, and the second in which regional expanding-circle Englishes develop which have unique features due to their own substrates, etc., like the outer-circle varieties.

There is a great deal of evidence for the first: English learnt in countries where British Standard English has been the school norm and television offers undubbed US films and series is often in practice 'mid-Atlantic' in the sense that features of British and American usage are mixed, because learners are exposed to both varieties. The vocabulary of cars and leisure seems to be acquired from the media and learners say US/General *trunk* rather than British *boot* and *candy* rather than *sweets*, but Scandinavian mid-Atlantic at any rate has British *autumn* for US *fall* and *cinema* for *movie theatre*. A survey by Söderberg and Modiano (2002) of Swedish schoolchildren showed that US lexis predominated while spelling and pronunciation were merely mixed, and this is, as we said, probably typical of parts of the world where British norms prevail in the educational system and there is access to US varieties through the media.

6.3.2 Spelling

Informal written International English may come to be marked by a mixture of British (Commonwealth) and American spellings, with the latter presumably predominating. On the other hand, spelling is not standardized in electronic media like chats, and in formal contexts may increasingly be determined by one's spellchecker.

6.3.3 Phonology

In many environments expanding-circle English is characterized by a mixture of British-type and US-type pronunciations, but its main phonological characteristics derive from the speaker's mother tongue, so that standardization is unlikely. However, it is easy to identify features typical of many inner-circle English accents which are marked in terms of the world's languages and likely not to be met with in international accents. The <th> consonants are obvious examples, and others are voiced final stops, the distinction between /ɪ/ and /iː/, the dark/clear /l/ distinction, specific intonation patterns, and perhaps stress-timing. We discuss these issues below under 'choice of a model'.

6.3.4 Lexis

As in spelling and pronunciation expanding-circle Englishes are typically characterized lexically by mixture of heteronyms from different sources ('Should I say *sweets* or *candy?*').

Marked features of inner-circle English lexis are also eliminated as they are in many outer-circle varieties (5.2.4). Examples might be the irregular semantics of *funny* in relation to *fun* (resulting in *It's funny* for Brit/US, etc. 'It's fun' as in the pop group Abba's *Money, money, money, must be funny?*) and the unpredictable alternation of the suffixes *-ic* and *-ical* which leads to forms like *ethnical* 'ethnic'. The distinction between *opportunity* (collocating with *have, give, take, offer, miss*, etc. and followed by an infinitive in US/UK, etc.) and *possibility* (collocating mainly with *be, exist* and followed by an *-ing* form in US/UK, etc.) is evidently unusual and expanding-circle English often has *I have the possibility to do this.*

There may also be influence from the speaker's first language (native speakers of expanding-circle varieties exist but are not common). First, key words may simply be borrowed from the mother tongue when it is supposed that the interlocutor knows the country well enough to recognize them. Thus 'Thai English' includes words 'borrowed' from Thai like *farang* 'Westerner', *sanuk* 'fun' and *tuk-tuk* 'cross between a taxi and a bus'. Clearly the speaker has to judge how appropriate these are in the situation, and this kind of judgement is a key feature of International English competence, as we shall illustrate below.

Second, similarity between mother-tongue words and English ones leads to the type of tautonymy called 'false friends' and can lead to heteronymy and to local lexicalization as well. False friends are words whose form in the mother tongue suggests an English word which actually has a different meaning. The result is that the English word acquires a new meaning in 'local English'. The *Cambridge International Dictionary* gives the following 'false friends' for Thai: *bill* meaning 'receipt' (Thai /bin/), *van* meaning 'station wagon/estate car' (Thai /wɛɛn/). These examples result from changes or specialization in the meaning of loanwords from English into Thai. False friends more often cause tautonymy when the mother tongue is more closely related to English. In most European languages there are words that look like *genial* (inner/outer circle = 'friendly and cheerful'), *actual* and *eventual* but mean 'very clever, like a genius', 'current' and 'possible' respectively, so that 'European English' can contain expressions like *a genial photographer* meaning 'a photographic genius' or *This is not actual* meaning 'This is not an issue at present'.

6.3.5 Syntax

Expanding-circle English has a wide lectal range, a wide range of varieties from the pidgin-like example quoted from James in 6.3.1 to highly sophisticated lects characterized only by minor regularizations and other idiosyncratic features of syntax. These can be illustrated from a speech by the former EU Commissioner Ritt Bjerregård (from Denmark):

- ■ adverb position and focusing – *also* can move more freely to indicate its focus than in other varieties, for example:

    My last point in relation to the environmental benefits is that the enlarge-ment is important for the environment also in the existing Member States.

- ■ verb complementation patterns may be different, (cf. 5.3.2.3) and may be generalized across possible meanings of verbs. Thus the distinct meanings of *appreciate you doing it* 'be glad about' and *appreciate that you have to do it* 'understand' are merged in:

    I am particularly pleased to be able to address you today … I appreciate that we can exchange views and increase our mutual understanding on our common goal.

- ■ prepositions may be different: *prices on raw materials, I do not agree to the charges on the EU that it . . .* = 'agree with the charges against'.
- ■ minor morphological irregularities may be regularized: *trees have no leafs* (cf. *thiefs* in unedited native-speaker writing in 3.4.3).

We shall argue below that tolerance and comprehension of such features is an aspect of international English competence.

6.3.6 Pragmatics

Pragmatic transfer from other cultures is often quite pervasive. For example, forms of address will naturally be chosen in terms of the speaker's own norms. When writing or speaking to someone called Pablo Gonzales, Chinese, Japanese, and German speakers may choose title plus last name (*Mr Gonzales*) where Arabic speakers prefer title plus first name (*Mr Pablo*), and Scandinavians prefer first name alone (*Pablo*). Phatic communion is equally culture-bound. For example, meeting in the street, Europeans may give a perfunctory *How are you?* and a comment on the weather, but Arabs may enquire in some detail about family members' health, and East Asians may ask *Where are you going?* or *Have you eaten yet?* This kind of pragmatic influence is easily misinterpreted by people from another culture and again we shall argue that International English competence includes the ability to handle pragmatic variation.

6.4 HOW ENGLISH MIGHT BE AFFECTING OTHER LANGUAGES

Many books have been written on the influence of English on other languages and we can only outline a few points here. Melander (2001) suggests three possibilities. First, English affects the code of other languages, above all their vocabulary. Second, whole populations might give up their own language and go over to English, as they have done in Wales, Scotland, and Ireland. Third, languages might 'lose domains' – cease to be used in particular areas.

6.4.1 Effects on the code of other languages

The most obvious effect of English on other languages is borrowed lexis. The borrowing may be functional – in that terminology for new inventions or genres (like hip-hop) is borrowed along with the invention, for example – or merely fashionable, in that an English word is borrowed for a concept which is already adequately lexicalized in the borrowing language. Thus Melnyk (2002) observes that Russian and Ukrainian have borrowed some computing words from English unchanged: *upgrade*, *browser*, *e-mail*, while others are constructed from English roots and Russian affixes, like *smailik* from *smile* as a sign in e-mail and others again appear to be Russian words with a new meaning, so that *mylo* 'soap', has acquired the meaning 'e-mail'. Capitalism has brought *bizniz*, *coupon*, *voucher*, *broker*, etc. Other borrowings into Russian/Ukrainian seem, however, to be due to fashion rather than function: *cool*, *dance*, or *free love*.

When Newton Paiva asked his students to note the English words they heard and saw in Belo Horizonte, Brazil, they came up with words from computing (*mouse*, *e-mail, hacker, online, offline*), foreign food (*milk-shake, banana split, hamburger, fast food, light, diet*), and English words used in shop names, adverts, etc. (*self-service, drive-thru, drive-in, country*).

Since loan words are often adapted to the phonology of the borrowing language, they can appear very un-English, as we saw in the Thai 'false friends' above. This is striking in Japanese. Millet (1999) gives *Wa puro* 'word processor', *Apaato* 'apartment', *Choco* 'chocolate', *Paso kon* 'personal computer' as examples.

In some languages there are many pseudo-loans – words that look English but do not correspond to any actual English item. The German for 'mobile phone/cell phone' is *handy*, there is a German word *pullunder* 'undershirt' based on English *pullover* and many languages have *smoking* 'dinner-jacket / tuxedo'.

Pseudo-loans seem particularly popular in Japanese, perhaps because the language has traditionally been open to borrowing. English has a high status, and the language is not very well known, so that native-speaker norms have little currency. Examples are (see Millet 1999, Ishiwata 1986):

Japanese	English
baacodo oyaji	a bald man who combs the few strands of hair that he does have to cover the maximum amount of head possible looks like an old man (*oyaji*) with a 'barcode'
sumaato	a 'sumaato' woman has a good figure
chenji-rebaa	To change gear, use the 'change lever,' or gearshift
goo-stoppu	traffic light

It is interesting that *sumaato* and *baacodo* reflect a nonrhotic source and that *sumaato* must derive from British (etc.) English *smart* 'well-dressed' rather than US 'clever', showing that even in Japan influence has not only been from US varieties.

The borrowings above are at the level of content words or short phrases, but some borrowings show deeper influence from English. An unusual example of a borrowed infixing process is this utterance from a review on the most 'serious' Swedish radio channel: *en ny tid, utan Carmina fucking Burana.* This would be best translated 'a new era, without *Carmina* bloody *Burana*' because foreign-language swearwords usually have an attenuated force.[2] More typical 'deep' effects arise from words and constructions in the local language being influenced by English usage (grammatical calquing). People start to say *in deutsch*[3] 'in German' instead of *auf deutsch, il est une disgrâce* on the model of 'it's a disgrace' and *Fue por eso que lo hice* instead of *Fue por eso por lo que hice* 'It was for this reason that I did it' (Truchot 1990:221). Practices in the EU can encourage this tendency because it is a requirement that legal documents in all languages have the same sentences in the same order. Since the original documents are nearly always written in English or French, the requirement forces speakers of other language to adopt the sentence lengths and rhetorical ordering typical of the English or French traditions (Trosborg 1997).

Words in the mother tongue that are formally similar to English ones can be influenced in their meaning – an effect called 'loan shift'. Truchot (1990:209) cites *régulier* representing AmE *regular* (French *normal)* in fast-food shops, unidiomatic uses of general terms like *système* and *nécessiter* in the IT domain and uses of the passive that are new to French.

Loanwords, foreign terms in advertising, and to a lesser extent syntactic and semantic influence, are common in many languages, but codeswitching of the type seen in

---

2 There was a Swedish film, in Swedish, called *Fucking Åmål* – Åmål is a typical small town – which was circulated in Britain as *Hungry for Love.*

3 For example on the website of Karlsruhe University *Auch in deutsch verfügbar.*

many outer-circle countries is much less so. Occasional English functional phrases – *okay, bye-bye, so what,* etc., have often been borrowed, but switching from language to language in mid-sentence is rather uncommon. This is true even in communities where English proficiency is high (Sharp 2001).

6.4.2 Language switch

Languages are dying out all over the world as, domain by domain, their speakers go over to languages perceived as more powerful or useful. In the inner and outer circles it is often English or pidgin they go over to. Welsh and Gaelic speakers, Native Americans, Australian Aborigines, and Maoris have switched to English. Speakers of 'small' languages in south-east Nigeria and New Guinea are certainly going over to pidgin, and there must be many other cases. It is not obvious, however, that language shift to English is happening or is likely to happen in the expanding circle, where the local official language is usually essential for work and education, and English merely a desirable extra. Fears that people will give up speaking Thai or German, or even Danish or Slovenian, seem unrealistic (Melander 2001).

6.4.3 Domain loss

Domain loss, on the other hand, is quite likely, and seems to have happened in certain cases. The modern official languages of Europe and Asia have struggled to gain domains from classical languages like Latin, Arabic, Sanskrit, and Chinese, and by the twentieth century many of them were usable in virtually all domains. But the pressures described earlier mean that there are many domains in which English competes with the official languages, and some (like medical research reporting) in which some official languages are no longer used. If official languages came to be used less and less in domains like education, law, business, and politics, a process would have started which might actually lead to parents ceasing to speak their own language to their children because it seems useless, and thus to language switch. Governments which want to maintain their own language therefore have to be vigilant in limiting domain loss as far as possible.

6.5 IMPLICATIONS FOR THE CHOICE OF SCHOOL VARIETY

In the context of globalization, one could ask what kind of English should be taught by schools in the expanding circle. This is actually three questions: what *exposure* should we give the learners, what production *model* should we choose and what production *target* should we aim for? We need first to distinguish these three concepts. Exposure is the English learners listen to or read. (Whatever the school gives, pupils in many countries will be exposed to predominantly US English through the media.) The model is above all the teacher's usage, but also the tapes or written material they are supposed to imitate. The target is what we aim for pupils to learn and produce themselves. We might well want to expose learners to Shakespeare, but we will hardly set his language as a model for them to learn, still less expect them to actually produce Shakespearean English.

To answer the question we also have to consider the purpose of the English education. Is it for *national use (language education)* – are we teaching Vermonters to use English well in the USA or Nigerians to use it well in Nigeria? Or for *foreign language learning* which has the aim of introducing children to a different culture and means of expression? Or for *international language learning* which has the aim of allowing the learners to communicate across cultures and language boundaries? Or some combination of these?

In the expanding circle, it is increasingly considered that learners will need English to communicate with almost anyone in the global community, rather than merely learning it as a foreign language studied for personal development and cultural awareness. In this context one might aim at English as an international language (Smith 1983). Here the aim would be for students to have the maximum scope of proficiency (3.4.6). They should be able to understand as many accents and varieties as possible, so there would be wide exposure. The general model would be the effective international communicator, so it would be important to learn cross-cultural communication strategies. Learners would have to avoid culturally specific references and behaviours in their own speech and pragmatic behaviour.

The code taught for production would be whatever is most likely to be comprehensible to speakers of different varieties – probably the syntax of Standard English with the lexis of its American variety, omitting items like *condominium* and *left field* which are culturally specific (Modiano 1999a). For reception we would probably want to make learners aware of the major alternatives to American lexis. Above all we would seek to make them aware that there may be unexpected lexis and indeed usage on all levels, and give training in strategies to deal with it (as in the 'blowing cheese' example in 6.3.1). A project at the University of Vienna (Seidlhofer 2001) aims to establish the norms actually used for English in international communication, with a view to codifying a standard independent of native speakers.

The target for the accent would be merely that the key distinctions made in most varieties were maintained. Jenkins (2000) has produced a minimum list of features for the pronunciation of International English. Her list proposes a target pronunciation that is quite unlike British or American patterns. Stress-timing is not on the list, for example, because it is difficult to learn and is in any case not a feature of major Asian and African varieties. But the aim is a common core, not uniformity. Speakers of Germanic languages will naturally sound more like American or British speakers, Chinese speakers more like Singaporeans, etc. Whatever the model, teachers would only focus on some features for practice, imitation, and correction.

It is clear that, except with reference to accent, these recommendations apply to speakers of inner- and outer-circle varieties as well as to expanding-circle learners, and we can expect that some training in International English would be part of the education of American, British, Nigerian, and Indian young people as well as German, French, and Japanese.

So International English should be an artificial variety, with no particular accent, but related above all to a set of communicative practices designed to make it comprehensible to speakers of all varieties.

To return to our stereotypes from 3.4.1, we are unmasked as liberals here. The conservatives will probably think that cultural aims of foreign language teaching are important, and that native varieties are the only 'real thing' and so the model and target for school learning should be a single native variety. The liberals will think that English belongs to everyone, so some kind of 'International English' is a good aim. The radicals will regard 'International English' as concealing the fact that it is the USA (and Britain/Australia) that gain from everyone learning English, and would use the money for something else.

7 What's next?

No sweetie im gonna b a good girl n stay in! lol! well 1 got no feckin money spent it al in Liverpool 2day i realy should of gone clubbin! lol! :) n 2) got work in mornin need 2 get in2 shower! ;) l8a huni luv ya luv Suz xxxxx[1] (message in British chat-room)

Dave: lots of white guys like asian girls.
just don't be so fobbish, they'll like abc-like asians[2]
Cindy: What does 'fobbish' mean????
Andy: FOBBISH = usually dressed as hong kong-like or chinese-like. not like american style.
Cindy: Someone told me before, FOB = Fresh Off Boat, that mean new immigrant loh. am I right ah?
Andy: yeah you're rite cindy. FOB = fresh off the boat. fob usually refer to asians coming to america the first time. we also refer foreigners as the european and we call the mexicans, the beiner or people who cross the border. (exchange from US Asian-American chat room)

The varieties of English around the world are changing in form, in their environments of use, in their mutual relations, and in their relations to other languages. In this chapter we try to summarize some of the processes we have seen at work in this book, and to speculate about the future.

We can identify three interrelated root causes of many of the developments we describe: US power, globalization, and information technology. US power in the domains of economics, politics, the military, science and academe generally, and culture, especially entertainment, has been maintained at a very high level over the last 50 or more years. Globalization means that more and more activities which used to be carried on at a national or local level (business, academic publishing, politics, military co-operation, and many others) are now carried on at an international level and require the use of link languages. Information technology, e-mail, chatrooms, and so forth, increase international contact and these media, along with word processing, make informal and unedited language publicly available (Crystal 2001).

---

1 There are two reasons why she is not going out: (1) she has no money, and (2) she has to work tomorrow. Otherwise 2 = 'to', *lol* = 'lots of laughs'?, and *l8a* = 'later'
2 *fobbish*, see below; *abc-like* ABC = American Born Chinese.

The overall changes in the environments in which English is used mean that the language is used more and more for practical purposes by people with very varied norms and scopes of proficiency. Many interactions in English are between participants who do not control standard grammar and whose lexis and pronunciation do not conform to any recognized norm. We could describe this as a process of internationalization and destandardization. Nonstandard, unedited English is becoming more and more visible.

In fact a number of new technologies, such as mobile-phone text messages and online chat, make renewal and adaptation of the language code almost inevitable, although specific forms may be a teenage fad, of which only a few become established. Text and chat-room messages are full of abbreviations, some international like *l8* 'late' and *2* 'two, to, too', some probably local or individual like British *moz, soz* 'tomorrow', 'sorry'. In this chapter's motto *l8a* 'later' seems to represent a local non-rhotic pronunciation and *feckin* 'fucking' may represent a northern English pronunciation of STRUT with [ə] (4.1.5.1). In other chatrooms *l8r* and *fuckin* are more common.

Correspondingly, the hierarchy of the standard varieties is tending to break down – if no one cares whether they are writing or speaking Standard English they are not likely to care much if they are using a British or Indian variety. Of course people still see and hear more edited and standardized US English than other kinds, and they still in general attach prestige to it, but the trend is towards more variety, less standardization, and more International English, and so to some reduction of the authority of the inner-circle native speaker. If this trend continues, it could affect the code and lead to simplification and elimination of what Trudgill (2002:92) calls 'afunctional grammatical categories', at least in international usage. On the other hand, as Graddol (1997) points out, the main agency for spreading English is the school and until now this has usually supported Standard English and resisted simplification and variety. The school might have a different effect if proposals for a codified 'lingua franca' English become influential.

This loosening of standardization pressure has resulted from, among other things, more and more use of English by speakers with another first language. This is both 'lingua franca' use between people with different mother tongues and codeswitching, for example in electronic communication among members of the Chinese and Indian diaspora in Asia, North America, and Europe, as in this chapter's second motto. At the same time local awareness and self-confidence on all scales around the world, from Australia to Jamaica to Shetland, has increased. Both these developments mean that the various local and ethnic norms are more free to develop independently of one another. However, the continuing power of the USA (and media availability of US English) means that US varieties have more prestige than others and exercise an influence on all other varieties. The amount of that influence depends on many factors, but it is clearly related to the extent to which the variety sets its own norm. US influence seems to be greater on expanding-circle English, which can simply switch standards from Britain to the USA, than on outer-circle and inner-circle varieties. However, since in general speakers of outer-circle varieties are ambiguous about the status of the local norm, they are more likely to adopt high-prestige outside variables than speakers of inner-circle varieties. All through Chapter 5 we noted comments from outer-circle countries with British-type varieties that American pronunciation and vocabulary were being heard more, though not yet predominantly.

The process of Americanization is least obvious in the inner circle. Trudgill (2002: 149) points out that inner-circle accents are actually diverging from one another rather than converging (4.1.5.1): the /æ/ phoneme in TRAP words is being lowered in southern England at the same time as it is being raised in the USA and the southern hemisphere; the /e/ phoneme in DRESS words is being raised and tensed in New Zealand, but it is being centred in the northern USA; and /ʌ/ in STRUT is being fronted in the south of England while it is being backed in the northern USA. As we noted in Chapter 4, similar divergent tendencies appear in the pronunciation of English within the larger inner-circle countries. Nevertheless, at the level of lexis Americanization is proceeding quite steadily, with many forms like British *lorry* and Indian *wafer* replaced by US *truck* and *potato chip* and a similar process can sometimes be observed in syntax.

The three factors – US power, internationalization, and information technology – will also have effects on the relationships between English and other languages. Continuing American predominance is likely to mean continuing borrowing of lexical items and other types of influence on the codes of other languages. Internationalization is likely to encourage the use of link languages, which will not always be English. Graddol (1997) suggests that Chinese, Malay/Indonesian, Hindi/Urdu, Arabic, Russian, and Spanish have the potential to be local link languages supplementing rather than replacing English. But English is likely to continue to displace French and German in this type of role. Computing and the Internet will have complex effects on the 'ecology of languages'. In so far as chatrooms and e-mail are sites of international and intercontinental interaction they are likely to use English and to contribute to the extension of its domains. But the system is increasingly language-neutral and provides cheap opportunities for publication and communication in any language. The proportion of pages which are in English has declined steadily since the Internet was initiated. Crystal (2002) says that 90 per cent of web pages based in Japan are in Japanese nowadays, and quotes an estimate of 50 per cent English-language web pages worldwide for 2002. Many chatrooms are bilingual and full of code-switching like those quoted in 5.5.3 and 5.5.4. So electronic communication is not in itself an agency that supports the spread of English, and it may even be supportive of minority languages. But the other two factors support the spread of English (and other link languages).

Wide use of English is a natural consequence of the way the world is now. It benefits inner-circle countries in many ways. It helps them spread their conscious or unconscious ideologies, and offers opportunities for their education systems, publishers, entertainment industries, newspapers, and magazines to exploit wider markets. This process may well be damaging to the survival and scope of other languages, as we noted in Chapter 6, but it is probably not realistic to expect the USA, Britain, and Australia to act to hinder something which is so advantageous to them. The governments of other countries have to strive to manage language use in their own countries so as to maintain linguistic diversity and the vitality of their own languages. Some countries, even small ones like Iceland, are remarkably successful in this type of policy, but English is so popular and so much in demand worldwide, that many democratic systems do not seem to be able to do more than tinker at the margins. One effect of globalization is to weaken national governments and make it more difficult for them to carry out language policies that resist its trends. Furthermore, we have seen that in many outer-circle environments use of English actually favours the groups who constitute the government. Concerted action to manage the spread of English is a long way off.

Appendix 1: a presentation of the speakers on the accompanying CD

The 17 men and women whose voices can be heard on the CD represent the three categories of users of English described in Chapters 4–6 and come from various parts of the world. We have not aimed for complete coverage but certainly for variation, not only in specific linguistic features but in age, gender, degree of standardness, and style of delivery. The speakers are presented in the order they appear on the CD, beginning with an inner-circle speaker from England and ending with an expanding-circle speaker from Sweden.

1. *Philip Shaw*, one of the authors of this book, comes from England but has lived in many different areas, in Britain as well as Europe and the Far East. He is currently a senior lecturer at the Department of English, Stockholm University.
2. *Caryl Phillips*, who talks about his experiences as a newcomer to Oxford, including class distinctions based on accents, is a well-known writer of fiction (*A State of Independence, Cambridge*). He was born on the island of St Kitts in the West Indies, but came to England as an infant and grew up in Leeds, Yorkshire.
3. *Deborah Lewis*, a young student, was born in Manchester but moved to Sheffield for her studies. As you can hear from her way of speaking and some of the views she expresses, she does not look up to RP as a superior form of speech.
4. *Alexandra Simpson*, who comes from Edinburgh, is a teacher of English. In addition to being an excellent informant, representing a Scottish accent, she supplies insightful comments on the distinction between Scots and ScotE.
5. *James Moody* is another Scottish speaker, but his accent is rather different although he comes from Glasgow, which is actually not at all far from Edinburgh.
6. *George Jamieson* is a former teacher and headmaster, living in Shetland. He, too, speaks a variety of ScotE – or Scots, rather – but with a sizeable Scandinavian element. One aspect of this Scandinavian heritage is the retention of two forms of address, namely *du* (less formal) and *you* (formal), about which he is interviewed.
7. *Frank Millsopp* comes from Belfast and is a typical speaker of NIrE. In the recording he comments on his experience of cross-dialectal miscomprehension.
8. *Paul Schreiber* is an American who has moved about a great deal. He makes interesting comments about his own linguistic accommodation, e.g. to EngE/RP.
9. *Katie Misener* is a student from Ontario, Canada. She makes interesting comments about some of the aspects that make CanE such a special and complex variety: the search for identity and the British-American 'rivalry'.

10. *John Clark* is an Australian phonetician (cf. the motto of 4.7). In the recording he demonstrates in great detail the classification on which Mitchell and Delbridge based their large-scale description of social variation in Australia in the early 1960s.

11. *Rebekah Hyde* is a student from Wellington, New Zealand. In her speech, the characteristic vowel qualities of NZE are richly demonstrated.

12. *Nelson Preville* comes from the island of St Lucia in the West Indies. Although English is his first language, Nelson is also conversant with the local dialect, which is a French-based creole (*patois*).

13. *Ishrat Lindblad*, a senior university lecturer in English literature, was born in India but when she was seven her family moved to Pakistan where she first went to school. She was later sent to a British boarding school but returned to Pakistan for her tertiary education.

14. *Cresantas Nombo Biamba* is a PhD student within the field of comparative education. He comes from Cameroon, a bilingual country, and speaks French as well as English.

15. *Lu Hong* is a teacher of Chinese and English from the People's Republic of China.

16. *Elise Beyst* is a young Belgian student.

17. *Gunnel Melchers*, the other author of this book, is a retired professor, who has lived in Sweden virtually all her life.

Appendix 2: reading questions

QUESTIONS ON CHAPTER I

Prereading

1. When did Germanic-speaking people (who became the first English) come to Britain?
2. Who was living there before?
3. What languages do these words come from?

   street, crag, candle, sky

4. When did French have most influence on English?
5. Dr Johnson's dictionary is often thought of as the first one to 'fix' English. Which century was it published in?

Postreading

1. Why would the Germanic peoples have borrowed *pepper* and *camp* from the Romans?
2. Why was it easy for the English and the descendants of Scandinavians to communicate?
3. In what way did French 'endanger' English after the Norman Conquest? Where might English be 'endangering' other languages at present?
4. The modern (Paris) French for *guardian* is *gardien*. Where does *warden* come from?

QUESTIONS ON CHAPTER 2

Prereading

1. Which of the following territories was settled first from Britain, and which last? Australia, Canada, New Zealand, South Africa, the USA
2. Many people in Africa use English for some purposes and other languages for others. Why and for what purposes?
3. Which languages have more native speakers than English?

Postreading

1. Where did most of the early English-speaking settlers in Canada come from?
2. Why did the early British settlers go to Australia?

3. Why might Indian English be called a *New English*? Given that it probably dates back to 1800 or so, what objection might be made?
4. Why do estimates of the numbers of people who know English vary so much?
5. Why is English a world language?

QUESTIONS ON CHAPTER 3: 3.1 AND 3.2

Prereading

1. What is the difference between an accent and a dialect?
2. In your own English:
    a. Do you use the spelling *color* or *colour*?
    b. Do you say *better* with a glottal stop in the middle like *be'er*, or with a voiced sound (a tap or flap) like *bedder*, or with a voiceless alveolar stop as suggested by the standard spelling?
    c. Does *lawn* rhyme with *corn*?
    d. Does *mirror* rhyme with *nearer*?
    e. Does *good* rhyme with *mood*?
    f. Would you say *Did you call her yet?* or *Have you called her yet?* or *You already call her?*
    g. What do you call the piece of furniture where you keep your clothes? What about a phone you can carry in your pocket?
    h. What does *pavement* mean? What about *braces?*
    i. Have you ever been called *dear* by a stranger? What would it mean?

Postreading

Define *accent* and *dialect*.

1. Define *rhoticity, a tap, centralization of vowels.*
2. Australian English differs from RP mainly in realization. So how are the phonemes /aɪ/ and /ɑ:/ in *say* and *father* realized differently in the two varieties?
3. Australian English (and RP) differ from General American in the phoneme inventory. How many different vowel phonemes do Australian/RP have in the following words? What about GA?

    Thought   cloth   lot   palm   near   mirror

4. Which of the following are true and which are not?
    ■ All the words in a lexical set usually share the same vowel phoneme, in any accent.
    ■ Each lexical set has a different vowel phoneme.
    ■ If two words have the same vowel phoneme, they must belong to the same lexical set.
    ■ If the realization of a vowel in a word is different in two varieties, the word belongs to different sets in the varieties.

5. Which of the following illustrates an epenthetic vowel?
   ■ New Zealand pronunciation of *bet* as [bɪt].
   ■ Punjabi pronunciation of *school* as 'sakool'.
6. What is the difference between syllable-timing and stress-timing (assuming they exist at least as ideal targets)?
7. Which of the following illustrates a variant tag?
   ■ *You saw him, no?*
   ■ *You saw him, isn't it?*
   ■ *You saw him, didn't you?*
8. Think of a fairly new word in English, perhaps a term for a technical innovation or for sport. Is it a new use of an old word (a conversion or transfer), a new coinage (compound or derivation), or a borrowing?
9. Use the terms *localism, tautonym,* and *heteronym* to describe these situations:
   A. A certain type of sandwich is called *hoagie* in Philadelphia but *submarine* elsewhere.
   B. A particular shape of roll is found only in Newcastle on Tyne and is called a *stottie* there.
   C. The term *biscuit* refers to a type of bread in the USA but to cookies and crackers in Britain.
10. Which of these situations (as described here) illustrates the occurrence of a linguistic variable?
    A. People in northern and south-east England do not pronounce the orthographic <r> in words like *heart*; people in the western and central states of the USA do pronounce it.
    B. Many people in London sometimes pronounce words like *heart* with /h/ and sometimes without. Frequency of pronunciation with /h/ varies with class and style.

QUESTIONS ON CHAPTER 3: 3.3 AND 3.4

Prereading

1. What do you think Standard English is?
2. Do you have to have learnt English as a young child to speak correctly?
3. Is there a difference between the role of English in India, and its role in France?
4. Is there a difference between the role of English in India, and its role in Britain?

Postreading

1. Match the terms on the left to the definitions on the right.
A. *Substratum*	1. Countries in which English is not generally used either as a home language or in national politics, or the law courts, or the education system.
B. *Norm*	2. The range of situations over which a speaker can communicate effectively.

C. Standard English	3. The 'regular' syntactic, lexical, etc., usage of a group of people, irrespective of whether it is codified, standardized, etc.
D. Covert prestige	4. The variety normally found in edited written English all over the world.
E. Codified variety	5. Liking a variety because it represents solidarity to one's own group or warmth even if it sounds uneducated or vulgar.
F. Expanding circle	6. A variety whose features are described in accepted and authoritative sources like dictionaries and grammars.
G. Scope of proficiency	7. A language currently or formerly spoken by a population, which influences another language it currently speaks.

2. In general, do you sympathize most with the 'conservative', 'liberal', or 'radical' viewpoints on world English?
3. If you had power in an inner-circle country what order of priority would you put these issues in, in terms of increasing their budget allocations?
    - ▪ improving the teaching of standard English
    - ▪ improving the status of other varieties of English
    - ▪ improving the teaching and use of other languages, either foreign or local minority.
4. If you had power in an outer-circle country what order of priority would you put these issues in, in terms of increasing their budget allocations?
    - ▪ improving the teaching of standard English
    - ▪ improving the status of local varieties of English
    - ▪ improving the teaching and use of local languages.
5. If you had power in an expanding-circle country what order of priority would you put these issues in, in terms of increasing their budget allocations?
    - ▪ improving the teaching of English
    - ▪ improving the teaching of other foreign languages
    - ▪ translating more books, etc. into the local official language.

QUESTIONS ON CHAPTER 4

Prereading

In this chapter we look at varieties of English from England, Scotland, Wales, and Ireland, and from the USA and Canada, the Caribbean, Australia, New Zealand, Liberia and one variety from South Africa (the speech of the descendants of British settlers).

1. English came to England and south-east Scotland between the fifth and seventh centuries. Do you know when it came to any or all of the other territories?
2. Which of these varieties do you expect to be rhotic (pronouncing the orthographic <r> in words like *heart*)?

3. Which varieties do you associate each of these words with?

fortnight   *wee*   *bach*   *chesterfield*   *goober*   *billabong*
pakeha   *jalopy*   *bioscope*

Postreading

4.1 England

1. How can different writers have different opinions about the number of varieties of English?
2. Listen to an English-language television programme and see if speakers are consistent within themselves in pronouncing all words you expect to belong to the LOT set (*stop, sock, dodge*, etc. 3.22) with the sound you expect? Do all words you expect to belong to the THOUGHT set (*taught, sauce, hawk*, etc. 3.2.2) actually have the sound you expect? Does the same apply to BATH and TRAP?
3. What is the relationship between Standard English English and RP? Are there speakers of Standard English who do not use RP? Are there users of RP who do not speak Standard English?
4. Why is Estuary English attractive? Where do its features come from?
5. Can you pronounce the traditional and more modern Derby GOAT vowels?
6. How do you suppose *talk, port,* and *hurt* are pronounced in Geordie/Newcastle?
7. How do they pronounce *singer* in the West Midlands?
8. In Barnsley in South Yorkshire (the north of England) people say *doesta? ('dost thou?')* to some people and *do you?* to others. Which form do they use to friends and children?
9. Where do they say *we is* and *we be?*
10. Local accents in England seem to be quite strong, but local lexis is dying out. Why do you think this is happening?

4.2 Wales

1. Which characteristics in 4.2.3 are likely to derive from Welsh substratum features? Which might be left-overs from learning English as a foreign language?
2. Say *strut, nurse,* and *square* in Welsh English.
3. How can you tell a posh Welshman from a rough one with START/PALM?
4. Where did most Welsh people learn English (in the past!)?
5. What does a Welsh person mean by *There's posh!*?
6. There are quite a lot of Maori words in NZE and rather few Welsh ones (other than place names) in WelshE. What does this say about borrowing from a lower-status language? Was there a need for Maori words?

4.3 Scotland

1. What social forces support the survival of Scots Gaelic, and which tend to make it die out?

2. Why might some people object to treating Ulster Scots, or any other variety of Scots, in a discussion of English?
3. Read the Caroline Macafee Scots text aloud.
4. What is the difference between Scots and Scottish English?
5. What might be Scandinavian in Shetland dialect?
6. Where else has dark /l/ been vocalized?
7. Pronounce *cheers* with rhoticity, and without a centralized diphthongal element.
8. Explain Aitken's Law (the SLVR) in relation to the words *mess, mace, maze* and *rod, road, rove.*
9. Explain the difference between *this, that,* and *yon.*
10. What is the difference between borrowing and substratum in terms of the Scandinavian element in mainland Scots and Shetland dialect?
11. What influence did the Franco-Scottish alliance have? Why is it important historically?

4.4 Ireland

1. What is the main function of the Irish language in Ireland today?
2. Which of the terms in 4.4.2.2 is used for English with a substrate of Irish Gaelic, analogous to 'Welsh English'? Distinguish between Anglo-Irish, Ulster Scots, and Hiberno-English. Why do you think so many terms have emerged?
3. Say *a foul silly film* with clear /l/ throughout.
4. Look at the attached extract from a Rudyard Kipling story and identify Irish English features in the character's speech. Dialect representations like this usually indicate some features genuinely characteristic of the variety and a number of features which are common in many varieties of spoken English but different from the written language.

   The Army's mate and dhrink to me bekaze I'm wan av the few that can't quit ut. I've put in sivinteen years. . . Bein' fwhat I am, I'm Privit Mulvaney, wid no good-conduc' pay an' a devourin' thirst.

   (The Army's meat and drink to me because I'm one of the few that can't leave it. I've put in seventeen years . . . Being what I am, I'm Private Mulvaney, with no good-conduct pay and a devouring thirst) (Kipling 'The Taking of Lungtungpen', from *Plain Tales from the Hills* 1888)
5. 'The dental sounds are still firmly fricative' in the north. What does this mean and why is it so?
6. Why does Hiberno-English have so many more 'odd' grammatical constructions than US English, for example?

4.5 USA

1. How do you interpret the motto at the beginning of the section?
2. Read the following text from 'When there's an R in the mouth' *English Today* 6 1986. What does it tell us about accents of English in Britain, New England, New York, and the South. Is the writer British or American?

To a Londoner, the strawbreez at Wimbledon ah veddy good with clotted-cream . . .

We all know the American Cantabrigian [from Cambridge, Mass, outside Boston], who packs his *ca neah Havvad Squayah* . . .

When I lived in my native heath, Brooklyn, I vose oily on Satiday mawning, put erl in my cah – not the same as the New Englander's ca – and dvove to the synagogue on Pennsylvaniav-Avenue to hear the vabbi's soimon . . .

Scahlett, my friend with the raid haia, says she was bawn in Jawja . . .

3. Why is there less variety of accent in the west than in the east?
4. US LOT is unrounded. and there is yod dropping. Where have you heard things like that before? (Check 4.1!)
5. What characteristic linguistic features can you find in the AAVE text in 4.5.4.1?
6. What alternative explanations might there be for features such as double modals occurring both in US nonstandard varieties and in British or Irish ones, but not in the standard dialect?
7. If you can find a speaker of American English (native or otherwise) ask about regional variation in terms like *faucet/spigot/tap* or terms for types of sandwich like *hoagie/submarine.*
8. Are any of the lexical items described as US in 3.2 unfamiliar to you? Why?

4.6 Canada

1. What are the 'two immigrations' that have contributed to Canadian English? Are there more than two?
2. Canadians write *fulfill* but *enrol* and they say /mɪsəl/ and /fjuːˈtaɪl/ Why?
3. How do BATH and CLOTH in Newfoundland differ from their US, Canadian, and RP equivalents?
4. Why could Canadian raising actually be failure to lower? (What's going on here?)
5. What is going on with h in the Newfoundland poem?
6. Explain the relation of yod dropping to US, British, and Canadian pronunciation.
7. What is meant by difference in lexical incidence? (Check 3.1.2) How does it relate to the pronunciation of *leisure?*
8. How does Canadian *eh?* relate to Welsh *isn't it?* Why are tag forms so varied in English?
9. Can you classify any of the vocabulary in 4.6.3.4 in terms of tautonymy and heteronymy?

4.7 Australia

1. Summarize the differences and similarities between AusE and NZE.
2. What does John Wells mean when he writes: 'Phonologically, all Australian English is very close to RP, phonetically, it is not'?
3. 'Australian English is just like Cockney'. Discuss.

4. Read the six 'test sets' distinguishing between the three varieties of AusE.
5. Give phonetic definitions of these sets.
6. What is remarkable about the use of *she* in AusE as mentioned among the salient features?
7. Why is there so little regional variation in AusE?
8. Make an attempt at classifying some AusE vocabulary according to the typology laid out in Chapter 3:3.2.

4.8 New Zealand

1. Say *kit, trap dress, near, square,* and *bath* in NZE.
2. NZE seems to have some rhoticity left from West Country, Scottish, and Irish immigrants. In which set of words?
3. Can you demonstrate a 'High Rise Terminal' in a paragraph like that quoted from Jane Smiley in 3.2.2 (page 21)?
4. Which varieties use the subjunctive in mandative sentences? What does BrE use?
5. How would you classify *bach, rellie, stair-dancer, creek,* in the terms of section 3.2.4?

4.9 South Africa

1. Why does this variety of South African English have many similarities with Australian English? What similarities can you list?
2. What is the KIT split? How would the following be pronounced?

    tick, pig, dish, dip, tin, bit

3. Which loanwords from Afrikaans do you remember? Can you imagine why Afrikaans has had so much more influence on South African English than French has on Canadian English?

4.10 Liberia

1. Why does Liberian English have more vowel distinctions than other West African (non-settler) varieties?
2. Liberian Settler English is of great interest to historians of AAVE. Some features seem to be similar to modern AAVE, but others (such as *ain't* for standard *didn't*) are less frequent in LSE than in AAVE. What might this suggest about the development of AAVE?

4.11 The Caribbean

1. It now seems likely that African slaves worked alongside nonstandard-English-speaking (Scottish and English) and Gaelic-speaking (Irish) indentured labourers in the West Indies. How would this have affected the linguistic forms available to second-generation Africans in developing a variety of native English?
2. Jamaica has a continuum from acrolect (Standard English with a local accent) to basilect (strongly nonstandard creole). Why is a 'new standard' developing?

3. To what extent, if at all, does this reggae lyric represent Jamaican basilect?

> Si We Dem Nuh Know We Transcribed by: Azzdem and Nerd
> Murder bwoy ...
> Si wi dem nuh know we dem nuh know we pon dem si wi
> One come arrest me and charge me wif da murder
> They take me to the station one lock me down
> I want a phone call to link up with me lawyer
> Me say who adopt the bwoy me say look what they took

4. What Trinidadian linguistic features can you identify in these extracts from Samuel Salvon's short story 'Calypsonian'?

> 'Wait until the calypso season start,' he tell Chin 'and I go be reaping a harvest. You remember last year how much money I had?'. . .
>
> 'Don't worry with that kind of talk, is so with all-you fellars, you does borrow a man money and then forget his address.'. . .
>
> Well the shoemaker in the back of the shop and it only have few people sheltering rain on the pavement. It look so easy for him to put down the old pair [his own old pair of shoes] and take up another pair [steal a new pair] this time so he done have his eye fix on a pair that look like Technic, and just his size too, besides.

QUESTIONS ON CHAPTER 5

Prereading

1. In your experience – visits, television, reading, etc. – of one or more ex-colonial countries, which languages are used in which domains?
2. Refer back to Chapter 3:3.2 and collect examples of grammar and vocabulary from 'outer-circle' varieties from Asia or Africa. Do they have any features in common?

Postreading

5.1 and 5.2

1. If you were a citizen of a multilingual postcolonial country, where would you stand on using English versus the national language(s) for education and politics? What would your position be influenced by?
2. What influence might aid policies have had on the choice of language in postcolonial countries? As an aid donor, what language-in-education policy would you recommend and what difficulties would the policy face?
3. To what extent can we identify the 'New Englishes' of the outer circle as a coherent group? That is, do they have common features, and if so of what sort?
4. Who speaks basilect to whom and why? Does it depend on the country?
5. Why do most outer circle varieties have monophthongs realizing /eɪ/ and /ou/?

6. Read question 5 first with syllable-timing, then with stress-timing.
7. Is the development of invariant tags in some outer-circle Englishes due to a feature of English or a feature of the substrate? Can we decide?
8. What are the pragmatics of *well done* in the US/UK, and in West Africa, that is, when do you say the phrase in either culture?

5.3 South Asia

1. Why did the Westernizers introduce education in English into India?
2. Can you relate the language-of-education problem in Pakistan to the 'language pyramid'?
3. Say *date* with a retroflex /d/ and monophthongal vowel.
4. If we find differences between British and Indian newspaper usage, they could be due to different standardization/editing processes, different local norms, or limited proficiency. What do these terms mean? Which do you think is the most likely source of differences?
5. What is the difference in meaning between *lungi* and *crore* as typically Indian words? What are the differences in form or origin between the compounding elements *-lifter* and *-wallah?*

5.4 Africa

1. What are the arguments for and against calling Ghana an English-speaking country?
2. In The Gambia everyone can speak Wolof. Why did creole/Krio/pidgin not flourish there?
3. Why is there no English-based pidgin in East Africa? What other factors make East African English different from West African?
4. In fact English is still very widely used in education, business, and government in Kenya and Tanzania. The inhabitants of both countries speak many different languages. Far more people know Swahili than English – there is a thriving literature in the language, and primary education generally uses it, especially in Tanzania. On the other hand, Swahili is a lingua franca which is not the mother tongue of many people. Those who have it as mother tongue are not particularly the elite, and the countries are poor. In these circumstances could Swahili take over more domains from English, and what would cause this to happen?
5. Are there common features between the language situation in, say, Jamaica, and that in Nigeria?
6. Why do African parents want their children taught in English? Should aid donors do something about this?
7. How would the English-language vowels of a South African, a Kenyan, and a Ghanaian differ?

5.5 South East Asia

1. English seems to have penetrated most in Singapore, a good deal in the Philippines, and less in Hong Kong. Why?

2. In what way is the situation in Singapore comparable to a postcreole continuum?
3. What does the language pyramid for the Philippines look like?
4. Can you interpret the representation of uncool Singlish pronunciation in 5.5.2.2 into Standard English?
5. What features of Singapore/Malaysian English do you see in the examples of *kiasu* behaviour in 5.5.3.4?
6. Explain why the Hong Kong v-split means that Hong Kong English has different phonological representations from Standard English.
7. Where do you think the Philippine meaning of *standby* comes from?
8. Can you give examples of style mixing from the 'bedspacer' article?

5.6 Others

1. Why has Spanish survived so much better in Puerto Rico than local languages in the Philippines and Guam, given similar assimilationist colonial policies in all three?
2. Why is pidgin English so widespread in the Pacific Islands?
3. What are the prospects for English and French in Vanuatu and Mauritius?
4. Why has official use of the dominant indigenous language been less effective in Fiji than in Malaysia?

CHAPTER 6

Prereading

1. If you have travelled to countries where English has no official status, what use could you make of English there? Did you see English in the media or in shops, etc.?
2. What sort of 'threat' do you think English represents to relatively small national languages like Danish or Estonian? What about large national languages like Thai or Italian? Does it represent a threat to 'international' languages like Portuguese or Bahasa Indonesia/Malaysia?

Postreading

1. Do you think it is true that English has a 'special' status in every country in the world? In which countries do Chinese, Russian, or Spanish have a 'special' status? Why?
2. Why has the need for a world lingua franca emerged in the twentieth century?
3. Crystal (1997) expresses the common view that loanwords do not 'damage' a language. Do you agree? How might they do 'damage'?
4. How much material is available on the Internet in languages you know other than English?
5. Look at an EU Internet site. Is all the material on this site available in all EU languages? Which languages have least material available?
6. Can you summarize the processes which reduce the multilingualism of the EU? Do you think more action could or should be taken to limit them?

7. Why do Asian international organizations use English as a medium? Would it be healthier if they invested more in translation, like the EU?

8. What is the effect on the language of the media in Japan or Turkey of international news being supplied in English by Reuters and AP?

9. Can you give examples of the role of English in covert-status subcultures you are familiar with? Which subcultures do not make use of English? Is this English as a language or just loan words?

10. Market forces work against the Americans/British/Australians being good at foreign languages, so government action is the only way of achieving this goal. Is it desirable? Do you think British people would know foreign languages better if the government introduced foreign languages early in primary school?

QUESTIONS ON CHAPTER 7

Prereading

What technological, social, economic, or political factors do you think will determine the nature of English in the first decades of the twenty-first century?

Postreading

1. Can you speculate as to why accents of English are diverging while vocabulary is converging? What attitudes might these processes express?

2. Graddol makes the point that trends rarely continue as they are at present. What factors will tend to slow or even reverse the spread of English – economic, demographic, political? What roles will Mandarin Chinese, Spanish, and Arabic play?

References

Abdulaziz, M. (1991) 'East Africa (Tanzania and Kenya)'. In J. Cheshire (ed.), *English around the World: Sociolinguistic Perspectives*. Cambridge: CUP, 391–401.

Adegbija, E. (1989) 'Lexico-semantic variation in Nigerian English'. *World Englishes* **8**(2), 165–77.

Adekunle, M. (1995) 'English in Nigeria: attitudes, policy, and communicative realities'. In A. Bamgbose, A. Banjo, and A. Thomas (eds), *New Englishes: a West African perspective*. Ibadan: Mosuro, 57–86.

Aitken, A. J. (1984) 'Scots and English in Scotland'. In P. Trudgill (ed.), *Language in the British Isles*. Cambridge: CUP, 94–114.

Aitken, A. J. (1985) 'Is Scots a language?' *English Today* **3**, 41–5.

Arthur, J. (1997) '"There must be something undiscovered which prevents us from doing our work well": Botswana primary teachers' views on educational language policy'. *Language and Education* **11**(4), 225–41.

Bailey, R. W. (1982) 'The English Language in Canada'. In R. W. Bailey and M. Görlach (eds), *English as a World Language*. Ann Arbor, MI: The University of Michigan Press, 134–76.

Baker, C. (1992) *Attitudes and Language*. Clevedon: Multilingual Matters.

Bamgbose, A. (1995) 'English in the Nigerian environment'. In A. Bamgbose, A. Banjo, and A. Thomas (eds), *New Englishes: a West African perspective*. Ibadan: Mosuro, 9–27.

Banda, F. (1996) 'In search of the lost tongue: prospects for mother tongue education in Zambia'. *Language, Culture and Curriculum* **9**(2), 109–19.

Banjo, A. (1993) 'On codifying Nigerian English: research so far'. In A. Bamgbose, A. Banjo and A. Thomas (eds), *New Englishes: a West African Perspective*. Ibadan: Mosuro, 203–31.

Bansal, R. (1990) 'The pronunciation of English in India'. In S. Ramsaran (ed.), *Studies in the Pronunciation of English: A Commemorative Volume in Honour of A. C. Gimson*. New York: Routledge, 219–30.

Barber, K. (1998), (ed.) *Canadian Oxford Dictionary*. Oxford: OUP.

Barkhuizen, G. and V. de Klerk (2000) 'Language contact and ethnolinguistic identity in an Eastern Cape army camp'. *International Journal of the Sociology of Language* **144**, 95–117.

Bauer, L. (1994) 'English in New Zealand'. In R. Burchfield (ed.), *The Cambridge History of the English Language, V*. Cambridge: CUP, 382–429.

Bauer, L. (2000) 'The dialectal origins of New Zealand English lexis'. In A. Bell and K. Kuiper (eds), *New Zealand English*. VEAW G25. Amsterdam: Benjamins, 40–52.

Baumgardner, R. J. (ed.) (1993) *The English Language in Pakistan*. Karachi: OUP.

Baumgardner, R. J. (ed.) (1996) *South Asian English*. Urbana, IL: University of Chicago Press.

Bayard, D. (2000) 'The cultural cringe revisited: changes through time in Kiwi attitudes toward accents'. In A. Bell and K. Kuiper (eds), *New Zealand English*. VEAW G25. Amsterdam: Benjamins, 297–324.

Bell, A. (2000) 'Maori and Pakelia English: a case study'. In A. Bell and K. Kuiper (eds), *New Zealand English*. VEAW G25. Amsterdam: Benjamins, 221–48.

Bell, A. and J. Holmes (eds) (1990) *New Zealand Ways of Speaking English*. Clevedon: Multilingual Matters.

Bell, A. and K. Kuiper (eds) (2000) *New Zealand English*. VEAW G25. Amsterdam: Benjamins.

Benson, P. (2000) 'Hong Kong words: variation and context'. *World Englishes* **19**(3), 373–80.

Bernsten, J. (1998) 'Runyakitara: Uganda's "new" language'. *Journal of Multilingual and Multicultural Development* **19**(2), 93–107.

Bhatia, V. K. (1993) *Analysing Genre*. London: Longman.

Bhatia, V. K. (1997) 'The power and politics of genre'. *World Englishes* **16**(3), 359–71.

Bisong, J. (1995) 'Language choice and cultural imperialism'. *ELT Journal* **49**(2), 122–32.

Bobda, A. Simo (1993) 'English pronunciation in Cameroon: conflicts and consequences'. *Journal of Multilingual and Multicultural Development,* **14**(6), 435–46.

Bobda, A. Simo (1994) *Aspects of Cameroon English Phonology*. Bern: Peter Lang.

Bobda, A. Simo (2000a) 'Comparing some phonological features across African accents of English'. *English Studies,* **81**(3), 249–66.

Bobda, A. Simo (2000b) 'English pronunciation in sub-Saharan Africa as illustrated by the NURSE vowel'. *English Today* **16**(4), 41–8.

Bobda, A. Simo (2001) 'East and Southern African English accents'. *World Englishes,* **20**(3), 269–84.

Bolton, K. (2000). 'The Sociolinguistics of Hong Kong and the space for Hong Kong English'. *World Englishes* **19**(3), 265–86.

Bolton, K. (ed.) (2002) *Hong Kong English: Autonomy and Creativity*. Hong Kong: Hong Kong University Press.

Branford, W. (1994) 'English in South Africa'. In R. Burchfield (ed.), *The Cambridge History of the English Language V*. Cambridge: CUP, 430–96.

Branford, J. and Branford, W. (1991) *A Dictionary of South African English*. Cape Town: OUP.

Britain, D. (1992) 'Linguistic change in intonation: the use of high rising terminals in New Zealand English'. *Language Variation and Change* **4**, 77–104.

Brown, G., Currie, K. L. and Kenworthy, J. (1980) *Questions of Intonation*. London: Croom Helm.

Burridge, K. and Mulder J. (1998) *English in Australia and New Zealand*. Melbourne: OUP.

Carver, C. M. (1987) *American Regional Dialects: A Word Geography*. Ann Arbor, MI: University of Michigan Press.

Catford, J. C. (1994) *A Practical Introduction to Phonetics*. Oxford: Clarendon Press.

Chambers, J. K. (1991) 'Canada'. In J. Cheshire (ed.), *English around the World: Sociolinguistic Perspectives*. Cambridge: CUP, 89–107.

Chambers, J. K. (1994) 'The Demise of the Canadianism Chesterfield'. In G. Melchers and N-L. Johannesson (eds), *Nonstandard Varieties of Language*. Acta Universitatis Stockholmiensis, Stockholm Studies in English LXXXIV. Stockholm: Almqvist & Wiksell International, 1–10.

Chambers, J. K. (1995) *Sociolinguistic Theory*. Oxford: Blackwell.

Chambers, J. K. (1998) 'Canadian English: 250 years in the making'. In *The Canadian Oxford Dictionary*. Oxford: OUP, IX–X.

Cheshire, J. (ed.) (1991) *English around the World: Sociolinguistic Perspectives*. Cambridge: CUP.

Chirrey, D. (1999) 'Edinburgh: descriptive material'. In P. Foulkes and G. Docherty (eds), *Urban Voices. Accent Studies in the British Isles*. London: Arnold, 223–9.

Chisanga, T. and Kamwangamallu, N. M. (1997) 'Owning the other tongue: the English language in Southern Africa'. *Journal of Mulitilingual and Multicultural development* **18**(2), 89–99.

Clampitt-Dunlap, S. (1995) *Nationalism, native language maintenance and the spread of English: a comparative study of the cases of Guam, the Philippines and Puerto Rico*. Unpublished D.Ed, University of Puerto Rico, Rio Piedras.

Clarke, S. (ed.) (1993) *Focus on Canada*. VEAW G11. Amsterdam: Benjamins.

Clarke, S. *et al.* (1995) 'The third dialect of English: some Canadian evidence'. *Language Variation and Change* **7**(2), 207–28.

Cochrane, R. (1992) 'No u-turn on "-or" spellings'. *The Globe and Mail*, 1 February.

Cramley, S. (2001) *The Vocabulary of World English*. London: Arnold.

Cruttenden, A. (1997) *Intonation*. (second edn) Cambridge: CUP.

Crystal, D. (1995) *The Cambridge Encyclopedia of the English Language*. Cambridge: CUP.

Crystal, D. (1997a) *English as a Global Language*. Cambridge: CUP.

Crystal, D. (1997b) *The Cambridge Encyclopedia of Language* (second edn). Cambridge: CUP.

Crystal, D. (1999) 'The future of Englishes'. *English Today* **15**(2), 10–20.

Crystal, D. (2000) *Language Death*. Cambridge: CUP.

Crystal, D. (2001) *A chat with David Crystal*. Wordsmith.org chat transcript. Available http:/www.wordsmith.org/chat/dc.htm.

Crystal, D. (2002) *Language and the Internet*. Cambridge: CUP.

Cummins, J. (1983) 'Language proficiency and academic achievement'. In J. R. Oller (ed.), *Issues in Language Testing Research*. Rowley, MA: Newbury House, 108–126.

Cummins, J. (1986) 'Linguistic interdependence: a central principle of bilingual education'. In Cummins, J. and Swain, M. *Bilingualism in Education: Aspects of theory, research, and practice*. London: Longman.

Davenport, M. and Hannahs, S. J. (1998) *Introducing Phonetics and Phonology*. London: Arnold.

Davidson, B. (1984) *Africa in History,* (second edition). London: Paladin.

DeCamp, D. (1971) 'Toward a generative analysis of a post-creole speech continuum'. In D. Hymes (ed.), *Pidginization and Creolization of Languages*. Cambridge: CUP, 349–70.

de Klerk, V. (ed.) (1996) *Focus on South Africa*. VEAW G15. Amsterdam: Benjamins.

Deverson, T. (2000) 'Handling New Zealand English lexis.' In A. Bell and K. Kuiper (eds), *New Zealand English*. VEAW G 25. Amsterdam: Benjamins, 23–39.

Diamond, J. (1998) *Guns, Germs, and Steel*. London: Vintage.

Docherty, G. and P. Foulkes (1999) 'Derby and Newcastle: instrumental phonetics and variationist studies'. In P. Foulkes and G. Docherty (eds), *Urban Voices. Accent Studies in the British Isles*. London: Arnold, 47–71.

Dorian, N. (1981) *Language Death. The Life Cycle of a Scottish Gaelic Dialect*. Philadelphia: University of Pennsylvania Press.

D'Souza, J. (1998) 'Afterword to special issue on "standards and world Englishes"'. *World Englishes* **1**(2), 271–74.

Eagleson, R. D. (1983) 'English in Australia and New Zealand'. In R. W. Bailey and M. Görlach (eds), *English as a World Language*. Ann Arbor, MI: University of Michigan Press, 415–38.

Early, R. (1999) 'Double trouble, and three is a crowd: languages in education and official languages in Vanuatu'. *Journal of Multilingual and Multicultural Development* **20**(1), 13–33.

Ebot, W. A. (1999) 'Phonological peculiarities in Cameroon English'. *English Studies* **80**(2), 168–79.

Edwards, J. (1984) 'Irish and English in Ireland'. In P. Trudgill (ed.), *Language in the British Isles*. Cambridge: CUP, 480–98.

Firth, A. (1990) '"Lingua Franca" negotiations: towards an interactional approach'. *World Englishes* **9**(3), 69–80

Fisher, A. (2000) 'Assessing the state of Ugandan English'. *English Today* **16**(1 (61)), 57–61.

Fishman, J. (1968) 'Nationality-nationalism and nation-nationism'. In J. Fishman, C. Ferguson and J. Das Gupta (eds), *Language Problems of Developing Nations*. New York NY: John Wiley, 39–51.

Foulkes, P. and Docherty, G. (eds) (1999) *Urban Voices. Accent Studies in the British Isles*. London: Arnold.

Gebhard, S. (2001) 'Building Europe, or back to Babel?' *Communicate, Journal of ALLC*. November–December, 1–3.

Gill, S. K. (1999) 'Standards and emerging linguistic realities in the Malaysian workplace'. *World Englishes* **18**(2), 215–31.

Gill, S. K. (2002) *International Communication: English Language Challenges for Malaysia*. Selangor. Universiti Putra Putra Malaysia Press.

Gimson, A. C. (1994) *An Introduction to the Pronunciation of English* (fifth edition). London: Edward Arnold.

Gonzalez, A. (1991) 'Stylistic shifts in the English of the Philippine print media'. In J. Cheshire (ed.), *English around the World: Sociolinguistic Perspectives*. Cambridge: CUP, 333–61.

Gonzalez, A. (1998) 'The language planning situation in the Philippines'. *Journal of Multilingual and Multicultural Development* **19**(5&6), 487–525.

Gordon, E. (1994) 'Reconstructing the past: written and spoken evidence of early New Zealand speech'. *New Zealand English Newsletter* **8**, 5–10.

Gordon, E. and Deverson, T. (1998) *New Zealand English and English in New Zealand*. Auckland: New House Publishers.

Gordon, E. and Trudgill, P. (1999) 'Shades of things to come: embryonic variants in New Zealand English sound changes'. *English World-Wide* **20**, 1.

Görlach, M. (1991) 'Scotland and Jamaica – bidialectal or bilingual?' In M. Görlach (ed.), *Englishes*. Amsterdam: Benjamins, 50–73.

Görlach, M. (1995a) 'Heteronymy in International English'. In M. Görlach (ed.), *More Englishes*. Amsterdam: Benjamins, 93–123.

Görlach, M. (1995b) Text types and Indian English. In M. Görlach (ed.), *More Englishes*. Amsterdam: Benjamins, 192–219.

Graddol, D. (1997) *The Future of English?* London: British Council.

Gramley, S. (2001) *The Vocabulary of World English* (The English Language Series). London: Arnold.

Gunnarsson, B.-L. (2001) 'Swedish, English, French or German – the language situation at Swedish universities'. In U. Ammon (ed.), *The Dominance of English as a Language of Science*. Berlin: Mouton de Gruyter, 287–316.

Gupta, A. S. (1992) 'The pragmatic particles of Singapore colloquial English'. *Journal of Pragmatics* **17**(3), 39–65.

Gupta, A. S. (1994) *The Step Tongue*. Clevedon: Multilingual Matters.

Gupta, A. S. (1997) 'Colonisation, migration and functions of English'. In Edgar W Schneider (ed.), *Englishes around the World* 1: General Studies, British Isles, North America Studies in Honour of Manfred Görlach. Amsterdam: Benjamins, 47–58 .

Gupta, A. S. (1999) *Singapore Colloquial English*. Paper presented at the Workshop on mixed languages, Aarhus.

Gupta, A. S. and Yeok, S. P. (1995) 'Language shift in a Singapore Family'. *Journal of Multilingual and Multicultural Development* **16**(4), 301–13.

Hancock, I. F. and Angogo, R. (1982) 'English in East Africa'. In R. W. Bailey and M. Görlach (eds.), *English as a World Language*. Ann Arbor, MI: University of Michigan Press, 281–305.

Harris, J. (1984) 'English in the north of Ireland'. In P. Trudgill, (ed.), *Language in the British Isles*. Cambridge: CUP, 115–34.

Harris, J. (1991) 'Ireland'. In J. Cheshire (ed.), *English around the World: Sociolinguistic Perspectives*. Cambridge: CUP, 37–50.

Harris, J. (1993) 'The grammar of Irish English'. In J. and L. Milroy (eds), *Real English*. London: Longman, 139–86.

Harrison, T. (1986) *Selected Poems*. Harmondsworth: Penguin.

Hickey, R. (1999) 'Dublin English: current changes and their motivation'. In P. Foulkes and G. Docherty (eds), *Urban Voices. Accent Studies in the British Isles*. London: Arnold, 265–81.

Hickey, R. (ed.) (2002) *The Legacy of Colonial English. A Study in Transported Dialects*. Cambridge: CUP.

Holm, J. (1994) 'English in the Caribbean'. In R. Burchfield (ed.), *The Cambridge History of the English Language V*. Cambridge: CUP, 328–81.

Holmes, J. (1998) 'A Kiwi cocktail: current changes in New Zealand English'. In H. Lindquist, S. Klintborg, M. Levin and M. Estling (eds), *The Major Varieties of English*, Acta Wexionensia Humaniora No.1. Växjö: Växjö University, 37–48.

Honey, J. (1989; 2nd edn 1991) *Does Accent Matter?* London: Faber & Faber.

Honey, J. (1997) *Language is Power*. London: Faber & Faber.

Horvath, B. M. (1985) *Variation in Australian English: The Sociolects of Sydney*. Cambridge: CUP.

Hundt, M. (1998a) 'It is important that this study (should) be based on the analysis of parallel corpora: on the use of the mandative subjunctive in four major varieties of English'. In H. Lindquist, S. Klintborg, M. Levin and M. Estling (eds), *The Major Varieties of English*, Acta Wexionensia Humaniora No.1. Växjö: Växjö University, 159–76.

Hundt, M. (1998b) *New Zealand English Grammar: Fact or Fiction? A Corpus-based Study in Morphosyntactic Variation*. Amsterdam: Benjamins.

Hung, T. T. N. (2000) 'Towards a phonology of Hong Kong English'. *World Englishes,* **19**(3), 337–56.

Iatcu, T. (1999) 'Teaching English as a third language to Hungarian-Romanian bilinguals'. In J. Cenoz and U. Jessner (eds), *English in Europe: the Acquisition of a Third Language*. Clevedon: Multilingual Matters.

INRA (2001) *Les Europeens et les langues* (Eurobarometer 54 Special) Brussels: EU (Directorate-General for Education and Culture).

Ireland, R. J. (1979) *Canadian spelling: an empirical and historical survey of selected words*. Ph.D. thesis. York University.

Irvine, A. (1994) 'Dialect variation in Jamaican English: a study of the phonology of social group marking'. *English Worldwide* **15**(1), 55–78.

Ishiwata, T. (1986) 'English borrowings in Japanese'. In W. Viereck and W-D. Bald (eds), *English in Contact with other Languages. Studies in honour of Broder Carstensen on the occasion of his 60th birthday*. Budapest: Akadémiai Kiadó, 159–77.

James, A. (1999) 'English as a European *lingua franca:* current realities and existing dichotomies'. In J. Cenoz and U. Jessner (eds), *English in Europe: The Acquisition of a Third Language*. Clevedon: Multilingual Matters.

Jenkins, J. (2000) *The Phonology of English as an International Language*. Oxford: OUP.

Kachru, B. (1983) 'Models for non-native Englishes'. In L. E. Smith (ed.), *Readings in English as an International Language*. London: Pergamon, 69–86.

Kachru, B. (1985) 'Standards, codification and sociolinguistic realism: the English language in the outer circle'. In R. Quirk and H. G. Widdowson (eds), *English in the World: Teaching and Learning of Language and Literature*. Cambridge: CUP, 11–36.

Kachru, Y. (1997) 'Cultural meaning and contrastive rhetoric in English education'. *World Englishes* **16**(3), 337–50.

Kallen, J. (1994) 'English in Ireland'. In R. Burchfield (ed.), *The Cambridge History of the English Language V*. Cambridge: CUP, 148–96.

Kandiah, T. (1998) 'Epiphanies of the deathless native user's manifold avatars: a post-colonial persopective on the native speaker'. In R. Singh (ed.), *The Native Speaker: Multilingual Perspectives*. New Delhi: Sage, 79–100.

Kanyoro, M. R. A. (1991) 'The politics of the English language in Kenya and Tanzania'. In J. Cheshire (ed.), *English around the World: Sociolinguistic Perspectives*. Cambridge: CUP, 402–19.

Katamba, F. (1989) *An Introduction to Phonology*. London: Longman.

Kennedy, A. E. H. (1993). 'Of dacoits and desperadoes: crime reporting in Pakistani English'. In R. J. Baumgardner (ed.), *The English Language in Pakistan*. Karachi: OUP, 69–82.

Krishnaswamy, N. and Burde, A. S. (1998) *The Politics of Indians' English*. Delhi: OUP.

Labov, W. (1966) *The Social Stratification of English in New York City*. Washington DC: Center for Applied Linguistics.

Labov, W. (1972) *Sociolinguistic Patterns*. Philadelphia: University of Pennsylvania Press.

Labov, W. (1994) *Principles of Linguistic Change*. Oxford: Blackwell.

Ladefoged, P. (1993) *A Course in Phonetics* (third edition). New York, NY: Harcourt Brace Jovanovitch.

Ladefoged, P. and Maddieson, I. (1996) *The Sounds of the World's Languages*. Oxford: Blackwell.

Lanham, L. W. (1984) 'English in South Africa.' In M. Görlach and R. Bailey (eds), *English as a World Language*. Ann Arbor, MI: University of Michigan Press, 324–52.

Lass, R. (1987) *The Shape of English: Structure and History*. London: J. M. Dent.

Laver, J. (1980) *The Phonetic Description of Voice Quality*. Cambridge: CUP.

Lawton, D. L. (1982) 'English in the Caribbean'. In R. W. Bailey and M. Görlach (eds), *English as a World Language*. Ann Arbor, MI: University of Michigan Press, 251–80.

Leith, D. (1996) 'English – colonial to postcolonial'. In D. Graddol, D. Leith and J. Swann (eds), *English – History, Diversity and Change*. London: Routledge, 180–221.

Liebst, B. (1996) 'Peoples and languages in the Danish West Indies in the 18th century'. In E.-U. Pinkert (ed.), *Language and Cultural Hegemony*. Aalborg: Aalborg University Press, 111–27.

Lindquist, H., Klintborg, S., Levin, M. and Estling, M. (eds) (1998) *The Major Varieties of English, Acta Wexionensia Humaniora No.1*. Växjö: Växjö University.

Macafee, C. (1994) *Traditional Dialect in the Modern World*. Bamberger Beiträge zur Englischen Sprachwissenschaft 35. Frankfurt am Main: Peter Lang.

Macafee, C. (ed.) (1996) *A Concise Ulster Dictionary*. Oxford: OUP.

Macafee, C. (2001) 'Scots: hauf empty or hauf fu?' In J. M. Kirk and D. P. Ó Baoill (eds), *Linguistic Politics. Language Policies for Northern Ireland, the Republic of Ireland, and Scotland*. Belfast Studies in Language, Culture and Politics 3. Belfast: Cló Ollscoil na Banríona, 159–68.

MacKinnon, K. (1998) 'Gaelic in Scotland'. In A. Ó Corráin and S. Mac Mathúna (eds), *Minority Languages in Scandinavia, Britain and Ireland*. Acta Universitatis Upsaliensis, Studia Celtica Upsaliensia 3. Uppsala: Almqvist & Wiksell International, 175–97.

Malan, K. (1996) 'Cape Flats English'. In V. de Klerk (ed). *Focus on South Africa*. VEAW G15. Amsterdam: Benjamins, 125–48.

Maloney, W. (1977) *The Jimmy Carter Dictionary*. New York, NY: Playboy Press.

McArthur, T. (ed.) (1992) *The Oxford Companion to the English Language*. Oxford: OUP.

McArthur, T. (1998) *The English Languages*. Cambridge: CUP.

McArthur, T. (2001) 'Error, editing, and World Standard English'. *English Today* **65**, 3–8.

McCafferty; K. (1999) '(London)Derry: between Ulster and local speech – class, ethnicity and language change'. In P. Foulkes and G. Docherty (eds), *Urban Voices*. London: Arnold, 246–64.

McClure, J. D. (1995) *Scots and its Literature*. VEAW G14. Amsterdam: Benjamins.

McConnell, R. E. (1979) *Our Own Voice. Canadian English and How It Is Studied*. Toronto: Gage Educational Publishing Ltd.

McCrum, R., Cran, W. and MacNeil, R. (1986) *The Story of English*. London: Faber & Faber.

Mees, I. and Collins, B. (1999) 'Cardiff: a real-time study of glottalization'. In P. Foulkes and G. Docherty (eds), *Urban Voices*. London: Arnold, 185–202.

Mehrotra, R. R. (2000) 'Indian Pidgin English: myth and reality'. *English Today* **16**(3): 49–52.

Mekacha, R. (1993) 'Is Tanzania diglossic? The status and role of ethnic community languages'. *Journal of Multilingual and Multicultural Development* **14**(4), 307–20.

Melander, B. (2001) 'Swedish, English, and the European Union'. In S. Boyd and L. Huss (eds), *Managing Multilingualism in a European Nation-State*. Clevedon: Multilingual Matters.

Melchers, G. (1972) *Studies in Yorkshire Dialects. Based on Recordings of 13 Dialect Speakers in the West Riding*. Stockholm Theses in English 9. Stockholm University: Department of English.

Melchers, G. (1988) 'Tags are used in English, world-wide?' In I. Henryson and G. Persson (eds), *Proceedings of the 4th Scandinavian English Studies Conference*. Umeå: University of Umeå.

Melchers, G. (1998) 'Fair ladies, dancing queens: a study of mid-Atlantic accents'. In H. Lindquist, S. Klintborg, M. Levin and M. Estling (eds), *The Major Varieties of English, Acta Wexionensia Humaniora No.1.* Växjö: Växjö University, 263–72.

Melnyk, Y. (2002) 'The Influence of English on Russian and Ukranian'. *Rice University Electronic magazine* Available http://www.rice.edu/projects/topics/Electronic/Magazine.html

Mesthrie, R. (1996) 'Language contact, transmission, shift: South African Indian English'. In V. de Klerk (ed.), *Focus on South Africa.* VEAW G15. Amsterdam: Benjamins, 79–98.

Meurman-Solin, A. (1999) 'Letters as a source of data for reconstructing early spoken Scots'. In I. Taavitsainen, G. Melchers and P. Pahta (eds), *Writing in Nonstandard English.* Amsterdam: Benjamins, 305–22.

Miller, J. (1993) 'The grammar of Scottish English'. In J. and L. Milroy (eds), *Real English.* London: Longman, 99–138.

Millet, D. (1999) *Communicating with the Japanese, Part 2 Japlish.* Tokyo: Cultural Savvy. Available http://www.culturalsavvy.com/Japan_part_2.htm

Milroy, J. (1981) *Regional Accents of English: Belfast.* Belfast: Blackstaff Press.

Milroy, J. and L. Milroy (1985) *Authority in Language: Investigating Language Prescription and Standardisation.* London: Routledge & Kegan Paul.

Milroy, J. and L. Milroy (eds) (1993) *Real English.* London: Longman.

Milroy, L. (1980) *Language and Social Networks.* Oxford: Blackwell.

Milroy, L. (1994) 'Sociolinguistics and second language learning'. In G. Brown, K. Malmkjer, A. Pollitt and J. Williams (eds), *Language and Understanding.* Oxford: OUP, 153–68.

Milroy, L. (1999) 'Standard English and language ideology in Britain and the United States'. In T. Bex and R. J. Watts (eds), *Standard English: The Widening Debate.* London and New York: Routledge, 173–206.

Mitchell, A. G. and Delbridge, A. (1965) *The Pronunciation of English in Australia* (revised edn). Sydney: Angus & Robertson.

Modiano, M. (1999a) 'International English in the global village'. *English Today* **15**(2), 22–34.

Modiano, M. (1999b) 'Standard English(es) and educational practices for the world's lingua franca'. *English Today* **15**(4), 3–13.

Morais, E. (1998) 'Language choice in a Malaysian car-assembly plant'. *International Journal of the Sociology of Language* **130**, 89–105.

Mufwene, S. (2000) 'Population contacts and the evolution of English'. *The European English Messenger* **IX**(2), 9–15.

Mufwene, S. (2001) *The Ecology of Language Evolution.* Cambridge: CUP.

Mufwene, S., Rickford, J. R., Bailey, G. and Baugh, J. (eds) (1998) *African American Vernacular English.* London/New York: Routledge.

Mühlhäusler, P. (1984) 'Tok Pisin in Papua New Guinea'. In R. W. Bailey and M. Görlach (eds), *English as a World Language.* Ann Arbor, MI: University of Michigan Press, 439–66.

Mühlhäusler, P. (1991) 'Watching girls pass by in Tok Pisin'. In J. Cheshire (ed.), *Englishes Around the World: Sociolinguistic Perspectives.* Cambridge: CUP, 637–46.

Nair-Venugopal, S. (2000) 'English, identity, and the Malaysian workplace'. *World Englishes* **19**(2), 204–13.

Nash, R. (1983) 'Pringlish: still more language contact in Puerto Rico'. In B. Kachru (ed.), *The Other Tongue.* Oxford: Pergamon, 250–69.

Nettle, D. and Romaine, S. (2000) *Vanishing Voices. The Extinction of the World's Languages*. Oxford: OUP.

Newbrook, M. (1999) 'West Wirral: norms, self-reports and usage'. In P. Foulkes and G. Docherty (eds), *Urban Voices*. London: Arnold, 90–106.

Niedzielski, N. A. and Preston, D. R. (2000) *Folk Linguistics*. Berlin: Mouton de Gruyter.

Nihalani, P. R., Tongue, K. and Hosali, P. (1979) *Indian and British English*. Oxford: OUP.

Oladejo, J. A. (1993) 'How not to embark on a bilingual education policy in a developing country: the case of Nigeria'. *Journal of Multilingual and Multicultural Development,* **14**(1&2), 447–62.

Orkin, M. (1997) *Canajan, eh?* (revised edn). Toronto: Stoddart.

Orsman, H. W. (ed.) (1995) *The Dictionary of New Zealand English*. Auckland: OUP.

Paddock, H. J. (1982) 'Newfoundland dialects of English'. In H. J. Paddock (ed.), *Languages in Newfoundland and Labrador*, (second version). Department of Linguistics, Memorial University, St John's, 71–89.

Paradis, M. (1998) 'Neurolinguistic aspects of the native speaker'. In R. Singh (ed.), *The Native Speaker: multilingual perspectives*. New Delhi: Sage, 205–19.

Penfield, J. and Ornstein-Galicia, J. L. (1985) *Chicano English: An Ethnic Contact Dialect*. VEAW G 7. Amsterdam: Benjamins.

Peng, L. and Ann, J. (2000) Stress and duration in three varieties of English. *World Englishes,* **20**(1), 1–27.

Pennycook, A. (1994) *The Cultural Politics of English as an International Language*. London: Longman.

Peters, P. (2001) 'Kaleidoscope: A final report on the worldwide langscape project'. *English Today* **65**, 4–20.

Phillipson, R. (1992) *Linguistic Imperialism*. Oxford: OUP.

Pilos (2001) *Foreign Language Teaching in Schools in Europe* (Statistics in Focus KS NK 01 004 EN I) Brussels: EU (Eurostat).

Platt, J. T. (1984) 'English in Singapore, Malaysia, and Hong Kong'. In R. W. Bailey and M. Görlach (eds), *English as a World Language*. Ann Arbor, MI: University of Michigan Press, 384–414.

Platt, J., Weber H. and Ho, M. L. (1984) *The New Englishes*. London: Routledge & Kegan Paul.

Poussa, P. (1999) 'Dickens as sociolinguist: dialect in *David Copperfield*'. In I. Taavitsainen, G. Melchers and P. Pahta (eds), *Writing in Nonstandard English*. Amsterdam: Benjamins, 27–44.

Poplack, S. and Tagliamonte, S. (2001) *African American English in the Diaspora*. Oxford: Blackwell.

Pratt, T. K. (1988) *Dictionary of Prince Edward Island English*. Toronto: University of Toronto Press.

Preisler, B. (1999a) 'Functions and forms of English in a European EFL country'. In Bex, T. and R. Watts (eds), *Standard English: The Widening Debate*. London: Routledge, 239–67.

Preisler, B. (1999b) *Danskerne og det engelske sprog*. Roskilde: Universitetsforlag.

Proctor, P. (1995) (ed.) *Cambridge International Dictionary of English*. Cambridge: CUP.

Quirk, R. (1985) 'The English language in a global context'. In R. Quirk and H. G. Widdowson (eds), *English in the World: Teaching and Learning of Language and Literature*. Cambridge: CUP, 1–6.

Quirk, R. (1990) 'Language varieties and standard language'. *English Today* **21**, 3–10.

Quirk, R., Greenbaum, S., Leech, G. and Svartvik, J. (1985) *A Comprehensive Grammar of the English Language*. London: Longman.

Rahman, T. (1997) 'The medium of instruction controversy in Pakistan'. *Journal of Multilingual and Multicultural Development* **18**(2), 146–54.

Richards, J. C. (1977) 'Variation in Singapore English'. In W. Crewe (ed.), *The English Language in Singapore*. Singapore: Eastern Universities Press, 68–82.

Roach, P. (2001) *English Phonetics and Phonology. A Practical Course* (second edition). Cambridge: CUP.

Robinson, M. (ed.) (1987) *Concise Scots Dictionary*. Aberdeen: Aberdeen University Press.

Romaine, S. (1982) 'The English language in Scotland'. In R. W. Bailey and M. Görlach (eds), *English as a World Language*. Ann Arbor, MI: University of Michigan Press, 56–83.

Romaine, S. (1988) *Pidgin & Creole Languages*. London: Longman.

Romaine, S. (1994) *Language in Society*. Oxford: Oxford University Press.

Schaefer, R. P. and Egbokhare, F. O. (1999) 'English and the pace of endangerment in Nigeria'. *World Englishes* **18**(3), 381–91.

Schlossmacher, M. (1994) *Die Amtssprachen in den Organen der Europäischen Gemeinschaft*. Frankfurt: Peter Lang.

Schmied, J. (1989) 'Second-language varieties across the Indian Ocean'. In J. Schmied, (ed.) *English in East and Central Africa*. Bayreuth: Bayreuth University Press, 85–96.

Schmied, J. (1991) *English in Africa*. London: Longman.

Schneider, E. W. (ed.) (1996) *Focus on the USA*. VEAW G16. Amsterdam: Benjamins.

Scobbie, J., Hewlett, N. and Turk, A. (1999) 'Standard English in Edinburgh and Glasgow: the Scottish vowel length rule revealed'. In P. Foulkes and G. Docherty (eds), *Urban Voices. Accent Studies in the British Isles*. London: Arnold, 230–45.

Sebba, M. (1997) *Contact Languages*. London: Macmillan.

Seidlhofer, B. (2001) 'Closing a conceptual gap: the case for a description of English as a lingua franca'. *Journal of Applied Linguistics* **11**(2), 133–58.

Sharp, H. (2001) *English in Spoken Swedish: A Corpus Study of Two Discourse Domains*. Acta Universitatis Stockhomiensis. Stockholm Studies in English XCV. Stockholm: Almqvist & Wiksell International.

Silva, P. (1998) 'South African English: oppressor or liberator?' In H. Lindquist, S. Klintborg, M. Levin and M. Estling (eds), *The Major Varieties of English*, Acta Wexionensia Humaniora No.1. Växjö: Växjö University, 69–77.

Singh, R. (ed.) (1998) *The Native Speaker: Multilingual Perspectives*. New Delhi: Sage.

Singh, R., D'Souza, J., Mohanan, K. P. and Prabhu, N. S. (1998) 'On 'new/non-native' Englishes: a quartet'. In R. Singh (ed.), *The Native Speaker: Multilingual Perspectives*. New Delhi: Sage, 45–61.

Singler, J. (1987) 'Where did Liberian English *na* come from?' *English World-Wide* **8**, 69–95.

Singler, J. (1991) 'Liberian Settler English and the ex-slave recordings: a comparative study'. In G. Bailey *et al.* (eds), *The Emergence of Black English: Text and Commentary*. Amsterdam and Philadelphia: Benjamins, 249–74.

Skandera, P. (1999) 'What do we really know about Kenyan English: a pilot study in research methodology'. *English World-Wide* **20**(2), 217–35.

Smit, U. (1998) 'South African English lexemes for South Africans – a case in point for a developing multicultural standard of English.' In H. Lindquist, S. Klintborg, M. Levin and M. Estling (eds), *The Major Varieties of English. Acta Wexionensia Humaniora No.1*. Växjö: Växjö University, 79–82.

Smith, L. E. (ed.) (1983) *Readings in English as an International Language*. London: Pergamon.

Söderlund, M. and Modiano, M. (2002) 'Swedish upper secondary school students and their attitudes towards AmE, BrE, and mid-Atlantic English'. In M. Modiano (ed.), *Studies in Mid-Atlantic English*. Gävle: Gävle University Press, 147–71.

Språkvård (1998) 'Förslag till handlingsprogram för att främja svenska språket'. *Språkvård* **2**(1), 7–23.

Strevens, P. (1983) 'What is "Standard English"?' In L. E. Smith (ed.), *Readings in English as an International Language*. London: Pergamon, 87–93.

Stuart-Smith, J. (1999) 'Glasgow: accent and voice quality'. In P. Foulkes and G. Doherty (eds), *Urban Voices: Accent Studies in the British Isles*. London: Edward Arnold, 201–22.

Stubbe, M. and Holmes, J. (2000) 'Talking Maori or Pakeha in English: signalling identity in discourse'. In A. Bell and K. Kuiper (eds), *New Zealand English*. VEAW G 25. Amsterdam: Benjamins, 249–78.

Sure, K. (1989) 'Attitudes towards English among Kenyan students'. In J. Schmied (ed.) *English in East and Central Africa*. Bayreuth: Bayreuth University Press.

Taavitsainen, I. and Melchers, G. (1999) 'Writing in nonstandard English: introduction'. In I. Taavitsainen, G. Melchers and P. Pahta (eds), *Writing in Nonstandard English*. Amsterdam: Benjamins, 1–26.

Tent, J. (2000) 'English lexicography in Fiji'. *English Today,* **16**(3), 22–8.

Thiong'o, Ngũgĩ wa (1986) *Decolonising the Mind: the Politics of Language in African Literature*. London: James Currey.

Thomas, A. R. (1994) 'English in Wales'. In R. Burchfield (ed.), *The Cambridge History of the English Language, Vol. 5*. Cambridge: CUP, 94–147.

Thomson, R. L. (1984) 'The history of the Celtic languages in the British Isles'. In P. Trudgill (ed.), *Language in the British Isles*. Cambridge: CUP, 241–58.

Times Atlas of the World (1990). London: Bartholomew.

Todd, L. (1982a) *Cameroon*. VEAW G2. Heidelberg: Julius Groos.

Todd, L. (1982b) 'The English language in West Africa'. In R. W. Bailey and M. Görlach (eds), *English as a World Language*. Cambridge: CUP, 281–305.

Todd, L. (1989) 'Cultures in conflict: varieties of English in Northern Ireland'. In O. Garcia and R. Otheguy (eds), *English across Cultures, Cultures across English: A Reader in Cross-cultural Communication*. New York, NY: Mouton de Gruyter, 335–55.

Todd, L. (2000) *Green English. Ireland's Influence on the English Language*. Dublin: The O'Brien Press.

Tollefson, J. W. (1992) *Planning Language, Planning Inequality*. London: Longman.

Tongue, R. K. (1974) *The English of Singapore and Malaysia*. Singapore: Eastern Universities Press.

Tottie, G. (2002) *An Introduction to American English*. Oxford: Blackwell.

Trosborg, A. (1997) 'Text typology: register, genre and text type'. In A. Trosborg (ed.), *Text Typology and Translation*. Amsterdam: John Benjamins, 3–23.

Truchot, C. (1990). *L'anglais dans le monde contemporain*. Paris: le Robert.

Trudgill, P. (1983) *On Dialect: Social and Geographical Perspectives*. Oxford: Blackwell.

Trudgill, P. (ed.) (1984) *Language in the British Isles*. Cambridge: CUP.

Trudgill, P. (1986) *Dialects in Contact*. Oxford: Blackwell.

Trudgill, P. (1995) *Sociolinguistics: An Introduction to Language and Society* (third edition). London: Penguin Books.

Trudgill, P. (1998a) 'Standard English: what it isn't'. *European English Messenger* **7**(1), 35–9.

Trudgill, P. (1998b) 'World Englishes: convergence or divergence?' In H. Lindquist *et al.* (eds), *The Major Varieties of English, Acta Wexionensia Humaniora No. 1*. Växjö: Växjö University, 29–34.

Trudgill, P. (1999a) *The Dialects of England*. (second edition). Oxford: Blackwell.

Trudgill, P. (1999b) 'Norwich: endogenous and exogenous linguistic change'. In P. Foulkes and G. Docherty (eds), *Urban Voices. Accent Studies in the British Isles*. London: Arnold, 124–40.

Trudgill, P. (2000) 'Sociohistorical linguistics and dialect survival: a note on another Nova Scotian enclave'. In M. Ljung (ed.), *Language Structure and Variation*. Acta Universitatis Stockholmiensis, Stockholm Studies in English XCII. Stockholm: Almqvist & Wiksell International, 193–201.

Trudgill, P. (2002) *Sociolinguistic Variation and Change*. Edinburgh University Press.

Trudgill, P. and Hannah J. (1994) *International English* (third edition). London: Edward Arnold.

Trudgill, P. and Watts, R. (eds) (2002) *Alternative Histories of English*. London: Routledge.

Turner, G. W. (1994) 'English in Australia'. In R. Burchfield (ed.), *The Cambridge History of the English Language V*. Cambridge: CUP, 277–327.

Upton, C. and Widdowson, J. D. A. (1996) *An Atlas of English Dialects*. Oxford: OUP.

Viereck, W. and Bald, W.-D. (eds) (1986) *English in Contact with other Languages. Studies in Honour of Broder Carstensen on the Occasion of his 60th birthday*, Budapest: Akadémiai Kiadó.

Vine, B. (1995) *'Anyway, we're not British': a social dialect study of two features of the speech of thirty Pakeha women from Wangauni*. MA thesis. Victoria University of Wellington.

Wakelin, M. (1986) 'English on the Mayflower'. *English Today* **8**, 30–3.

Wales, K. (1989) *A Dictionary of Stylistics*. London: Longman.

Wales, K. (2002) '"North of Watford gap": a cultural history of Northern English (from 1700)'. In P. Trudgill and R. Watts (eds), *Alternative Histories of English*. Routledge: London and New York, 45–66.

Warren, P. and Britain, D. (2000) 'Intonation and prosody in New Zealand English'. In A. Bell and K. Kuiper (eds), *New Zealand English*. VEAW G25. Amsterdam: Benjamins, 146–72.

Watermeyer, S. (1996). 'Afrikaans English'. In V. de Klerk (ed.), *Focus on South Africa*. VEAW G15. Amsterdam: Benjamins, 99–124.

Waugh, D. (ed.) (1996) *Shetland's Northern Links*. Lerwick: Scottish Society for Northern Studies.

Wells, J. C. (1982) *Accents of English, vols I–III*. Cambridge: CUP.

Wells, J. C. (1994) 'The Cockneyfication of RP?' In G. Melchers and N-L. Johannesson (eds), *Nonstandard Varieties of Language*. Stockholm Studies in English LXXXIV. Acta Universitatis Stockholmiensis. Stockholm: Almqvist and Wiksell International, 198–205.

Wells, J. C. (2000) *Longman Pronunciation Dictionary* (new edn.) London: Longman.

White, R. (1981) *Inventing Australia*. Sydney: Allen & Unwin.

Williams, E. (1996) 'Reading in two languages at year five in African primary schools'. *Applied Linguistics* **17**(2), 182–209.

Wilshire, C. (2002) Paper given at the World Englishes conference, Urbana, IL, October 2002.

Wolfram, W. and Schilling-Estes, N. (1998) *American English*. Oxford: Blackwell.

Woods, N. (2000) 'New Zealand English across the generations: an analysis of selected vowel and consonant variables'. In A. Bell and K. Kuiper (eds), *New Zealand English*. VEAW G 25. Amsterdam: Benjamins, 84–110.

Index